PENGUIN BOOKS

SHUTOUT

Brian Kendall is a Toronto writer. His previous books are
*Ace: Phil Marchildon*, *100 Great Moments in Hockey*, and
*Great Moments in Canadian Baseball*.

# SHUTOUT

## THE LEGEND OF TERRY SAWCHUK

## BRIAN KENDALL

Penguin Books

PENGUIN BOOKS
Published by the Penguin Group
Penguin Books Canada Ltd, 10 Alcorn Avenue, Toronto,
Ontario, Canada M4V 3B2
Penguin Books Ltd, 27 Wrights Lane, London W8 5TZ, England
Penguin Books USA Inc., 375 Hudson Street, New York,
New York 10014, U.S.A.
Penguin Books Australia Ltd, Ringwood, Victoria, Australia
Penguin Books (NZ) Ltd, cnr Rosedale and Airborne Roads,
Albany, Auckland 1310, New Zealand

Penguin Books Ltd, Registered Offices:
Harmondsworth, Middlesex, England

First published in Viking by
Penguin Books Canada Limited, 1996

Published in Penguin Books, 1997
1 3 5 7 9 10 8 6 4 2

Copyright © Brian Kendall, 1996

Manufactured in Canada.

**Canadian Cataloguing in Publication Data**

Kendall, Brian
Shutout: the Terry Sawchuk story

ISBN 0-14-025385-8

1. Sawchuk, Terry. 2. Hockey goalkeepers – Biography. I. Title.

GV848.5.S3K45 1997      796.962'092      C95-933399-1

Visit Penguin Canada's web site at **www.penguin.ca**

*To the memory of*
Ron Butler
(1927–1996)

# Contents

Prologue — "A Time of Triumph"    1

One — Kid From East Kildonan    5

Two — Rookie of the Year    29

Three — The Greatest    47

Four — Trouble Ahead    73

Five — Back on Top    93

Six — The Whammy    113

Seven — Boston Blues    135

Eight — Walk-Out    151

Nine — The Homecoming    171

Ten — The Mask    191

Eleven — A New Leaf    213

Twelve — Centennial Project    235

Thirteen — Overtime    263

Fourteen — Final Days    279

Epilogue — The Legend Grows    291

ACKNOWLEDGMENTS    293

INDEX    295

# "A TIME OF TRIUMPH"

ON the morning of Friday, June 5, 1970, more than two hundred mourners gathered at Our Lady of LaSalette Catholic Church in suburban Berkley, Michigan, to bid farewell to hockey's greatest goalie and one of its most enigmatic heroes.

Gordie Howe arrived with his left arm in a cast, the result of recent wrist surgery. Sid Abel, Red Kelly, Johnny Wilson and Marcel Pronovost who, like Howe, were Terry Sawchuk's teammates during the glory years with the Detroit Red Wings, filed in. They were joined by Johnny Bower, Frank Mahovlich and Punch Imlach, who shared his last Stanley Cup in Toronto.

Rev. E.A. Vecchio began the service by pointing to his white vestments and saying that it was not a time of mourning, but of expectation and triumph. Sawchuk's seven children, age three to fifteen, and his former wife, Pat, the woman he had loved unequivocally, though faithlessly, since they'd first met seventeen years before, wept quietly in the front pew.

"The Lord is my Shepherd; I shall not want..." Ron Stewart, Sawchuk's teammate that winter with the New York Rangers and an honorary pallbearer, joined with the others in reciting the 23rd Psalm. Perhaps the most uncomfortable man at the service, Stewart was under investigation for his role in what a grand jury would describe as the "tragic, senseless, bizarre death of Terry Sawchuk."

The goalkeeper's passing stunned the hockey world and made headlines across North America. "It's just shocking," said Sid Abel, the Red Wing general manager, whose reaction was typical. "The last time I saw Terry was when we were in New York for the last game of the season. Health-wise, I'd never seen him look better."

"Terry Sawchuk's death is a tragic loss to hockey in general and the New York Rangers in particular," offered a visibly shaken Emile Francis, general manager and coach of the Rangers, who had been with the goalie almost to the end. Francis had performed the grisly duty of identifying Sawchuk's body in the New York morgue.

The exact cause of death and the role Ron Stewart had played would remain a heated topic of speculation and gossip on sports pages pending the outcome of the official inquiry. Accusations flew that Francis and the Rangers had even tried to cover up Stewart's involvement.

Most hockey historians agree that the game has never seen a finer goaltender than Terrance Gordon Sawchuk, better known to teammates as "Uke" or "Ukie," nicknames recalling his Ukrainian heritage. During Sawchuk's first five NHL seasons, his goals-against average never climbed above 1.99, an achievement that still astonishes. There were four Stanley Cup championships along the way—three with the powerhouse Red Wings of Howe and Lindsay and Kelly, and a final, heart-breakingly heroic stand with the Maple Leafs during Canada's Centennial spring of 1967. He won the Calder as the league's top rookie as well as four Vezina trophies, was elected to seven post-season All-Star teams, and in 1964 he surpassed George Hainsworth to become the all-time shutout leader.

Like so many of the greats, Sawchuk brought something new to the game. He was the first to adopt the crouch, bending so deeply that his chin almost touched his padded knees. He found that he was quicker from this position, especially when he had to kick out a leg to stop a shot. From down low he was able to catch sight of the puck through the legs of opponents who tried to screen him in front of the net. The famous "Sawchuk Crouch" was copied by a generation of young goalies.

He was an acrobat on ice; every incredibly rapid movement an explosion of action and a release of pent-up tension. Before Sawchuk finally donned the Frankenstein face mask in 1962, it almost hurt to watch his face during a game. Every save appeared to cost him so much.

But all this is only part of the Sawchuk legend. "He was the greatest goalie I ever saw, and the most troubled athlete I ever knew," recalled Joe Falls, sports editor of the *Detroit Free Press* at the time of Sawchuk's death. "The first time I met Terry Sawchuk he was raging with anger and shouting obscenities and throwing his skates at a reporter. This was in 1953. In all the years to follow, he never really changed."

Someone else said that Sawchuk could stop everything but trouble. His life was a procession of family tragedies, injuries and accidents. Long before the end, he became as famous for the jinx that plagued his existence as he was for his brilliance between the pipes. And yet, through it all, he remained the most durable of goaltenders. No member of his profession has ever played more NHL league games.

"I'll say this," observed Marcel Pronovost, Sawchuk's closest friend in hockey. "If I'd been bothered by his physical problems, I'd have thrown the rope over the beam long ago."

Pronovost was one of a handful of teammates he let get close. This select circle, whose membership included former Wings Johnny Wilson and Benny Woit, say that Sawchuk's surliness and aloofness were just his way of insulating himself from the pressures of his profession, that he was really a terrific guy underneath it all. Still, most teammates took the hint and gave him the privacy he so clearly desired, believing that anyone that great was entitled to his eccentricities.

Sawchuk had a classic love-hate relationship with the game. From his earliest days in the NHL, he would threaten to quit whenever the pressures mounted. On one memorable occasion, while at the height of his fame, he did walk out—and right onto the front pages of newspapers in cities around the old six-team league. The cycle never ended. By attempting to duck the spotlight, he only increased the harshness of its glare.

As the end of his career drew near, those who knew him best worried about what life after hockey might hold for Sawchuk. Drinking heavily, his personal life in a shambles, he seemed at his most restless and morose during the long off-season. The game, which so often in the past he had viewed as the enemy, became his sanctuary. "The only time Sawchuk was happy," wrote Joe Falls, "completely, totally happy...was when he was in those big, brown, bulging pads, with his legs dangling over the trainer's table and a cigaret dangling from his lips, and he was exchanging insults with his teammates.

"This was the life he was born for, the life he lived for...."

## Chapter One

# KID FROM EAST KILDONAN

IF it's true that an individual's personality is shaped almost entirely during childhood, then a great deal can be explained about the man Terry Sawchuk became. His early years were dogged by tragedies and responsibilities too heavy for anyone so young to bear without there being permanent scars. These experiences may have robbed him of the ability to ever be truly happy; to trust that life could offer something other than disappointment and pain.

Or perhaps all that is too easy an answer to the riddle. Despite everything, Sawchuk held mostly fond memories of his youth spent in the working-class Winnipeg suburb of East Kildonan, where he was born on December 28, 1929. On the streets of the old neighbourhood, he is remembered as a gregarious, happy youngster who made quick friends with just about everyone.

Both his parents, Louis and Anne, were members in good standing of the city's thriving Ukrainian community, which in those days was the largest in Canada. A slight, quiet man, Louis, who was born in Austria but raised in Canada, earned his living as a tinsmith. In almost all matters he deferred to Anne, a robust, heavy-set native Winnipegger who ruled both her husband and the family with a loving but iron hand.

Terry was the third son, after Mike, seven years older, and Roger, who died of pneumonia when Terry was in diapers. Still to come were a younger brother, Gerald, and an adopted sister, Judy.

East Kildonan was an ethnic stew of Ukrainians, English, Irish and Germans, many of them recent arrivals to the country. Like most who lived in the neighbourhood during the Great Depression, the Sawchuks struggled to survive on the sporadic wages earned by Terry's father. But Terry recalled that he never felt poor. "We weren't wealthy or anything, just average," he said. "But I always had everything I ever wanted."

Terry adored his mother, whose love and patience seemed limitless. She put him in his first pair of ice skates when he was four years old and took him to the local outdoor rink, where she waited patiently for hours in the freezing cold until Terry was ready to come home. The routine continued every day for several more winters until she trusted that he could be safely left on his own.

"What a terrific lady she was," remembers Terry's boyhood chum Biff Fliss. "She was very strong-willed. Whenever Terry and the rest of us got into mischief, she'd get on us like you wouldn't believe. But you couldn't help but like her. She had a heart of pure gold."

The neighbourhood enjoyed a proud tradition of producing hockey stars. NHLers Pete Langelle, Alfie Pike, Wally Stanowski and John McCreedy had all gotten their starts on the natural rinks that dotted East Kildonan. The dream shared by thousands of Canadian boys of one day making hockey their career was easier to hold onto here.

On Saturday nights Terry and his brothers would gather around the radio set in the living room of their modest, two-storey house on Bowman Avenue to listen to the legendary Foster Hewitt broadcast Maple Leaf games live from Toronto. A rabid Leaf fan, Terry's favourite player was goalie George Hainsworth. "I never saw him play and never met him," he recalled of his hero. "I had one picture of him, a card I traded four other players' pictures for." Later on, after Hainsworth's retirement, Terry idolized stylish New York Ranger backstop Charlie Rayner.

Big brother Mike showed considerable promise as a

goalie, rapidly working his way up the ranks of the Winnipeg Recreational League. At home, Terry would put on Mike's goal pads and slide across the floor, making imaginary saves in emulation of Hainsworth and the brother he worshipped. Sometimes Mike, who had been given the pads by an uncle, even let him try them out at the local rink.

Terry's world was shattered when Mike suddenly died of a heart attack at age seventeen. There had been no warning that his brother had a weak heart. "I couldn't believe it when it happened," said Terry, who was ten at the time. "He used to take me out in Dad's car and let me drive, and we played cards together all the time. I missed him for a long time afterwards." Friends remember that after Mike's death, Terry seemed almost obsessed with the idea of succeeding in hockey—not just for himself, but for *both* of them.

He began playing organized hockey the year his brother died. Terry was in goal that first season. But the following autumn when he tried out for another local team, one of his pals, Lenny French, beat him out at the position. So Terry became a centreman and won the league scoring championship.

The next year he moved up a competitive notch from Bantam A into the Midget class. By now Lenny had shifted to another team and his coach, Bob Kinnear, was looking for a new goaltender.

"Terry was one of a hundred or more boys who were around the outdoor rink," recalled Kinnear, who doubled as a scout for the Detroit Red Wings. "He was about eleven or twelve, husky and chubby. I remember he was a defenceman with his school team. We always needed equipment for the rink and I recall Terry telling me that he had a pair of pads at home. I told him to bring them on down and I think I suggested, 'You try them.' He was great from the time he put the pads on."

Already Sawchuk had earned a reputation as one of the best young athletes in the district. He excelled in all sports. During football season, he regularly arrived home covered in scrapes and bruises. Terry's mother finally forbade him to play the game. But the twelve-year-old continued on the sly until one day he severely injured the elbow of his right arm.

Fearing the reception that awaited him at home, Terry kept his injury a secret. For a while the elbow seemed to get better and he soon forgot all about it. But one morning two years later he awoke and found he could barely raise his arm. In the years to come more than sixty bone chips would be taken from his elbow during three operations that left Terry with a right arm at least two inches shorter than the left.

"I guess I would have been better off had I told my parents and suffered the consequences," Terry said. "But I wasn't exactly looking forward to a thrashing, although it would have been a lot less painful than what followed."

Terry was a power-hitting, smooth-fielding first baseman on junior Legion baseball squads during the hot prairie summers. A left-handed hitter, Sawchuk cocked his bad elbow high in the air when he swung. One season he batted over .500 and scouts for both the St. Louis Cardinals and Cleveland Indians offered him professional try-outs.

But his first love was hockey. Placed in net by Bob Kinnear, Terry stood out from the start, the best young goalie anyone could ever remember seeing. One of his opponents was Don Rope, who went on to play for Canada's national hockey squad in two Olympics. Rope remembers Sawchuk's abilities with something close to awe. "When Terry's team was well ahead in the second period, he'd take his goal pads off, leave on his goal skates and play defence," Rope says. "That amazed me, that he could play with those skates on."

Rope recalls once breaking in alone on Sawchuk, who was already working out of his famous crouch, a style he developed on his own. "I never even saw the bloody net," Rope says. "There was nothing I could do. He had absolutely every angle covered."

Determined to one day sign him for the Red Wings, Kinnear kept close tabs on Terry's progress. He remembered writing so many glowing reports about the Winnipeg prodigy that Wing coach and general manager Jack Adams finally told him to bring Terry to Detroit for a look.

"We took the train down and Terry was only fourteen then," Kinnear said. "He was so good in the workout that the All-Star defenceman Jack Stewart came up to Adams afterward and said, 'That boy is going to be a great one.'"

Terry knew that a professional hockey career would enable him to provide desperately needed financial help at home. For as long as he could remember, his parents had struggled to make ends meet. Things got even tougher in the Sawchuk household about a year later when Terry's father broke his back in a twenty-foot fall from a scaffold. His recovery, though eventually complete, would be a slow one.

Now the eldest son, Terry tried to help out his parents in any way he could. Before the age of fourteen, he had laboured in a foundry and for a sheet-metal company installing canopies over massive ovens in bakeries. Every payday he took his cheque home to his mother, who gave him twenty-five cents spending money for the week.

Still there was no sign of his spirit growing darker. Terry always seemed to be laughing, loved practical jokes and had a dry, quick wit. In those days almost everyone called him Butch, a nickname hung on him when he was a little boy and which somehow suited his energy and confidence. Less frequently he was Taras, after the famous Cossack warrior Taras Bulba. The monikers Uke and Ukie didn't come until later, after he'd turned professional.

No trouble was too great for a friend. Biff Fliss remembers

how later in their teens Terry kept talking up Fliss's abilities as a football player to a member of the Canadian Football League's Winnipeg Blue Bombers. "Terry hadn't even seen me play for two or three years," Fliss says. "But as far as he was concerned I was the best damn player in Winnipeg and he wouldn't stop hounding the guy until he arranged for me to have a try-out with the Bombers."

Terry's act of faith changed his friend's life. Fliss went on to play four years for the Blue Bombers as a fullback.

Only fifteen when the 1945-46 season opened, Terry starred that winter in Junior A hockey (where the age limit was twenty) for the Winnipeg Rangers, a team of Memorial Cup calibre. Despite Kinnear's best efforts on behalf of Detroit, Terry remained a free agent. Louis had stubbornly refused to allow his son to sign the standard C-Form, which in those days could bind a boy as young as twelve to one team for life. Every year when it came time for Terry to sign a registration card, his father, determined that his son should keep his options open for as long as possible, insisted that a clause be inserted releasing Terry at the end of the season.

By now interest in Terry was heating up. One night that season Baldy Northcott, the ex-Montreal Maroons star who scouted the area for Chicago, called at the Sawchuk home. "He offered me a bonus to sign an agreement with his club," Terry remembered. "But my dad advised me against it, said Chicago had no future then.

"The next day Bob Kinnear visited us and asked me to sign. This time my dad said yes."

Terry thus joined the organization that he would help lead to the proudest moments in its storied history. Though he played for four other teams during an NHL career that spanned twenty-one seasons, in his heart Terry Sawchuk was always a Red Wing.

By the time of Terry's signing, Detroit had widely come to be regarded as the classiest act in hockey. Sawchuk, like every other new recruit, would be painstakingly tutored and indoctrinated in the Red Wing way. Every practice session at every level of the organization included an hour of mandatory drills personally prescribed by Jack Adams. There were weekly analyses of every player that not only covered his progress on the ice, but also his ability to take instruction and the manner in which he comported himself away from the rink. Detroit's farm system routinely developed more NHL-calibre players than the Wings could themselves use. This allowed Adams—famous as Trader Jack for his eagerness to cut deals—the luxury of trading off the surplus for cash or for veteran players who might help the Wings in the short term.

Detroit's success had been built on the fortune of the team's owner, shipping magnate James D. Norris, Sr., and on the cunning and determination of Jack Adams, one of the most colourful characters in the history of the game. Rotund, pink-complexioned and bespectacled, the mercurial little Napoleon had been running the Red Wings since 1927. He would continue to rule the team with an iron fist for sixteen more years.

Born in Fort William (now Thunder Bay), Ontario, Adams starred as a scrappy, high-scoring centre in the NHL and the old Pacific Coast Hockey Association (then a major league) for ten years starting from 1918. In his debut with the Toronto Arenas late in the 1917-18 season, Adams suffered so many cuts and scrapes to his face that his own sister—who happened to be the attending nurse at the Montreal hospital he was taken to after the game—failed to recognize him.

"Adams was an awful slasher," remembered Alfie Skinner, a one-time opponent. "Some fellows could slash you and you'd hardly feel it through your pads. But when Adams swung his stick at a vulnerable part of your anatomy, he swung hard. He meant to hurt. On the other hand, he'd take punishment without a murmur. He'd never complain when anyone whacked him. A guy like that you had to admire."

At the end of his playing career, Adams caught on as the coach and general manager of the fledgling Detroit Cougars, who had lost $84,000 in their inaugural NHL season just past, and had already gone through two general managers. Adams did his best to sell hockey south of the border, personally handling the club's publicity and promotion. He even penned a newspaper column, "Following the Puck," in an effort to teach Detroit fans the finer points of the game.

But after four seasons with Adams at the helm, the club, hit hard by the Great Depression, stood on the brink of bankruptcy. Things got so bad that the Wings sometimes had to borrow hockey sticks from their opponents. On several occasions, Adams dipped into his own bank account to meet the payroll.

Enter Canadian-born but Chicago-based multi-millionaire James Norris, who purchased the team in 1932. Norris gave the team a new logo (the winged wheel) and a new name (the Red Wings) and told Adams that he had a year to prove himself. Money was no object, Norris said, spend what you need to build a winner.

In 1933-34, Detroit won its first league title. The next season, the Wings swept to both the league championship and the Stanley Cup, and then repeated the feat the following year.

That was when Jack Adams learned what he considered the most vital lesson of his long career. "The next year we stood pat and finished last in our division," he recalled. "That taught me you can't be sentimental in hockey and still be a winner." In the years since, which had included a third Stanley Cup in 1942-43, Adams had built a reputation as hockey's most flamboyant wheeler-dealer, a man willing to part with even fan favourites and perennial All-Stars if the price was right. And he had just gotten started. At the time of Sawchuk's signing, most of Adams's biggest deals still lay ahead.

As much as such great Red Wing stars as Gordie Howe and Ted Lindsay, Adams came to personify hockey in the Motor City. He earned the loyalty of most of the local sportswriters by always making the time to answer their questions and by giving colourful quotes that enabled them to write endlessly about the game. As an added bonus, Adams provided the chronically underpaid reporters with cold beer and free meals when they travelled with the team on the road.

"Adams, like many hockey people, privately loathed most sportswriters but thought of his generosity as throwing a little bread upon the water," wrote David Cruise and Alison Griffiths in their best-seller *Net Worth*. "In return, writers overlooked questionable trades and the periodic appearance of the dark side of his personality. They nicknamed him 'Jolly Jack' and 'Genial Jawn' and described him as an 'overweight cherub,' a 'jolly fellow' or a kind and 'genial guy.' They felt honoured to be the conduits for Adams's criticism of individual players. Comments attributed to 'sources close to the Wings' invariably came from Adams himself."

Adams's "dark" side included one of the game's most volcanic tempers. When the Wings played badly, Adams would stomp into the dressing room during intermission and start tossing and kicking around the oranges provided for the team. One of his players recalled that Adams "could stand over a guy for five minutes and never use the same curse word twice."

"He wanted to win and he put tremendous pressure on

all of us," remembers Johnny Wilson. "He didn't stand for bad performances. You had to be sharp every day. Even in practice you had to go all out. If you won, he was your best friend. He'd hug you and muss your hair. But, man, if you lost two or three games, he'd walk by you and never even say hello."

Every one of his players feared him. In his pocket Adams carried an envelope filled with one-way train tickets to the farm clubs in Indianapolis and Omaha. One bad game was sometimes enough to put a player on the shuttle. Unlike modern managers, he never felt the need to coddle superstar egos, nor did he brook arguments from his subordinates on the Red Wing staff. In all matters, the not always so jolly Jack Adams was the boss.

That autumn Detroit shipped Sawchuk east to the Ontario town of Galt, where they sponsored a squad in the Ontario Junior Hockey League, considered the top junior loop in Canada. Terry stuffed a red flannel jacket and two pairs of pants into an old cardboard suitcase. Then his mother handed him a ten-dollar bill—money he knew she couldn't afford—to cover expenses during the train ride to Galt.

Out on his own for the first time, Terry began his education shortly after boarding the train. "There was a crap game in the smoker," he recalled to sportswriter Trent Frayne. "After a long battle with my conscience I decided to get in. After an hour I'd won a hundred bucks, and I crouched there with the bills sweating in my hand, wanting to quit while I was ahead but being afraid to because I had most of the money. Finally, there was only one guy left who I hadn't cleaned out, and we rolled. He won it all."

Sawchuk settled into a rooming house and enrolled in grade 11 at Galt Collegiate Institute and Vocational School. The Red Wings paid him a living allowance of twenty dollars a week. "Well, actually, I got eight bucks a week," he told Frayne. "The other twelve went to the landlady. I remember seeing a pair of shoes that I wanted desperately. They were twelve bucks. I faithfully gave the guy two dollars a weeks for six weeks, staring in the store window every day.... Finally, I made the last payment, put on my new shoes, and walked proudly out of the store. I discovered walking down the street that I didn't like them any more, and never wore them again."

He played in Galt a year and moved on with the team the next season when the Wings shifted their junior sponsorship from Galt to Windsor, across the river from the big club's home base at the Detroit Olympia. That fall Terry, now seventeen, was the talk of the Wings' training camp. Writers called him Detroit's greatest amateur goaltending prospect since 1930s standout Johnny Mowers had played for the local Pontiac Indians.

Jack Adams fancied himself a connoisseur of goaltending talent. "If they don't have it when they're eighteen, they'll never have it," he often said. Harry Lumley, the Wings' incumbent goalie, had made his NHL debut at the age of seventeen and clearly Sawchuk was similarly gifted. Adams began casting about for a spot for Terry in Detroit's minor-pro system.

The Wings were already set at their top farm team, the Indianapolis Capitals of the American League, where Ralph Almas guarded the cage. Almas had shone the previous spring when he replaced the injured Lumley in five Stanley Cup playoff matches. At first glance the Wings appeared equally well served at their second-tier club in Omaha, where the Knights played in the United States Hockey League. There the regular netminder, the popular Harvey Jessiman, had been named a first-team All-Star the previous two seasons.

But Adams had already concluded that Jessiman would never make the big-time. Shortly after the start of the new season when Jessiman came down with a bad leg, Adams sold him to the American League's Philadelphia Rockets. By that point Terry had played four standout matches for the Windsor Spitfires. On November 3, 1947, Adams called Sawchuk into his office at the Olympia and handed him a ticket on a train leaving the next morning for Omaha. Another envelope contained a cheque for $2,000 as a signing bonus.

Terry recalled being so excited he could barely speak. Just seventeen and already a pro! The story of what happened next is the most charming in the Sawchuk canon. Rushing back across the river to a Windsor bank, where the exchange rate then favoured the Canadian dollar, Terry had his cheque converted into the equivalent of about $2,100 in one-dollar bills. Then he lugged his fortune back to his boarding house. Alone in his room, he unloosed the seals and tossed the bundles into the air, creating a shower of green. He remembered it as one of the happiest moments of his life.

In those days a lovely, virtually crime-free city of 282,000, Omaha sprawled along the west bank of the Missouri River, surrounded by some of the most prosperous farm land on the continent. Nowhere in the American heartland had hockey been more passionately embraced. The Knights, who had gone to the league finals the year before, routinely sold out the 7,000-seat Aksarben (Nebraska spelled backwards) Coliseum and every home game was broadcast by all four Omaha radio stations, as well as the one across the river in Council Bluffs, Iowa.

The eight teams comprising the USHL stretched from Houston in the south to the northernmost outpost of

Minneapolis–St. Paul and were broken into two divisions, the Southern and the Northern, which included Omaha. It was a tough, highly competitive circuit, where many of the Wings on the current NHL roster, including Gordie Howe, had gotten their start in professional hockey.

"I was so tense that I let the first shot on goal go in without making a single move—right in the first forty seconds," Sawchuk recalled of his professional debut, which came on the road against the Dallas Texans. But that was all that got by him and the Knights rolled on to a 5-1 victory.

Omaha coach Modere "Mud" Bruneteau kept Sawchuk on after every practice for a half-hour or more of personal instruction. Bruneteau, a patient, personable man known for his ability to communicate with young players, had been an outstanding right winger with Detroit for eleven seasons. One of the most deadly snipers to that point in Red Wing history, he was particularly adept at snap shots from about thirty-five feet out.

"He'd keep me out after practice and shoot, shoot, shoot," remembered Terry. "He fired all types of shots from all different positions." Bruneteau taught him that goaltending was not just a skill, but a science. Later on Sawchuk earned raves for his ability to sneak out and take away the angles from shooters. He gave most of the credit for this to Bruneteau.

Terry quickly made the Omaha fans forget all about Harvey Jessiman. Only his consistently outstanding performances kept the injury-riddled Knights within sight of a playoff spot.

Almost overnight he became one of the most heralded young players outside of the NHL. Terry basked in the attention, not yet having developed his later aversion to publicity and reporters. All of it was heady stuff for a seventeen-year-old not long removed from the outdoor ice rinks of East Kildonan. Finished with school, out on his own and playing hockey for a living just as he'd always imagined— he didn't see how life could get much better than this.

Max McNab, a high-scoring young centre who many years later became the executive vice-president of the New Jersey Devils, roomed with Terry that season in an Omaha boarding house. He remembered the teenage Sawchuk as "a big, happy puppy dog. He was probably the best goalie I ever saw, and certainly the biggest sleeper—that's all he did back at the boarding house."

And then, during a game in Houston, Sawchuk's career almost ended before it had really begun. The date, ironically enough, was December 28, 1947, Terry's eighteenth birthday.

During a mix-up in front of the Omaha net, the stick of Houston forward George Agar rose up and caught Terry in the right eyeball. At the hospital a doctor told him that he might lose the eye. There was even an outside chance that infection could spread to the other one. As the horrified teenager watched through an arrangement of mirrors, his damaged eyeball was removed from its socket and sewn with three stitches.

"I bawled like a baby that night," Terry said. "I didn't want to lose an eye, much less give up my hockey career. I didn't sleep worrying about what I might do for a living."

But the news in the morning was good. After missing only eight games, Sawchuk returned to action and fearlessly led a late-season charge that saw the Knights climb to third place in the Northern Division. Then, in a hard-fought play-off, Omaha was eliminated by the second-place Minneapolis Millers two games to one.

Terry led all goalkeepers in the high-scoring loop with four shutouts and a 3.22 goals-against average. The USHL's eight coaches made him their overwhelming choice in the voting for rookie of the year. Out of a possible twenty-one points, Sawchuk registered sixteen to double the number tallied by his nearest rivals, Len Mutcheson of Fort Worth and Houston's Jack Giesebrecht. The prize included a cheque for $250 and an engraved puck.

His family barely recognized him when he returned to Winnipeg that spring. Since they'd last seen him, Terry had ballooned from 175 to 210 pounds. When he wasn't asleep back at the boarding house in Omaha, he'd been busy eating everything in sight. Sawchuk, though, thought it looked good on him. He felt stronger and healthier and happier than ever. That summer, giving free rein to all his appetites, he gained another eighteen pounds.

Outside of stopping pucks, Sawchuk's primary interest by this point was chasing skirts. "He'd phone from Omaha or wherever he was and say, 'I'm coming back, get some girls lined up,'" remembers Biff Fliss. "He always wanted to find a few girls, which of course was never a problem. They were falling at his feet because he was Terry Sawchuk, the hockey player."

The ready availability of attractive and willing women proved a temptation that Terry, like many professional athletes, found impossible to resist, even after he married. "Where're the broads?" was often his first question to friends waiting outside after a game.

Terry played baseball that summer for the Elmwood Giants, a local entry in the Man-Dak League, a semi-pro circuit comprised of squads from communities in Manitoba and North Dakota. The writer Scott Young, then a resident of Winnipeg, recalled watching Terry hit "booming home runs in community parks on warm prairie evenings.... He was happy then—not yet famous, but becoming so."

"I've never seen a young goalie with more ability," raved Detroit coach Tommy Ivan after watching Sawchuk work

out during training camp that fall. Adams, in order to safe-
guard a weak heart and to focus on his duties as general
manager, had appointed the popular Ivan to succeed him
behind the Wing bench the season before. "All he needs to
rank right at the top of the list," Ivan said of Terry, "is
added experience."

For the 1948-49 campaign, the Wings promoted Sawchuk to Indianapolis of the American League, where he
came under the tutelage of coach Ott Heller, a Hall of Fame
defenceman during fifteen seasons with the New York
Rangers. Still a standout when he occasionally suited up for
games, the thirty-eight-year-old Heller spent most nights
directing the Capitals from behind the bench. "The guys
just loved him," says Lefty Wilson, the team's trainer and
spare goalie, who later fulfilled the same dual role for the
Red Wings. "He was the type of guy who went around with
a big smile on his face. Heller was also one of the all-time
great teachers. He and Terry always had their heads together about improving some aspect of his game."

Heller's primary contribution to Sawchuk's evolving
technique lay in teaching him the importance of staying on
his feet. "Ott Heller and I had a pact between ourselves,"
Terry said. "When I used to fall, he'd always stand by me
and yell for me to get back up. We worked that over and
over again, me starting to fall and him hollering for me to
stand up. That's a very important thing because when a guy
is coming in on you, you have to try and stand up as long as
possible and keep him guessing. That way you might be
able to confuse him or get him to commit himself too early
or too late."

In Indianapolis, Sawchuk roomed with Benny Woit, a
brash, twenty-one-year-old rearguard from Fort William
whose thunderous body checks inspired the sobriquet
Bashin'. Woit recalls how eager they both were to experience

everything that every stop on the eleven-team circuit had to offer. They took in night clubs, popular stage plays, rowdy burlesque shows as well as the usual tourist sights in such glittering metropolises as Washington, Philadelphia, St. Louis and Cleveland. And after games and frequently during their explorations, the new friends would stop in at local taverns to slake their thirsts.

Terry could drink any of his teammates under the table. "He'd put it away all night long and most people would never even know he'd had a drink," says Woit. The tell-tale sign that Sawchuk may have exceeded his limit was an unpleasant change of tone in his voice and manner. At such times, he became insulting and took quick offence. Occasionally a brawl would break out and Woit, if not already dragged in as an active participant, would be forced to act as peacemaker.

But Woit makes it clear that in those early days Sawchuk was usually an ideal companion. "I really enjoyed Terry's company," he says. "Sure, he could be a pain in the butt when he had too much to drink, but he always made me laugh. Terry was such a quick-witted, sharp kid. I still think of him as one of the best friends I ever had."

The step up to the American League proved a smooth transition for Sawchuk. In a season that saw the Capitals finish second in their division before losing in the opening round of the playoffs, he was named the top rookie in his league for the second straight season. Sawchuk polled almost double the votes of his closest challengers, teammates Fred Glover and Gerry Reid.

Adams, Ivan, Heller and everyone else in the organization knew that Terry was ready to play in the NHL. But the path to the big team remained solidly blocked by five-year veteran Harry Lumley. A swaggering, apple-cheeked six-footer who favoured cowboy boots and large cigars, Lumley, at age twenty-two, was only just beginning to hit his stride. The future Hall of Famer had been runner-up to first Turk Broda and then Bill Durnan for the Vezina Trophy the past two seasons.

In frustration, Sawchuk briefly considered concentrating his efforts on a career in baseball. That spring he took Cleveland up on its previous offer and one day reported to their Indianapolis farm club for a try-out. Terry remembered being "scared to death" before going up to the plate for the first time. "I was afraid I wouldn't be able to hit their pitching," he said. "As I was waiting my turn to bat, this fellow named Chet Johnson, who pitched part of one season for the Browns, came up to me. He said, 'Listen kid, don't be scared of anything. I've had it pretty tough in my day and I've been pushed around a lot. But let me tell you, when I go out on that mound, I tell myself I'm the best pitcher alive. You do the same and you'll be okay.'"

Sawchuk performed well enough that manager Al Lopez offered to send him to a lower-level squad in New Orleans to get in shape, but he declined with thanks. Taking his cuts against Triple A pitching had convinced him that his future lay in hockey.

Terry was by no means the only promising young netminder impatiently awaiting his big break in the American League in the winter of 1949-50. Johnny Bower toiled with distinction for Cleveland. Gerry McNeil spent the year in Cincinnati. Gump Worsley broke in with New Hampshire. And Al Rollins split twenty-six games between Cleveland and Pittsburgh.

Each one of them would go on to star in the NHL. But even among such distinguished company, it was Sawchuk who had caught everyone's attention. "There are three big-league goalies in hockey, and one of them is in the minors,"

New York Ranger coach Lynn Patrick pronounced before the season was through. He was referring to Bill Durnan in Montreal, Charlie Rayner of New York and the by now twenty-year-old Sawchuk in Indianapolis.

"Terry was unbelievable all that season, at least half the team," Lefty Wilson says. "The kid was like a cat, even when his weight was up around 210 pounds. He had greatness written all over him." Adds Benny Woit: "I honestly believe that even then he was already the best goalie that anyone had ever seen. Even the goals that got by him never hit the back of the net. They just trickled over the goal line after he got a good piece of them. He *always* got a piece of the puck."

Finally, early in the New Year, the call came through for Sawchuk to join the Red Wings in Detroit. A twisted ankle had forced Harry Lumley to the sidelines for the first time in 157 regular-season matches. Terry squeezed into Lumley's too-tight jersey and nervously skated out for his NHL baptism, Sunday, January 8, 1950, against the Boston Bruins.

"With the stage set for a heroic debut in this emergency, the entire deal panned out in a way you don't find in fiction," observed Marshall Dann in the next edition of *The Hockey News*. "The breaks, the bobbles and the Bruins were all against him." Dann went on to call it "one of the weirdest games" seen at the Detroit Olympia in many seasons. Wing defenceman Clare Martin inadvertently deflected two shots past Sawchuk for Bruin goals, and a third bounced in off the skate of a Detroit player. Boston's 4-3 victory was their first over the Red Wings that season.

Terry blamed himself for the defeat, which was hardly necessary, but typical. Throughout his career he would usually step forward and shoulder the blame for a teammate's miscue. "Anytime I either screened him on a goal or had a puck deflect in off me," recalled Marcel Pronovost, "I'd go over and apologize and he'd say, 'Aw shit, I got a piece of the damned thing and should've stopped it.' He was a very good teammate in those situations."

"I won't be jittery Wednesday night," Sawchuk promised Tommy Ivan after the game. "I also learned up here the players don't try the same trick twice. Mistakes like that cost me a few goals tonight, but I won't make the same ones again."

Lumley hobbled into the dressing room to offer his condolences. He patted Terry on the back and said, "It's all right kid. It wouldn't have been any different if I was in there."

Lumley couldn't have known how right he was about that. Terry sparkled for the remainder of his seven-game stay, winning four (including his first NHL shutout, a 1-0 whitewash of the Rangers), losing two and allowing a total of twelve goals. When Lumley left the line-up he had stood two goals back of Montreal's Bill Durnan in the race for the Vezina Trophy. The gap was still two goals when Sawchuk returned to Indianapolis.

Rumours flew that Jack Adams would soon move either Sawchuk or Lumley in a major deal. Both were highly desirable properties in a sellers' market heating up by the day—or rather, by the birthday. Three of the NHL's six regular netminders that season were nearing the end of the line. Turk Broda of Toronto was thirty-six; Bill Durnan of Montreal, thirty-five; and Frankie Brimsek of Chicago, thirty-four. If the general managers in those rival cities weren't already looking for goaltending help, they soon would be.

The most persistent whispers had Chicago, the league's perennial doormats, as the probable destination. Adams was known to covet the Hawks' smooth young centreman Metro Prystai, who scored twenty-nine goals that season. The Detroit braintrust envisioned the twenty-two-year-old as an eventual replacement for aging Sid Abel on the famed

Production Line between Gordie Howe and Ted Lindsay. Another name being bandied about as part of a possible return package was that of veteran Hawk scoring star Billy Mosienko.

Meanwhile, down on the Indianapolis farm, Sawchuk finished the season in brilliant form, though he played the last games in excruciating pain. He began wearing a special cast to protect the right elbow he had injured as a twelve-year-old. Surgery to remove loose bone chips floating inside the joint, which had swelled to twice its normal size, was scheduled to be performed in Toronto at the end of the season.

The Capitals, whose aggressive, youthful line-up included future NHLers Fred Glover, Max Quackenbush and Benny Woit, finished second in the league's Western Division. They then whipped the St. Louis Flyers in two straight games in the best-of-three preliminary round, and did the same to the Providence Reds in the next heat to gain a berth in the Calder Cup final against the Cleveland Barons. Sawchuk, who by this point had been named the league's All-Star goalie, allowed just four goals in the first four games of the playoffs.

Older and more experienced than the Capitals, Cleveland had been the league's dominant team during the regular schedule. The big line of Bobby Carse, Pete Leswick and Les Douglas, each one a first-team All-Star, led a powerful attack. In net was the redoubtable Johnny Bower, or old China Wall as his Baron teammates came to call him.

Cleveland blasted forty-three shots at Sawchuk in the opener of the best-of-seven final. "Terry was fantastic," remembers Bower. "We outplayed them most of that game and the series, just like we had through the regular season. But Terry just wouldn't be beaten." The Capitals emerged with a 4-1 victory, their fifth straight of the playoffs.

It was the same story in the second game when Sawchuk

faced thirty-seven shots to twenty-two for Bower and the
Capitals still came out ahead, this time by a score of 6-2.
Indianapolis squeezed out a 4-3 win in game three. Then
the Caps wrapped up a perfect post-season and the Calder
Cup with a 3-2 victory April 13 on home ice. No other AHL
team had ever made a clean sweep of the playoffs.

The same night that Sawchuk and his teammates concluded
their triumph, the parent Detroit Red Wings suffered a 3-1
defeat at the hands of the Cinderella New York Rangers in
game two of the Stanley Cup finals. The Ranger victory
evened the series at one win apiece.

Detroit, after finishing atop the standings during the regular season, gained their berth in the Cup showdown by
eliminating the defending-champion Toronto Maple Leafs
in a savagely contested seven-game semi-final. Late in the
opening match, Gordie Howe suffered severe head injuries
following a collision with Leaf captain Ted Kennedy. An
operation was performed later that night to relieve pressure
on Howe's brain. It was several days before doctors were
able to reassure him that he would play again.

Sawchuk joined the Red Wings in Detroit to serve as
Harry Lumley's back-up for the remainder of the series.
From a seat in the stands, he watched the two evenly
matched squads battle through five more thrillers. The
Wings finally persevered in double overtime in the decisive
seventh game when Pete Babando, a teammate of Terry's in
Galt, beat the screened Chuck Rayner with a wrist shot
from the right circle.

Detroit gave every appearance of a team poised for
greatness following the fourth Stanley Cup championship
in franchise history. Five Wings—Sid Abel, Ted Lindsay,
Gordie Howe, Red Kelly and Leo Reise—were named to
either the first or second All-Star squad and plenty more

talent awaited promotion at Indianapolis and Omaha, where the Knights had claimed the regular-season title.

The most heralded of all the Red Wing aspirants temporarily postponed the operation on his elbow to return to Winnipeg in early May and help man the dykes during one of the most devastating floods in the city's history. The Red River climbed thirty-two feet above normal levels to form a huge lake one hundred miles long and twenty miles wide. The flood reached more than 10,500 homes and damage to the area was estimated at $115 million.

Sawchuk finally went under the surgeon's knife in Toronto on June 28. His doctor wanted to rebreak the elbow in an attempt to restore full mobility to the arm, which Terry could barely raise to shoulder level. But Sawchuk, fearful of making a bad situation worse, refused. In the end, three bone chips came out in a minor procedure that did little to alleviate the problem.

The trade winds were blowing that spring and, given Jack Adams's reputation, everyone knew that whatever was coming would be big. The year before, Trader Jack had rocked the hockey world by dealing All-Star defenceman Bill Quackenbush and forward Pete Horeck to Boston in return for a package that included defenceman Clare Martin and forwards Jimmy Peters and Pete Babando. Many credited the trade with providing the depth that allowed the Wings to sweep to the league crown and the Stanley Cup.

But even that paled in comparison to the swap that Adams finally announced on July 13. Harry Lumley was the centrepiece of a nine-player transaction—the largest in league history to that point—with the Chicago Black Hawks that flouted one of the most oft-quoted axioms in sport: Never Break Up A Winning Combination.

Heading to the Windy City along with Lumley were veteran defenceman Black Jack Stewart, Pete Babando and farm hands Al Dewsbury and Don Morrison. In return, the Wings received the much coveted Metro Prystai, left winger Gaye Stewart, defenceman Bob Goldham and goalie Sugar Jim Henry, who was slated to fill Sawchuk's spot at Indianapolis.

The consensus around the league was that Detroit had gotten the best of a deal that was essentially a transfer of defence for offence. "The Wings are stronger—even a great team such as we had could be better, and a better team is what we'll have now," said a confident Adams.

No one doubted that the key man in the trade was really Sawchuk. In moving out Lumley, Adams had handed the top job to a youth of twenty who, no matter how highly regarded, had just seven games of NHL experience. It was a gamble, but one that everyone in the Detroit organization felt confident in taking, especially after Terry's recent clutch performance in the Calder Cup.

Sawchuk displayed becoming modesty when asked to describe his reaction to his sudden promotion. "I certainly was surprised," he said. "I was figuring on playing at Indianapolis again, and I'm still not counting on simply walking into the job."

At the Ontario summer resort of Sauble Beach on Lake Huron, Harry Lumley had just left his cottage and was driving serenely along the waterfront to a softball game when he heard on the radio that he had been traded to the last-place Black Hawks. Seconds later he had run his car aground in a washout on the beach.

"I was so mad," Lumley said, "I could have thrown that car into Lake Huron."

## Chapter Two

ALL the early reviews were raves: "The quickest reflexes ever seen on ice," a New York writer marvelled; "Terry never gives bad goals and he seldom yields goals at crucial times in a game," lauded a reporter for a Toronto daily.

The buzz started to build during the annual pre-season All-Star Game at the Olympia on October 8, 1950, when Sawchuk and the Wings romped to a 7-1 victory. Several times Terry produced towering close-in saves to frustrate the great Maurice Richard. His shutout of most of the NHL's top marksmen remained intact until Toronto's Sid Smith converted a pass from Johnny Peirson of Boston with just 92 seconds remaining on the clock. Those who hadn't seen Sawchuk work before went away talking about his speed in moving from one side of the net to the other, and his unorthodox but obviously effective crouch.

Fifteen games into the season, Sawchuk's goals-against average of 1.67 was by far the best mark in the league. He had posted two shutouts, allowed just one goal in five games, and two goals in five more. Everyone agreed that he deserved the lion's share of the credit for Detroit's quick start of nine wins, four ties and only two defeats.

One of Terry's most satisfying victories had to have been his 3-1 decision over Harry Lumley and the Black Hawks in their first meeting of the season. Sawchuk completely outshone the man he had replaced in the Detroit cage.

Montreal coach Dick Irvin quickly became convinced that only some manner of trickery could explain so many miraculous saves. At the Detroit Olympia on the night of December 28, coincidentally Terry's twenty-first birthday, the Canadiens trailed 6-0 after two periods when Irvin asked referee

Red Storey to check the width of Sawchuk's leg pads. After dutifully, though somewhat sheepishly, applying his tape measure to Terry's gear, Storey declared that both pads fell safely within the official limit of ten inches.

"Well, they looked big to me," replied Irvin.

"We'll give Irvin an inch or so of padding, if he needs it," chortled Jack Adams, "and we won't ask for players—a straight cash deal."

Who could blame Adams for gloating a little over Sawchuk's success? Everything was working out precisely as Trader Jack had planned when he pulled the trigger on the huge Lumley deal in July. Detroit went on to record an 8-1 victory the night of Irvin's bleat about the pads and grabbed first place from Toronto. The Wings had won ten and tied two of their past twelve games for twenty-two out of a possible twenty-four points.

Newcomers Metro Prystai, Gaye Stewart and Bob Goldham were all plugged seamlessly into the powerful Detroit machine. Prystai proved as valuable an addition as Adams and Tommy Ivan had hoped. Late in games he would apprentice on the Production Line, subbing for a tired Sid Abel. Because Prystai, who scored twenty goals for the season, could play any forward position with equal facility, Ivan used him wherever an injury or slump opened a spot. On power plays, he dropped back to take over one of the point positions.

Veteran sniper Gaye Stewart contributed eighteen goals, and the career of twenty-eight-year-old Bob Goldham, a stay-at-home defenceman with a unique talent for blocking shots, was miraculously rejuvenated the moment he pulled on a Detroit jersey. Goldham bolstered an already formidable Wing defence anchored by All-Stars Red Kelly and Leo Reise.

Detroit's blue-line corps provided Sawchuk with such rock-ribbed protection that some nights he actually complained of not having enough to do. In a match against the Rangers, he went a stretch of twenty-four minutes and forty-one seconds (including the entire second period) without seeing a single shot.

"Every guy on the club was giving me the razz afterwards about getting me a rocking chair so I'd be real comfortable," Terry laughed. "Funny thing, though, I was more nervous and scared as those twenty-four minutes ticked off than in any other game this season....

"Another thing, standing still for twenty-four minutes isn't so hot either. Try it yourself. Go stand on a chunk of ice that long without moving around. You get cold, no matter what you're wearing."

Jack Adams already felt confident that he had built the best team in hockey. But he might have suspected he was leading a group of supermen when he got the results of the tests conducted on the Wings that December by Toronto fitness guru Lloyd Percival. Adams had always been an innovator, willing to try anything that might give his team an edge. During the playoffs the previous spring, he had ordered an oxygen tank placed by the players' bench so they could fill their lungs with the good stuff between shifts.

Percival, whose pioneering work would one day earn him induction into Canada's Sports Hall of Fame, offered the services of the fitness experts employed at his Sports College to every club in the NHL. Adams was the only taker. Through an entire weekend the Wings were put through a barrage of tests designed to measure everything from shooting and skating speeds to co-ordination, body type and heart strength. Each player was given a physical exam and interviewed about his lifestyle.

The results showed the Red Wings to be the league's most physically imposing club—although Percival's estimates of the competition were by necessity made from afar.

Ted Lindsay worked harder during his time on the ice than any other Detroit player, skating a total of three miles in nineteen minutes of play; Leo Reise expended more energy than any other NHL defenceman; Gaye Stewart was the league's fastest skater.

On down the line it went. Almost to a man the Wings checked out as splendid physical specimens. One of the few exceptions was Sawchuk, whose bulging waistline met with Percival's displeasure. His report concluded that Terry had "a wonderful potential," but that achieving it would require "a special diet to keep him lean and his reflexes quick." Percival also wanted him to diligently perform a series of special exercises to strengthen his bad arm.

Unfortunately, Jack Adams would heed Percival's advice regarding his rookie all too well. During the next couple of seasons his growing preoccupation with Sawchuk's weight would precipitate problems that no one, including the fitness guru, could possibly have foreseen.

Of all the Wings, it was twenty-two-year-old Gordie Howe who most impressed Percival. "We've never looked at anybody like Howe," Percival said in awe. "He has remarkably good reaction time, co-ordination and ability to relax."

Howe did indeed have it all. During his breakthrough campaign the year before, he had finished third behind Lindsay and Abel in the scoring race. And now, fully recovered from the head injuries that had almost cost him his life, Howe was enjoying one of the greatest seasons in the history of the game. His final tally of eighty-six points (including forty-three goals) would shatter by four the old record set by Boston's Herbie Cain in 1943-44.

Howe was big and tough and strong. He skated effortlessly, stickhandled masterfully, and possessed a lethally accurate wrist shot that had been timed at 114.2 miles per hour. Most astonishing of all, Howe was ambidextrous, able to switch hands and shoot from either side as he broke in on befuddled goaltenders.

"Plain and simply, he's the greatest thing that has appeared in hockey in twenty-five years," Jack Adams pronounced at mid-season.

Predictably, Adams's statement set off a furor in Montreal, where fans were affronted that anyone could possibly question the supremacy of their long-time hero, Maurice "The Rocket" Richard. "When Howe scores as many goals as Richard has then I'll answer that," said Dick Irvin. "Of course, Howe is an exceptionally good hockey player but I wouldn't trade Richard for him at any time."

The Howe versus Richard debate raged for the rest of the decade and continues among many long-time fans to this day. But in 1950-51 there was no denying that Howe's star was in the ascendancy. The scoring title he would claim that season was but the first of an unprecedented four in a row.

Terry's carefree bachelorhood continued with even more abandon once he joined the Red Wings. In a hockey-mad city of more than two million, there were always pretty girls anxious to meet the famous goaltender. Many nights beginning around this time, Sawchuk went out carousing with a group of cronies that included two notoriously hard-drinking members of the Detroit Lions football club.

Most young Wings lived in one of several team-approved boarding houses within easy walking distance of the Detroit Olympia, which had stood at the corner of Grand River Avenue and McGraw since 1927. The most famous of these was run by Minnie "Ma" Shaw, a grey-haired matriarch who through the years had become a kind of surrogate mother to more than two hundred Red Wings, including Ted Lindsay and Gordie Howe. Terry made his winter home in the big, comfortable brick house owned by "Ma" Tannahill, a middle-aged charmer of whom he became so fond that he gallantly insisted on escorting her to the Olympia for Red Wing games.

Considering how frequently Trader Jack Adams changed his personnel, the Wings of those days remained a remarkably close-knit group. "There were no outsiders on our team," remembers Leo Reise. "Our captain, Sid Abel, was the catalyst. He wouldn't allow anyone to get a swelled head and start thinking they were better than anyone else. For all of us, the team came first."

Abel and, to an increasing degree, Ted Lindsay, who would one day succeed him as captain, showed their teammates the Red Wing way both on and off the ice. At age thirty-two, Abel was admittedly starting to slow down. But the ten-year veteran could still work his magic in the centre slot between Howe and Lindsay. "It was an instinctive thing," Abel recalled. "Gordie wasn't a positional player so you had to figure out where you were going to based on where he went. He made it easy for us. He'd just control the puck until one of us was open and he'd give it to us.

"One of my jobs was to get them going. Lindsay was so fiery. I had to get him to relax a little, to calm down and play. Gordie, every once in a while, you'd have to give him a little nudge. If he got riled up, they'd have to throw another puck on the ice for the rest of us to play with because Gordie wasn't going to let us have his puck."

On the train after the game, Abel would go over every detail of that night's performance with his teammates. What they'd done right and wrong. How they could be better the next time. A player suffering through a slump received a few private words of encouragement and advice. "I think I learned more on the trains than I did on the ice," Gordie Howe said later.

"Guys like him come along once every ten years," Jack Adams said of Abel.

In his own way, Ted Lindsay, who had joined the Wings at the age of nineteen in 1944, was just as rare a jewel. He spoke softly and had an almost courtly manner in his civilian life. "But when Ted Lindsay buckles on his hockey armor, grabs his stick and moves out on his skates," wrote a *Look* magazine reporter, "he drinks the devil's brew that transformed Jekyll into Hyde."

Lindsay's pugnaciousness and raw determination were possibly even more vital to the success of the team than his considerable talents as a playmaker and scorer. Red Wing rookies were taken aside and instructed to never skate in fear of the opposition because he, Terrible Ted, would be there to personally back them up. Any player unfortunate enough not to wear a Detroit jersey automatically became his sworn enemy.

"Lindsay," said Toronto defenceman Bill Juzda, "is just about the toughest character in the league. He always has an elbow or a stick in your face. He's as ornery as they come."

When trouble broke out, Lindsay led the charge over the boards and into battle. That January 25 at the Olympia, he capped his already fearsome reputation during a bloodbath with Boston's aptly named winger Wild Bill Ezinicki.

The gnarled, muscular Ezinicki slashed Lindsay above the left eye with his stick. Lindsay responded in kind, cutting his foe open from eyebrow to hairline. Then the two went at it with their fists, Lindsay landing almost all the punches before the officials finally pulled them apart.

But Ezinicki wasn't done yet. He broke away from his restrainers and circled back for Lindsay, who pretended not to notice. At precisely the right moment, Lindsay wheeled around and decked Ezinicki with a right that dropped him like a rag to the ice. Lindsay was on his unconscious opponent in a flash, his right arm raised to deliver another blow when a player pulled him off.

Those watching shuddered to think what might have happened if Lindsay had thrown that last punch. With Ezinicki's head against the ice, it could have been fatal.

"Aw, I never would have swung because after I raised my fist I saw he was unconscious," Lindsay said later.

Lindsay assisted Abel in organizing a variety of team activities that ranged from a bowling league and card tournaments (Sawchuk was an avid pinochle player in a group that included Abel and Red Kelly) to regular Monday-night socials at a local Italian restaurant to which attendance was considered mandatory. The restaurant's proprietors closed the doors to the public for the evening and brought in a dance band. These gatherings offered the players a chance to kick back with their wives and girlfriends away from the prying eyes of the public. Those who didn't show up had to answer to Lindsay, who would loudly demand to know why and insist that they pay their fair share of the tab anyway.

Red Wings of that era ate, drank, lived and did practically everything else together. Like Terry, most of them were bachelors having the time of their young lives, with every intention of maintaining their single status for as long as they could possibly hold out.

There were ten of them on the squad that winter, 35 per cent more single men than on any other NHL club. Paul Chandler of *The Detroit News* did the math for a story transparently calculated to arouse the interest of his newspaper's female audience. Chandler asked each of the ten eligibles—including Gordie Howe, Ted Lindsay and Sawchuk—their preferences between Canadian and American girls, brunettes or blondes or redheads, and whether marrying a good cook was more important than finding a mate with good looks.

Howe answered that he preferred Canadian women and predicted, "I'll be married five years from the time I first think about the big step." In fact, Howe would last just two more years before marrying a local American girl.

"I'll wait until my hockey days are ended," responded Ted Lindsay, who would marry even sooner than his buddy Howe.

When it came his turn, Terry protested, "I'm too young to get married. I'm going to wait until I'm thirty, no matter who comes along." He had no preference between Canadian and American girls, but he did want a good-looking wife. "You can always hire a cook," he said. "Brunettes for me."

From the start Sawchuk was generally conceded a shoo-in for the Calder Memorial Trophy, awarded to the league's outstanding rookie. His only serious competition came from another netminder, twenty-four-year-old Al Rollins, who had been promoted from the American League to platoon with veteran Turk Broda in the Toronto net. The Rollins-Broda partnership marked the first time that two NHL goaltenders had shared the job on a more or less equal footing for an entire season.

Four of the six teams introduced new goalies. Rookie Gerry McNeil took over in Montreal after reigning Vezina champ Bill Durnan shocked team officials by announcing his retirement. In Chicago, Harry Lumley replaced the retired Frankie Brimsek. Only Charlie Rayner of New York and Boston's Jack Gelineau, who had claimed the Calder Trophy the year before, returned to full-time duty at their old posts.

By New Year's Day, Detroit and Toronto had built a huge lead over the rest of the league. Montreal, Boston and New York were left to fight it out among themselves for the final two playoff spots. Even the presence of Harry Lumley failed to improve the fortunes of the hapless Hawks, who managed to win just two of their final forty-three contests.

Rollins and Broda proved a constant thorn in Terry's side. The lead in what many considered an unfair race for the Vezina Trophy bounced like a beachball between Sawchuk and the Toronto tandem until the final game of the schedule.

In those days, the Vezina went to the goalie who played the most games for the team allowing the fewest goals. This had always seemed fair enough in the past when every team employed just one backstop who, barring life-threatening injury, was expected to play every game of the schedule. But the new-fangled Rollins-Broda partnership changed the entire equation. Was it right for a goalie who might play far fewer games than a competitor to win the Vezina?

Red Wing management and the writers on the Detroit hockey beat began agitating for a change in the Vezina rules. They suggested that the trophy and the $1,000 league bonus that accompanied it should go to the goalie with the best goals-against average who had played a minimum of fifty-five games. Though their efforts were in vain, one day in the distant future Sawchuk would almost singlehandedly force the Vezina rules to be rewritten.

Only his teammates knew that Terry worked under a severe physical handicap the last two months of the season. Once again bone chips had formed in his right elbow and another operation was planned for shortly after the end of the playoffs, this time in a Detroit hospital. Had news of the injury been made public, brutish opponents would no doubt have targeted the sore spot with their sticks or elbows.

"Besides," said Sawchuk, "I'm not complaining, and I don't want anyone saying I'm alibiing." His surgeon said later that the pain he endured "must have been terrific."

The Wings clinched their third consecutive Prince of

Wales Trophy by downing Lumley and the Black Hawks 4-3 at the Olympia on March 18. Toronto gave a good fight, but by season's end Detroit was out in front by six points. The Red Wings finished with 101 points and 236 goals, both new league records.

Hockey may never have seen a more loaded squad. Sawchuk, Gordie Howe, Ted Lindsay and Red Kelly all made the first All-Star squad, while Sid Abel and Leo Reise were second-team picks. Howe broke Herbie Cain's scoring record and Kelly's seventeen goals and thirty-seven assists set a new standard for defencemen. The soft-spoken Kelly, whose red hair belied his pacifist nature, collected his first of four Lady Byng trophies, awarded to the player best combining skill, sportsmanship and gentlemanly conduct.

By the time the season wound down to its final weekend, Sawchuk led the Vezina race by a single goal. But on Saturday night in Montreal, the Canadiens fired three goals past him for a 3-2 triumph. That same evening in Toronto, Al Rollins notched a 4-1 victory over the Bruins in his thirty-ninth game of the season. The contest had thus narrowed to the two rookies, with Rollins, who had played the majority of the Leaf games, now out ahead by one goal.

According to one press account, Sawchuk played his heart out the next night in Detroit, making "half a dozen superb saves" in blanking Montreal 5-0. But in Boston, Rollins produced his own 1-0 whitewash to seal his Vezina victory. Toronto ended the season with 138 goals scored against, one fewer than Detroit.

Terry knew he had lost the race about five minutes before the final buzzer when the Olympia crowd of 13,753 was informed by loudspeaker of the result in Boston. He briefly dropped his head in disappointment before completing his eleventh shutout of the season.

His teammates tried their best to lift his spirits. "He's

been great all season," praised one, "but these last few games when the team was going all out for the NHL championship and he was after the Vezina he played even better than we thought it was possible for a goalie to play."

Al Rollins may have won the Vezina, but few in hockey doubted which goaltender had enjoyed the better season. Sawchuk's shutout count of eleven was the most by any goalie in the modern era. Despite his bum elbow, he played all seventy games of the schedule while recording an outstanding goals-against average of 1.99. Though Rollins's GAA was lower, at 1.77, he had played in thirty fewer matches than Sawchuk. Otherwise, the best marks of the past decade had been Turk Broda's 2.06 in 1940-41 and Bill Durnan's 2.10 in 1948-49.

Any lingering disappointment Terry may have felt over the Vezina defeat was softened by the announcement that the Wings would pay him $1,000 to replace the bonus money he had lost, but which everyone in Detroit felt was rightfully his.

Detroit entered the playoffs as overwhelming favourites against the third-place Montreal Canadiens, who finished a whopping thirty-five points back in the standings. In truth, the Canadiens, who introduced ten rookies into their line-up during the course of the season, surprised everyone by placing as high as they did. Many pundits had picked them to finish last.

But a team whose line-up included the incomparable Maurice Richard posed a potential threat to any rival. When the money was on the line, the Rocket turned up the voltage and almost always found a way to win.

Most who saw him play agree that he was hockey's greatest performer from the blue line in. Sometimes he would carry resisting defencemen on his back right up to the goal mouth and still score. Hapless goaltenders couldn't even begin to guess his final move, for there was no pattern to his genius. "I never knew what I was going to do when I went in until I did it," said Richard, who scored forty-two goals that season. "If I didn't know what I was going to do, how could the goaltender?"

"What I remember most about the Rocket were his eyes," said Glenn Hall. "When he came flying toward you with the puck on his stick, his eyes were all lit up, flashing and gleaming like a pinball machine. It was terrifying."

Despite their unimpressive season record, Montreal entered the playoffs on a roll. The Canadiens vaulted from fifth place to third in March and finished off the schedule by winning six and tying two of their last nine games.

And they were loose. Hab coach Dick Irvin figured all the pressure was on Detroit. "We're along for the ride," Irvin said, "everything to win and nothing to lose. The burden is on the mighty Red Wings, and what a disgrace it would be if they should lose."

By this point Irvin and his men might well have believed that a Montreal upset of Detroit was all part of some mysterious Divine Plan. One night that winter, as they travelled by train back to Montreal following a 6-1 drubbing in Toronto, their car suddenly derailed while crossing a bridge over the frigid waters of the Ottawa River. Had the car been flung to the right instead of to the left in the derailment, which threw several Canadiens from their berths, the entire team would have plunged into the river.

"I'd been planning a shakeup," Irvin joked, "but not quite as drastic as all that."

Facing Sawchuk in the Montreal net was twenty-four-year-old Gerry McNeil, rated by almost everyone as the league's worst goalie. The rookie didn't receive a solitary vote in All-Star balloting. Dick Irvin, worried that all the negative talk was getting McNeil down, started rooming and eating with his goalie in an all-out attempt to bolster his confidence. Forget the critics, Irvin constantly told him, and concentrate on the Red Wings.

It must have worked because few goalies have ever come up bigger than McNeil in the series opener at the Olympia. The Wings had it all over the Habs from the start, outshooting Montreal 14-1 in the first twenty minutes only to see the period end with the score knotted at 1-1. Both teams scored once in the second period. Then began a heart-thumping, end-to-end marathon that eventually extended into a fourth overtime. Sawchuk made forty-two saves, twenty-two of them in extra play. He foiled Richard and Cal MacKay on breakaways. At the other end, McNeil was even busier, making thirty-eight of his sixty-two saves in the extra sessions. McNeil tallied fifteen saves in the second overtime period alone. Twice he robbed Ted Lindsay of what seemed certain goals.

"It was like running into one-hit pitching your first time out," Jack Adams said. "The greatest goalkeeping this team ever faced."

Ever the innovator, Adams ordered his men to change their soaking wet underwear between the second and third overtime sessions. That, he estimated, would relieve each player of at least two or three pounds of excess weight.

Finally, at 1:10 a.m., Rocket Richard ended the suspense. Stealing the puck from Leo Reise, he burst in alone on Sawchuk. Richard pulled up short when he saw Terry go down. Coolly, almost casually, the Rocket flipped the puck high into the twine to put the game away 3-2.

The Red Wings retreated to their hotel hideaway in nearby Toledo to lick their wounds. Like an army on campaign, the Wings always left their families behind and encamped together for the duration of the playoffs. Adams wanted his

men far away from the distractions of wives and children,
and friends who called asking for tickets. In Toledo,
between games, they indulged in long strolls, did a little
gym work and held bowling tournaments. When the series
switched to Montreal, the Wings hid out at a rustic retreat
in Quebec's Eastern Townships.

McNeil still hadn't cooled off by the start of game two.
Time and again, Gerry the Magician, as the Wings had taken
to calling him, foiled the best efforts of Lindsay, Howe, Abel
and Kelly. It barely seemed creditable that this was the same
man whom Detroit snipers had beaten for forty-seven goals
in fourteen regular season matches.

And yet, if possible, Sawchuk played even better than
McNeil this night. He stopped forty-six shots, four more
than his rival. The rookies battled through a scoreless deadlock that stretched into a third overtime before lightning
struck Detroit a second time. Just after midnight, Richard
and centre Billy Reay swept in on Sawchuk. Reay faked a
shot, leaving Terry off balance, and then passed to the
Rocket. Richard saw an opening and fired for the game's
only goal.

"He's the greatest I've faced since I started playing hockey," Sawchuk said of Richard. "I've got no excuses. When
you're all alone with him you just don't know what to do.
When he beat me in the first game he made me make the
first move. In the second game I came out a bit to cover the
angle and he still beat me with a low shot into the corner. I
still don't know how he could have found that corner."

Jack Adams remained undaunted by the prospect of his
Wings having to win four of the next five games to move
on to the Cup final. "McNeil has been hot as a pistol in the
first two games," said Adams. "He'll have to stay that way
if Canadiens are going to beat us and I don't think he can.
Nobody could."

But the Montreal fans had their blood up. One newspaper columnist described the city as completely hockey mad; "madder than at any time in the history of hockey here." Scalpers were asking fifty dollars for a pair of tickets before the start of game three on Saturday night.

Gordie Howe had observed his last birthday while lying in a Detroit hospital bed recovering from life-threatening head injuries. His twenty-third birthday celebration on Saturday night proved a more festive occasion. Howe waltzed in on McNeil late in the second period, faked a shot that dropped the goalie to his knees, and then fired the goal that put Detroit back in the series. Sid Abel brought the final score to 2-0 in the third period when he beat McNeil with a smoking drive from about twenty feet out.

Sawchuk's first playoff shutout was well earned. The Canadiens outshot the Wings 31-24, forcing Terry to produce outstanding saves on Richard, Doug Harvey, Bert Olmstead, Billy Reay, Paul Meger and Floyd Curry. The action around the Wing net became so intense during the third period that Adams, mindful of his blood pressure, left the rink to wander the streets surrounding the Forum. He only returned when a taxi driver told him that Detroit had won.

The momentum appeared to have swung over to Detroit. The Wings won the next one 4-1 to square the series. Though Sawchuk faced just twenty-three shots, most of them routine, Adams magnanimously insisted on giving him credit for the victory. "It was the kid who pulled us through tonight," he told newsmen. "We're back in it again."

Adams was less pleased with Terry's performance when the series resumed in Detroit for game five. His whiff of a fifty-five-foot slap shot by rookie Bernie "Boom Boom" Geoffrion in the second period enabled the Canadiens to take a 3-2 lead. Geoffrion's goal turned the tide. Richard and Cal MacKay beat Terry in the third period to put away the game 5-2.

So far neither team had won on home ice, which was especially frustrating for the Wings. Detroit had lost only three times at the Olympia during the regular season. But the turnabout did raise their hopes heading into the crucial sixth game in Montreal, a match remembered by those who were there as one of the greatest hockey games ever played.

Not one penalty was called by referee Bill Chadwick. Through the first two scoreless periods, the advantage swung from one team to the other. The pace was breakneck, the checking hard but clean. Sawchuk and McNeil each produced a half-dozen or more unbelievable saves until suddenly, in the third period, there was an explosion of scoring. Montreal's Billy Reay struck first, at 6:49. Abel tied it less than a minute later. Soon after, the Habs regained the lead when Richard swung out quickly from behind the net and jammed the puck into the cage between the goalpost and Sawchuk's skate. Kenny Mosdell padded Montreal's advantage by scoring on a breakaway at 15:45.

Detroit desperately fought back. At 19:15, Lindsay scored during a scramble in front of the net. The roaring, frenzied audience of 14,448 was on its feet. Tommy Ivan pulled Sawchuk and Detroit continued to press until, with just six seconds left, a face-off was called in the Canadiens' zone. Elmer Lach beat Abel on the draw, feeding the puck back to defenceman Doug Harvey, who still held it when the buzzer sounded.

"It's unbelievable, but it's true," said Jack Adams, who sweated out the final few minutes of action alone in the Wing dressing room. "Who would ever have believed Montreal would knock us out of the playoffs after we finished eighteen games ahead of them over the season?"

Montreal would go on to battle Toronto in a fiercely contested five-game Cup final that saw every match go into overtime. The season ended on a spectacular goal by Toronto defenceman Bill Barilko, a moment made even more memorable by Barilko's death weeks later in an airplane crash.

Sawchuk, against all reason, would always blame himself for Detroit's defeat. He was crying by the time he got to the dressing room, where Adams put his arms around him and gave him a consoling hug. "It's not your fault, Terry," he said firmly. "You gave your best."

"Thanks, Mr. Adams," Sawchuk managed through his tears.

That May, the league office in Montreal announced the results of the voting for the Calder Memorial Trophy. Sawchuk was the near unanimous choice of the selectors, polling fifty-one votes out of a possible fifty-four. Al Rollins, with twenty-six points, placed second.

Terry thus completed what was described as a Rookie-of-the-Year Grand Slam. No one had ever before swept the freshman honours in hockey's top three professional leagues.

## Chapter Three

# THE GREATEST

"TILT!" Sawchuk joked when the scale in the trainers' room rested at 219 on the opening day of training camp in Sault Ste. Marie, Michigan.

That was at least ten pounds more than his playing weight during his sensational rookie campaign. "Something's wrong," he protested. "I weighed only 211 when I left home a week ago, and I've been eating like a sparrow since. Unless you count milkshakes."

Jack Adams didn't find the situation nearly so amusing as his netminder. If the kid was already having this much trouble keeping the pounds off, Adams wondered, how difficult would the struggle be in a few years' time?

Plump as the proverbial Thanksgiving goose himself, with jowls that fell in rolls over his shirt collar, Adams had never favoured chubby goaltenders. It was said that one of the reasons he'd finally decided to trade away Harry Lumley and make room for Sawchuk was Lumley's tendency to put on weight too easily. Good as Sawchuk already was, it seemed logical that he'd be even quicker and more agile if he were a few pounds lighter. Fitness expert Lloyd Percival, who had put Terry and the rest of the Wings through a barrage of tests the season before, was convinced that diet and exercise would help the boy fully live up to his extraordinary potential.

Adams ordered that Terry be put on a crash no-starch diet—no bread, no potatoes, no pastry. "In fact, not much of anything I like," Sawchuk soon complained. He said that what hurt most was having to forgo pizza pies, for which he had recently developed an insatiable appetite. To help curb his hunger pangs, he smoked a pack of cigarettes every three or four days.

The diet-or-else edict genuinely frightened Terry. There were 120 players employed in the six-team NHL, and not more than six or possibly seven of them were goalies. At that moment future Hall of Fame netminders Jacques Plante, Johnny Bower and Gump Worsley all impatiently awaited promotion in the minors.

Behind Sawchuk in the Detroit system was twenty-year-old Glenn Hall, a standout that year for Indianapolis in his first campaign as a pro. Terry's old coach Ott Heller was already saying that Hall was going to be one of the great ones.

Having himself been the cause of Harry Lumley's departure from the then reigning Stanley Cup champions to the worst team in the league, Sawchuk knew all too well that even the most highly regarded goalie could be replaced. He vowed that what had happened to Lumley wouldn't happen to him—at least not for the lack of willpower required to shed the pounds demanded by Adams.

Ten weeks later, with Detroit reporters on hand for the official weigh-in, a startlingly leaner Sawchuk stepped back onto the scales at the Olympia.

"See, Jack," he said proudly to a beaming Adams. "Why, these scales say 193, and I didn't think I was an ounce over 192 and a half today."

By this point early in the season it already seemed clear that Lloyd Percival had been right all along. Once the pounds started to fall away, Sawchuk did indeed appear to be quicker and more acrobatic than ever. His extraordinary goaltending helped the Wings jump out to a quick—and what would prove to be a permanent—lead in the standings. The new, streamlined Terry was headed for possibly the single greatest season ever enjoyed by a goaltender.

One of the unexpected benefits of the diet was that he no longer felt tired at the end of a game, as he sometimes had the season before when he'd carried the extra weight.

"I guess it must be for the best," Terry said resignedly of his new regimen. "I know I'm playing better hockey this year. But I get so darn hungry all the time."

Those who knew him well came to look back at the diet as one of the turning points in Sawchuk's life. That season a moodiness began to emerge that hadn't been seen before except, occasionally, when he was drinking. In the past he had almost always been good natured and carefree—a "big, happy puppy," as Max McNab described him. Now he was less likely to join in locker-room horseplay. His teammates' jokes didn't seem nearly as funny to him as they used to and, because he couldn't afford the calories, he didn't always accompany them for a beer and a sandwich after a game, as he had in his rookie year. More often he preferred his own company.

Reporters on the hockey beat also noted the changes. Terry began to ignore requests for interviews. Or he gave their questions terse one- or two-word answers. In the words of *The Toronto Star*'s Milt Dunnell, "his sunshine seemed to go with his suet."

Obviously, Sawchuk's rapid weight loss was not the sole factor in turning him into an often morose and unhappy man. Though the transformation was gradual, there can be no doubt that the diet triggered what eventually became a dramatic change in Terry's personality. Five years later, when Sawchuk was at one of the physical and emotional low points of his career, no less an authority than his mother traced the roots of his problems back to this period. Since the diet, Anne Sawchuk said with certainty, her son had never been the same.

To no one's surprise, Trader Jack responded to Detroit's upset loss to Montreal the previous spring with a vigorous reshaping of his line-up. In the years ahead Adams would be justly criticized for many of his trades. But the Wing boss had not yet lost his Midas touch. A rapid-fire series of summertime transactions combined with the addition of talented youngsters from Detroit's deep minor-league system transformed an already formidable hockey club into one that is now remembered as possibly the greatest in hockey history.

The dealing started with the departure of aging scoring star Gaye Stewart to the New York Rangers in return for combative little forward Tony Leswick. Then goaltender Sugar Jim Henry, who ranked no better than third in the organization behind Sawchuk and Hall, was sold to Boston. Next Adams negotiated the largest cash deal for players to that point in NHL history, shipping six familiar faces—George Gee, Jim McFadden, Jimmy Peters, Clare Martin, Max McNab and Clare Raglan—to Chicago for $75,000 in cash.

When the dust cleared, only six players remained behind from the club that had won the Stanley Cup in 1949–50. Replacements for the departed veterans included Terry's old roomie, defenceman Benny Woit, and forwards Johnny Wilson, Fred Glover and Alex Delvecchio, every one a home-grown product.

Adams considered Delvecchio, just nineteen, the prize of the litter, describing him as Detroit's best prospect since Gordie Howe. The year before, Delvecchio had scored forty-nine goals for the Junior A Oshawa Generals. After just two weeks of professional seasoning with Indianapolis, he was deemed ready for the big club.

The addition of the new attackers produced the balanced offence Adams had long sought. Up front the Production

Line was still expected to carry the load. The difference now was that Detroit had an excellent chance of winning even on those rare nights when Howe, Lindsay and Abel were shut down by the opposition. The second and third lines were faster and more gifted around the net than ever before.

Teamed with Metro Prystai and Marty Pavelich on the second unit, Leswick, who stood just five foot six and weighed 155 pounds, quickly became one of the sparkplugs of the club. Leswick specialized in needling opponents first into distraction, then fury and, finally, into the penalty box. And when he dropped his gloves, Tough Tony was one of the most feared brawlers in the game. During his six years in the league (all with New York), Leswick had fought the ferocious Maurice Richard an estimated fifteen times and, on balance, given as good as he received.

Even Jack Adams professed surprise at the club's quick start and by how quickly and smoothly his rookies fit in. "I never in my best dreams thought we'd get away this season as we have," he said after the Wings won ten and tied four of their first seventeen games. "I really thought we'd be feeling our way around in the early part, and if we did get hot it would be after the first of the year."

By the start of the New Year, Detroit enjoyed a twelve-point lead over second-place Toronto, a comfort zone that would never fall below eight and which by season's end became a twenty-two-point landslide over Montreal, who had moved past the Leafs into second spot.

Adams and Tommy Ivan were quick to give most of the credit for the club's success to their newly slimmed-down goaltender. Though growing hungrier and glummer by the day, Terry had never played better. Remarkably, his goals-against average remained under two the entire campaign. Neither Al Rollins nor anyone else gave him a serious chase in the Vezina race.

At twenty-one going on twenty-two, Sawchuk was often still an awestruck kid who sometimes had a hard time believing that he was tending goal for the famous Detroit Red Wings, and that there in the flesh at the opposite end of the rink stood Turk Broda or Charlie Rayner.

"Although he works at a man's job, Sawchuk has all the mannerisms and characteristics of a guileless, unsophisticated boy," a reporter wrote that winter. Early in the season an awesome performance by New York's Charlie Rayner produced a 1-0 shutout over Detroit that ended a record-tying string of fifteen consecutive road wins. At the final buzzer Sawchuk spontaneously broke through the swarm of Rangers hugging and pounding the back of their goaltender to personally congratulate his boyhood hero.

"Chuck Rayner is the best, that's all," Terry practically gushed in the dressing room. "When I was a boy, all I wanted to be was a Rayner. It's a great thrill playing against a man you used to idolize, and when he comes up with that kind of performance, well, you just feel you've got to say something."

As Rayner and Broda approached the end of their careers, Sawchuk clearly emerged as the top goaler in the game. Around the league his acclamation was nearly unanimous. Only Toronto boss Conn Smythe, who was loath to give credit to anyone who wore the hated winged wheel, offered a serious objection.

Detroit goalies *always* look better than the competition, Smythe insisted, because of the team's emphasis on defensive play. "You see, they teach a player how to stop the other fellow from scoring before they teach him to score himself. That's the way to do it. I'm not finding fault with the system; I just say that's why their goalies always look good."

Smythe made a strong point about the relationship between team defence and a netminder's success. One of hockey's biggest stories that winter was the sudden stardom of thirty-one-year-old netminder Sugar Jim Henry after Adams traded him to Boston. In two previous shots at the big time, with weak New York and Chicago squads, Henry was found wanting and sent back to the minors. Now, behind a solid Bruins defence of Bill Quackenbush, Gus Kyle, Hal Laycoe and Bob Armstrong, Henry looked like the reincarnation of Georges Vezina.

Sawchuk happily acknowledged his own good fortune. "Not only do we have five fine defencemen, but the ten forwards are just as important on defence with their backchecking," he said at mid-season. "In other words, keeping out goals is a sixteen-man job on this team."

If anything, the five defenders responsible for Sawchuk's personal safety performed even better than the year before. The blue-line quarterback, Red Kelly, was enjoying one of his finest seasons. Reliable as ever were wily veterans Leo Reise and Bob Goldham. Playing his first full season, Marcel Pronovost combined a love of the rough stuff with an ability to, like Kelly, instantly turn onto the attack and orchestrate thrilling rink-length rushes. Burly 192-pound Bashin' Benny Woit was a fearsome presence whenever Tommy Ivan sent him in to spell off one of the regulars.

"Sawchuk only got half the number of tough chances that other goalies did," remembers Leo Reise with pride. "We felt we hadn't done our jobs if the other team was able to break in for more than four or five good scoring opportunities a night."

"Even if they did get through," adds Benny Woit, "Sawchuk was so great that he almost always made the save."

By now Sawchuk and his defencemen enjoyed the benefit of having worked together for more than a full season. "The extra year of playing behind them has helped me a lot in knowing what to expect," Terry said. "It's a marvel the way they cover me now on passouts from the side and back of the net. Those are the most dangerous passes in setting up goals."

A code had been worked out that helped him direct the play inside the Detroit blue line. When he yelled "Go ahead," it meant the way was clear to carry out the puck. "Heads up" signalled that an opponent was coming up fast from the rear. "Hold it" told a defenceman that he was surrounded and should freeze the puck along the boards or against the back of the net for a face-off.

"Red and Marcel keep a lot of heat off me," Sawchuk said of his two rushing defencemen. "When they're on the ice, the other team has to worry about them as if they were forwards. Leo, Bob and Benny block a lot of shots which I never have to handle. Goldham is a real master at dropping to his knees to take those long shots head on."

Most nights, Goldham acted as almost a second goal-tender, blocking nearly as many shots as Sawchuk. His technique, taught to him ten years before by Bucko McDonald during Goldham's rookie season with Toronto, was to go down on both knees while extending his arms on either side.

"Bucko told me the main tip," recalled Goldham. "Watch a forward's shooting shoulder, and when it drops, he's going to shoot."

An old dispute involving Goldham's mentor Bucko McDonald was at the heart of Conn Smythe's hatred of the Red Wings and his cynicism about Sawchuk's goaltending abilities. The troubles began back in 1934 when Smythe and Adams shared a compartment during a train trip to New York. At first the two got along famously. Smythe, who had a gargantuan ego, appreciated how Adams constantly deferred to his opinions and laughed uproariously at all of his jokes. He felt certain he had found a new friend.

But the wily Adams was simply playing his pigeon. Lulled into carelessness, Smythe eventually let slip the name of a muscular young defenceman he had been keeping his eye on, the self-same Bucko McDonald.

When he returned to his office in Toronto, Smythe discovered to his everlasting fury that Adams had already wired the league office in Montreal and placed McDonald on Detroit's "list," which meant that no other team could sign him. McDonald went on to help Detroit win two Stanley Cups before Adams finally agreed to sell him to Smythe in 1938.

That initial skirmish sparked both the bitter personal feud between Smythe and Adams as well as the legendary rivalry between the Maple Leafs and Red Wings, which had now flamed for almost two decades.

Epic battles had been fought by the two teams down through the years. When they met in the 1942 Stanley Cup finals, Detroit won the first three games before the Leafs regrouped and charged back to tie the series. Adams became so upset by the turn of events that after one Leaf victory he hopped the boards and pummelled the referee in frustration.

Smythe, who had joined the Canadian Army with the acting rank of major and was then posted to a base in rural Ontario, urgently requested leave to travel to Toronto for the final game. His team down 1-0 after two periods, Smythe rallied his troops during a famous second-intermission harangue. The Leafs charged back to score three third-period goals and win the game, thus becoming the only team in history to capture the Stanley Cup after dropping the first three games of a final series.

Toronto downed the Red Wings again in the 1945 final, and beat them in the playoffs every spring while winning three straight Stanley Cups from 1947 to 1949.

The long struggle reached a climax of sorts during the bloody 1950 semi-final series won by Detroit in seven games. Those who were there say there has never been a more violent playoff series, or one in which two teams have so unabashedly displayed their mutual hatred.

The Red Wings had a saying in those days: "We play everybody else for the money we get, but the Leafs we'd play for free."

Toronto stood in second place, four points back of Detroit when, at the Olympia on Sunday, December 2 of Sawchuk's sophomore season, the battle began anew. A savage check by Toronto defenceman Gus Mortson sent Freddy Glover tumbling into the boards. Pushing led to shoving and then other players rushed to join in. Watching from his box seat just above the Detroit bench, Jack Adams was certain that through the mêlée he saw Mortson viciously kick out at Glover with his skate.

When it was announced that Mortson had been issued only a minor penalty for "roughing," Adams dashed clean around the perimeter of the rink to the penalty box where he interrupted the proceedings for several more minutes while he berated referee George Gavel.

"One of the most vicious and cowardly attacks I have ever witnessed during my years in the league," huffed Adams.

"A loser's squawk," countered Toronto coach Joe Primeau, whose Leafs held on to win this round by a score of 2-1.

Sawchuk, the most combative of goalies, always ready to mix it up with players who crashed into his crease or to climb into the stands after an abusive fan, made certain he got in his licks against the Leafs a few nights later during the rematch in Toronto. Terry and Ted Kennedy exchanged hot words after Sawchuk reached out his stick and hooked the Leaf captain to the back of the net. They squared off but were held back by teammates. Then Terry offered to meet Kennedy after the game to settle their differences.

It was the sort of challenge often issued during the heat of a hockey match—and almost always promptly forgotten. But never between Maple Leafs and Red Wings. At the conclusion of a 2-2 draw, Sawchuk and Kennedy went for each other in the corridor used by both teams to get to their dressing rooms.

Only the intervention of a burly Toronto policeman, a champion at tossing cabers and other heavy objects during the annual Police Games, spoiled the fun.

Conn Smythe was one of the few hockey bigwigs who sent his regrets for a testimonial dinner that January 22 in honour of Jack Adams's silver anniversary as general manager of the Red Wings. A sell-out at twenty-five dollars a plate, the gala packed 375 guests into the largest banquet hall at Detroit's plush Sheraton-Cadillac Hotel. Attendees included Montreal's Frank Selke, Chicago's Bill Tobin, Boston president Walter Brown, New York general manager Frank Boucher and league president Clarence Campbell.

Also on hand was the entire Detroit hockey club, whose record of three consecutive league championships and their soaring success to that point in the current campaign reflected so well on the guest of honour.

There were the usual corny jokes. Al Sutphin, a former owner of Cleveland's entry in the American Hockey League, recalled that Adams had promised to "save" hockey players to help stock his team. "And he did...he saved them until they were forty years old. But I want to say this about Jack, he always sent a wheelchair along with them."

Soon it was time for Adams, whose personality included

a wide streak of Irish sentimentality, to take the microphone and tearily reminisce about the years of toil that had gone into the building of the great franchise.

Adams said his time with the team could be divided into three phases. "First, there were four years of fair prosperity. Second, there was the Depression, and tough times for all of us. We rode day coaches and ate sandwiches. If Howie Morenz had been for sale for $1.87, we still couldn't have bought him."

Just when things looked their bleakest, he said, along came James Norris to save the franchise. "There has been reams written about what that has meant and our relationship. I know that hockey can never repay Mr. Norris for the way he has built up the Detroit team, and also for how he has dug into his pocket several times just to keep the game going in other cities."

Adams was in no way exaggerating the influence wielded by his boss, who had to miss the dinner when his flight from New York was cancelled by a snowstorm. While managing to keep a remarkably low public profile, Norris had quickly become the most powerful force in the NHL following his purchase of the Olympia and the bankrupt Red Wings for $100,000 in 1932.

Three years later Norris bought Chicago Stadium and, in 1944, added the Black Hawks to his portfolio. During the hard years of the Depression Norris also underwrote several mortgages taken out by Boston president Charles Adams (no relation to Jack), a favour that left Adams and the Bruins firmly in his sway. As well, Norris accumulated a major voting block of stock in Madison Square Garden, home of the New York Rangers.

Norris, then, had full or effective control over four of the six NHL clubs. "The NHL...expressly forbade multiple ownership," wrote the authors of *Net Worth*, "but the

League allowed a corporation rather than an individual to be named as owner. Conveniently, the rules didn't require the disclosure of who was behind those company names."

Loud, brash and huge, Norris stood six feet, two inches tall and weighed as much as three hundred pounds. His family had made its fortune by building a fleet of cargo ships that plied the Great Lakes. Norris based himself in Chicago and expanded into flour and roller mills, and speculated on the grain market and in real estate. His personal fortune was estimated to be one of the largest in the United States.

Big Jim, as he was widely known, had been a fair hockey player during his university days in Montreal. Although he never managed to muster much interest in the other clubs he controlled (of the four, only Detroit had thus far built a productive farm system), Norris lavished money and attention on his beloved Red Wings. In the early days he evaluated the rookies during training camps and oversaw the signing of contracts. Whenever his busy schedule permitted, Norris was in attendance during home games at the Olympia, his booming voice unmistakable among the cheers of the crowd.

Also prominent in the management of the Red Wings was Norris's eldest son, James Dougan Norris, known as Little Jim. A charming rogue cut in the same larger-than-life mould as his father, the younger Norris loved to play the horses and enjoyed the company of gangsters. His personal bodyguard was a former mob hitman, Sammy "Golfbag" Hunt, so-called because he carried his machine-gun in a golf bag and was said to holler "Fore" before every execution. Little Jim eventually became president of the Black Hawks and the most powerful fight promoter in the United States.

From about 1945 on when doctors ordered him to stay away from games because of a weak heart, Norris insisted that no matter where he was—working late in his Chicago office, at any one of several residences throughout the country, or cruising on his yacht in the Caribbean—Adams must telephone him after every game with news of how the team had fared. Often for hours into the night, they discussed everything from the club's chances of signing a hot junior prospect to an impending multi-player trade.

"In my whole life, I've never been criticized by him about a deal," said Trader Jack. "If it goes sour—and a lot of them do—he just shrugs it off and observes that we all agreed on it, so what."

By the time of Adams's silver anniversary, Big Jim's heart condition had worsened and he had less than a year to live. Most of his remaining energy was spent in planning the division of his estate among his four children—Jim Jr., Bruce and daughters Eleanor and Marguerite.

He had become almost a phantom figure around the hockey club, out of sight for months at a time. So there was considerable surprise when one night that January Norris was waiting to greet the players in the dressing room before a game in Chicago. He had driven through a snowstorm from his home in Lake Forest, Illinois, to spend just a few minutes with them. When they clomped out for the opening whistle, Norris slowly walked back to his car and drove home.

"Mr. Norris is seventy-two, but he knows every player on the roster," Adams said at his anniversary bash. "He gave me a great argument about eleven o'clock last night about why we should bring up a player now in the minors."

When he had finished talking, Adams received dozens of gifts, including a new Lincoln Continental and, from his players, a silver tea and coffee set. Making the presentation on behalf of the Wings was captain Sid Abel who, having married the boss's former secretary, had perhaps more reason than any of his teammates to be grateful to the star of the evening.

A position among the game's immortals is almost always achieved through years of sustained excellence. As the recipient of rookie-of-the-year honours in the top three professional leagues, Sawchuk had undeniably made a good start. Having been named the All-Star goalie in his first NHL season also boosted his growing stature.

But thanks to Frank Boucher, general manager of the New York Rangers, Sawchuk found himself launched on an unprecedented wave of media hype that all but secured his place in the pantheon.

Boucher said flat out that Sawchuk wasn't just a good goalie, or even a great one, but already the best who had ever played the game. "There simply isn't any question about it—Terry Sawchuk is the greatest goalie in history," Boucher said the night after Adams's testimonial. Boucher had stayed on in Detroit to watch the Maple Leafs play the Red Wings to a thrilling 2-2 draw, a game in which Sawchuk had been at his most phenomenal.

"Oh, I know what some of the old-timers are going to say," he continued. "That Sawchuk is just a kid and has to stand the test of time...that you have to judge over a period of years to determine greatness. But I'm sure that they'll be saying the same thing about Sawchuk years from now."

This wasn't just any man's opinion. Boucher had been involved in the game for thirty years as an All-Star player, a coach and an executive. It was at his insistence that the centre red line had been introduced in 1943-44, a brilliant innovation that dramatically sped up the tempo of the game.

Boucher marvelled at Sawchuk's innovative crouch, a technique he felt certain would be copied by a generation of young netminders. The crouch, he said, enabled Sawchuk to routinely block low shots that other netminders had to flop to the ice to cover. And when he did fall to his knees, Terry's reflexes were so quick that he could bounce right back into position.

Forget Vezina, Hainsworth, Brimsek, Durnan or any other goalie from the past, Boucher insisted. There was absolutely no doubt in his mind that Sawchuk was better. "As for the modern goalie stars, just look up their records and Sawchuk's and see what they say."

Reporters rushed to Sawchuk for his reaction. Naturally, he was surprised by Boucher's comments—and, predictably, a little uncomfortable and embarrassed by all the attention.

"Did he really say that?" Terry asked quietly. "It was nice of him to say so."

In a little over one and a half seasons in the league, Sawchuk had not only arrived as one of the game's marquee players, but he had been stamped as something unique, a goalie unlike any who had come before. Interviewers sought him out at every stop on the six-city circuit. That winter prestigious *Sport* magazine, which would name Sawchuk hockey's top performer for 1951-52, ran an in-depth profile entitled "Hockey's New Mr. Zero" in reference to his penchant for recording shutouts. Boston's Frankie Brimsek had been the old Mr. Zero.

The profile's author, Al Silverman, found Terry a difficult subject to warm to. "When you first meet Sawchuk, he is apt to impress you as being somewhat gruff, as if he were trying to get on top of you, beat you to the puck, if you like, the way he does on the ice."

Terry confided to Silverman that he stayed away from reading and the movies during the hockey season for fear of damaging his eyesight. After games, he said, he was usually unable to sleep for two or three hours from nervous tension. "Sometimes after a real tough game, I don't get to sleep at all."

Maurice Richard, Boston's Milt Schmidt, the Toronto line of Ted Kennedy, Sid Smith and Tod Sloan, and Don Raleigh of the Rangers were the shooters who gave him the most trouble. Of Richard, he said: "No matter where he shoots from, it's always on the net. His backhand's even tougher than his forehand, and he shoots a heavy puck. When you stop it, it feels like it's going through you."

Just days after Boucher made his comments, a survey of all six NHL coaches found Sawchuk their unanimous choice as the top goaltender. That wasn't a surprise. What was startling was another unanimous selection, Gordie Howe at right wing. Not one coach, not even Dick Irvin, chose Maurice Richard at the position. Just a year before, the debate over who was better had been regarded as a toss-up.

To be fair, it had been an unusually troubled campaign for the Rocket, who missed twenty-two games due to a combination of stress, exhaustion and a lingering groin injury.

Howe led the league again in scoring, with forty-seven goals and thirty-nine assists, and collected his first Hart Trophy as most valuable player. Sawchuk tied with Milt Schmidt for fourth in the Hart voting. Elmer Lach placed second, while Sugar Jim Henry, on the strength of his remarkable comeback, held down third spot.

There were no last-minute Vezina dramatics this year. Once again playing the full seventy-game schedule, Sawchuk posted a goals-against average of 1.90, compared to the 2.22 of runner-up Al Rollins. Terry's twelve shutouts bettered by one his own modern record set the year before.

When the writers and broadcasters cast their All-Star votes, they made Sawchuk their unanimous choice for the first squad, as were teammates Gordie Howe and Red Kelly.

Ted Lindsay also made the team—but Terrible Ted proved too unpopular in enemy cities to similarly sweep the ballots. All four Wings were holdovers from the season before.

There was tremendous pressure on the Red Wings to continue the success of their regular season on into the playoffs. Detroit's unexpected semi-final loss to Montreal the previous spring had been a bitter disappointment to the fans and everyone connected with the club. Despite the Stanley Cup victory in 1949-50, the Red Wings were gaining an unenviable reputation as a poor playoff team.

Of all the Wings, Sawchuk was perhaps the most anxious to prove himself in the post-season. In interviews he continued to insist that he had been primarily responsible for last year's upset.

Opposing Detroit in the opening round were the despised Maple Leafs. Toronto had finished in third place, four points behind Montreal and twenty-six points back of the Wings. Though the defending Stanley Cup champions had posted the best record of any club against Detroit during the regular season (four wins and four ties against six losses), the Wings knew they could easily beat Toronto if they refused to be goaded into losing their composure by old animosities.

As expected, the Leafs tried to bash Detroit into submission during a brawl-filled opener at the Olympia. Leaf Fern Flaman and Sid Abel tussled early in the 3-0 Detroit victory, prompting Conn Smythe to accuse the Wings of deliberately attempting to reinjure his defenceman, who was still recovering from a broken cheekbone.

"Why would we try to get him out? He's our best player—our seventh man," sneered Ted Lindsay of Flaman, who was on the ice for all three Detroit goals.

Already convinced the Leafs were overmatched and in need of a miracle to win the series, Smythe tapped thirty-seven-year-old Turk Broda to replace Al Rollins for the second game. Balding and overweight, Broda saw action in part of just one game during the regular schedule. But the other Toronto players regarded him as a good-luck charm. Through ninety-nine previous playoff matches he had backstopped the Leafs to five Stanley Cups while earning a reputation as the game's stingiest goalie when playoff money was on the line. At a testimonial dinner for Broda earlier in the season, Smythe had promised him a chance to conclude his career with an even one hundred post-season appearances.

Smythe's strategy very nearly worked. Toronto's defence erected an almost impenetrable wall around their pudgy talisman, who faced no more than five or six tough chances the entire game. Only Johnny Wilson managed to break through and beat him, at 15:33 of the first period.

The difference this night was the remarkable effort put forth by the considerably younger man in the opposite net. "Turk had to take second place to that fast-moving young giant, Terry Sawchuk," observed Red Burnett in *The Toronto Star*. "Terry acted like he was triplets. He swooped from side to side, jumped up and down as if on a pogo stick, and fielded shots like a Phil Rizzuto."

Sawchuk made twenty-two saves to preserve his second-straight shutout. In the second period he robbed Ted Kennedy twice, Harry Watson twice more, and produced a foot save on Sid Smith that came to be regarded as the most spectacular stop of the playoffs.

Speedy little Max Bentley started the play on the Smith save by darting over the blue line and slipping past a Detroit defender. At the same time, Smith streaked for the net. "I figured Max would try to deke me," Sawchuk recounted. "I made up my mind not to move. Bentley faked me, then passed across to Smith, who let a shot go. It was really labelled, but I managed to kick in time to stop it with my foot."

Terry confirmed what was already obvious to anyone who watched his performance. "I feel a lot better this year than I did in last season's playoffs," he said. "I felt nervous and jittery a year ago but feel right at home now."

Smythe sent Broda out again when the series resumed before a Saturday-night crowd in Toronto. But in the final game of his fourteen-year career, the Turk showed only his age and Detroit romped to a 6-2 victory.

Even with his team so clearly in control, Adams took nothing for granted, not when the Leafs were involved. He fretted publicly about the danger of his team becoming overconfident. "I still can't forget 1942 when we beat the Leafs in three straight, then lost the series."

The Wings put his fears to rest and completed the sweep with a 3-1 decision in Toronto. This time Sawchuk astonished the crowd by doing the splits and grabbing a sizzling drive off the stick of Tod Sloan. "That's my boy," Jack Adams shouted happily in the dressing room as he embraced Terry and playfully patted his hair for the photographers. "I'll tell you, it helps when you've got a kid like that out there. The greatest in hockey."

The Wings had looked awesome in becoming the first Detroit team to take out Toronto four-straight in playoff action. Sawchuk and his stingy defence yielded just three goals.

Perhaps even more impressive was the overall balance of the Red Wing attack, the added dimension that had emerged from Adams's line-up changes before the start of the season. It didn't matter so much that Gordie Howe was held scoreless in the series, not with rookie Johnny Wilson contributing four goals to lead both teams in scoring.

Detroit rested and waited nine days while the overmatched but dogged Boston Bruins extended Montreal to a seventh game in the other semi-final series. Then it took the most spectacular of all Maurice Richard's patented playoff miracles to finally settle the outcome.

Incredibly, Richard's heroics came after he had been knocked unconscious in a second-period collision with Bruin defenceman Bill Quackenbush. The score was tied 1-1 late in the third period when the Rocket returned to action. Blood streaming down his face, Richard took possession of the puck and outraced or bulled his way through every Bruin on the ice before cutting in front of Sugar Jim Henry and unleashing a low drive that caught the corner of the net.

While his teammates noisily celebrated around him, Richard sat in the Canadiens' dressing room holding his aching head in his hands. He claimed to have only a hazy memory of what had happened. "I heard the crowd yell," he said, "and by that time I was too dizzy even to see."

Richard's goal set the stage for the rematch fervently desired by every Red Wing. The memory of the six-game upset inflicted on them by Montreal the year before remained an open sore.

"They were knocked off by Canadiens last year and that's the blow that will send them roaring into the playoffs this year," Conn Smythe predicted. "They're not going to forget for a minute what happened last spring." Bookmakers pegged the Red Wings as 9 to 5 favourites, the same odds given at the start of the Toronto series.

And yet Montreal coach Dick Irvin maintained a haughty disregard for his Stanley Cup opponents. Earlier in the season he had announced that the Wings were the team he *hoped* to meet in the playoffs. He said his Habs would have a tougher time beating Toronto.

Irvin's optimism persisted even though the Canadiens were exhausted and their ranks decimated by injuries sustained in the gruelling Boston series. Centres Kenny

Mosdell and Johnny McCormack had both been knocked out of action and several other key players were among the walking wounded.

Irvin was convinced that Sawchuk—season-long rave reviews to the contrary—would prove to be Detroit's weakest link. He predicted that the youngster would crack under the spotlight of a final series, believing that Terry, like every other sensible goalie in the league, was spooked by the Rocket, who had beaten him for four goals in the series the year before.

The Canadiens' coach also claimed to have detected a potential weak spot in Terry's armour—up high on his right side, where his damaged elbow presumably slowed his reflexes.

Sawchuk neither cracked, nor spooked, nor displayed any sign of his so-called weakness on high shots when the series got underway in Montreal. Detroit had waived its right to the home-ice advantage due to a scheduling conflict at the Olympia.

While the Wings struggled to regain their game legs after the long layoff, Montreal pressed the attack from the opening face-off. But the Habs, playing on just forty-eight hours' rest, couldn't quite finish their set-ups. Dickie Moore muffed a goalmouth pass, Geoffrion shaved a backhander off the goalpost, and Richard lost control of the puck after breaking through the defence. Then Sawchuk robbed Billy Reay from close in and made several more outstanding saves before the close of the first period.

The eagerly anticipated renewal of the Howe-Richard rivalry proved a dud on opening night. The Rocket, though a constant threat, failed to score. Neither could Howe, whose playoff famine was extended to five games.

Soon the momentum swung over to Detroit. Tony

Leswick, who had a habit of saving his best games for the playoffs, fired two goals past Gerry McNeil before the Habs' Tom Johnson finally beat Sawchuk on a rebound midway through the third period.

The Canadiens maintained the pressure. Terry produced game-saving stops on Richard and Geoffrion. Finally, when Irvin pulled McNeil for an extra attacker, Ted Lindsay put an insurance goal into the empty Montreal net to complete a 3-1 victory.

Just one more goal would get by Sawchuk that season. Having by now shaken off the rust of their long layoff, the Wings took charge of the series in the second game. Blessed with balance, depth, skill and an ideal blend of youth and experience, Detroit possessed too much of everything to be beaten by a squad as worn down and ravaged by injuries as the Canadiens.

Montreal's final tally came on a power play late in the first period of game two when Elmer Lach converted Geoffrion's screened drive from the point. Lach's goal briefly tied the game following an earlier score by Marty Pavelich. After Lindsay put Detroit ahead 2-1 soon after the start of the second period, hockey's tightest defence closed ranks and the score remained frozen until the final buzzer.

At no point did any member of the Red Wings harbour even the slightest doubt about the eventual outcome of the series. "It was almost eerie," Johnny Wilson recalls. "Everything was meshing so perfectly. Everyone was so completely focused. When we'd get on that bus in Toledo to make the drive to the Olympia, you could hear a pin drop. We just *knew* we were going to win."

"The way we were playing," said Gordie Howe, "I think we could have won thirty-five straight."

Whatever remaining hope Irvin and his Canadiens had managed to cling to was dashed in game three at the

Olympia when Howe finally ended his scoring drought.

Howe scored twice and assisted on another by Ted Lindsay in leading the Wings to a 3-0 victory. His first goal early in the opening period was a work of sheer artistry. Moving in slowly from the point during a power play, Howe stickhandled his way around one Canadien player after another. Refusing to be moved off the puck, he waited patiently until McNeil was screened and then, from ten feet out, unloaded a backhander into an upper corner of the net.

Sawchuk made twenty-six saves in recording his first shutout of the final and his third in the seven games of the playoffs. At one point he robbed the line of Paul Masnick, Paul Meger and Bernie Geoffrion three times in a span of seconds.

Montreal mustered one last charge in an all-out effort to avoid the humiliation of a sweep and deny Detroit the distinction of becoming the first club to capture the Stanley Cup in the minimum eight games. For the first two periods of the fourth game, the Canadiens had the better scoring chances. But once again Sawchuk slammed the door.

In the first period, he somehow managed to get a pad on a Floyd Curry drive from five feet out. In the middle frame, with Alex Delvecchio off for tripping and the Habs swarming around his net, Sawchuk made tremendous saves on both Meger and Geoffrion.

That busy second period also saw the start of what would become a Detroit playoff tradition. For the first time, an octopus was flung onto the ice surface of the Olympia. The fishmonger who did the tossing later explained that the eight tentacles of the octopus were meant to symbolize the number of victories required to win the Stanley Cup.

Action resumed after the following announcement: "Octopi shall not occupy the ice. Please refrain from throwing same."

By the third period the Red Wings enjoyed a 3-0 lead on a pair of goals by Metro Prystai and a single by Glen Skov. As the clock ran out, Sawchuk was called upon to make one final, towering save to preserve his record-tying fourth playoff shutout. This time the threat came from Montreal's rookie winger Dickie Moore, who would later win two scoring titles.

First Moore fired a ten-foot drive that Sawchuk stopped with his chest. The rebound fell at Moore's feet. He slapped at the puck—but Sawchuk thrust out a toe and deflected it wide. Incensed, Moore repeatedly banged his stick on the ice as he rejoined the play.

Montreal's frustration and humiliation were also apparent at the final buzzer, when Dick Irvin, followed closely by Rocket Richard and Elmer Lach, made a beeline for the dressing room, refusing to offer the customary congratulations to the victors.

"Have your fun," Irvin shouted at the spectators who jeered them on their way. The coach petulantly ordered the Montreal dressing room door closed to all members of the Detroit press.

Jack Adams greeted Sawchuk first when the victory party finally shifted from the ice into the Red Wing dressing room. "You helped make a great finish to my twenty-fifth year in hockey, Terry. Thanks, kid."

Sawchuk's playoff performance that spring remains unmatched by any goaltender in the modern era. He surrendered just five goals during the two playoff series (none on home ice) for a minuscule goals-against average of 0.62. His four playoff shutouts equalled the record shared by Davey Kerr of the New York Rangers and Toronto's Frank McCool. But Kerr needed nine games to get his four in 1937, and McCool thirteen in 1945.

"What do you think of this club?" Adams kept repeating

to newsmen. "For balance, for depth, for anything you want to call it, this is the best Red Wing team I have ever had."

For once, Adams may have been understating his case. Many hockey historians regard the 1951-52 Red Wings as not just the greatest Detroit team, but possibly the greatest hockey club ever—at least over the course of a single season.

Adams couldn't resist a parting dig at Dick Irvin, who had claimed the Wings would be pushovers in the playoffs. "They asked for us and they got us," Adams crowed. "Wonder how they feel now!"

Ted Lindsay stuck the knife in a little deeper. "Didn't Irvin say Sawchuk wouldn't stand up under pressure? Wonder what he thinks of him now?"

Busy being mobbed by teammates, club officials and reporters, Terry was still in full uniform long after everyone else was showered and getting dressed for the victory party later that night at the Sheraton-Cadillac Hotel.

"I wasn't worried about equalling the playoff shutout record," he said. "All I wanted to do was to get this series over with."

Sawchuk modestly gave credit for his success to his defencemen, singling out for special praise Bob Goldham, who he said had blocked almost as many shots as he had.

Over in the Canadiens' dressing room, a weary Maurice Richard knew better. "He is their club," he said of Sawchuk, who had held him scoreless in the finals. "Another guy in the nets and we'd beat them."

## Chapter Four

# TROUBLE AHEAD

SAWCHUK entered the 1952-53 season popularly acclaimed as the greatest goalie in the history of the game. Yet the coming months would prove to be among the most puzzling and disappointing of his career. By season's end serious questions about his future as a Red Wing had been raised and then ominously left unanswered.

At training camp the year before, Jack Adams had read Sawchuk the riot act when he weighed in at a cherubic 219 pounds. Now Terry shocked everyone by tipping the scales at just 169, a full fifty pounds lighter than twelve months before, and about twenty pounds less than what the Detroit brass considered his ideal playing weight.

Sawchuk looked gaunt and tired, although he insisted that he felt fine. Even after he had stopped dieting early that summer the pounds continued to fall off. "I lost my appetite and couldn't get it back," Terry shrugged. Worries about his weight would plague him for the rest of his life. But, ironically, from this time forward the goal would always be to gain back some of the pounds he'd dropped so quickly.

The turnabout exasperated Adams, who complained bitterly that his goalie had taken the directive to lose weight to absurd lengths. All he had wanted, Adams said, was for Sawchuk to drop a few pounds, not report to training camp looking like a cadaver.

Terry underwent a complete physical examination to make certain there was no underlying medical reason for the weight loss. When the first exam showed nothing abnormal, Adams insisted on another just to be certain. At meal times Sawchuk's dinner tray was heaped with huge portions and extra desserts in a vain attempt to fatten him up.

Also of concern that September, as it seemed to be every year, was the status of Terry's crippled right elbow. Still more chips had broken off the bone the season before, causing him discomfort as the season wore on. For the third time in as many years, an operation was performed at the conclusion of the playoffs.

The Detroit surgeon who went in this time was determined to fix the problem once and for all. "He removed over sixty pieces of bone, taking everything he thought might break off and cause trouble later on," Terry reported. In early practice sessions he found that his arm had regained almost complete mobility, something he hadn't enjoyed since before the original accident when he was a youngster.

With two significant exceptions, the Red Wings opened the season with the same stacked line-up that had swept the league the season before. Not even Trader Jack could bring himself to seriously tamper with the Detroit juggernaut, although he did fret that maybe his boys "would be too complacent after winning it all last season."

Gone were captain Sid Abel and hardrock defenceman Leo Reise. Abel ended his twelve-year career as a Red Wing to assume the dual role of player-coach in Chicago. In his only significant trade of the off-season, Adams shipped Reise to New York in return for centreman Reg Sinclair, a gifted playmaker expected to fill Abel's old slot between Howe and Lindsay.

Appointed captain in Abel's place was the colourful, explosive, at times frightening and always inspirational Ted Lindsay, the obvious choice. "He's the guy who holds us together," Abel himself had said before departing. "He keeps us at a high pitch. He won't allow anyone to let down when he's on the ice."

Benny Woit remains awed by a particular memory of the

new captain's zealous attention to his duties. One morning around this time Woit was driving through downtown Detroit on his way to the hospital after breaking his nose in a road game the night before. A car in the next lane veered slightly toward him, forcing Woit to slow down and apply his brakes.

"Not a particularly close call," he remembers, "nothing to worry about. But as I drove on I saw another car come from out of nowhere and force the guy who'd veered into my lane up onto the sidewalk and almost into the wall of a building.

"It was Ted Lindsay," Woit says. "'Nobody,' Lindsay told me as he rolled down his window at the next stoplight, 'gets away with cutting off one of our players.'"

Everything seemed in place for a romp to another league championship and the Stanley Cup. But the powerful Red Wings surprised themselves and everyone else by sputtering out of the gate. One month into the season, Detroit stood an unaccustomed fifth in the standings.

No one was playing well, including Sawchuk. Twice he blew two-goal leads heading into the third period of a game, something that had never happened to him before. The low point came on October 25 in Montreal when Terry and the Red Wings suffered a public humiliation that he at least would never forget.

By the end of the opening period the Canadiens, who had scored just thirteen goals in seven games to that point in the season, led 4-0. Outskating, outhustling, outchecking and outshooting the Wings, Montreal ran up the damage to 7-0 by the end of the middle frame. Two more unanswered goals in the third period before an ecstatic Saturday-night Forum crowd produced a final score of 9-0.

It was Detroit's worst defeat since another Montreal squad whipped them 9-1 back in 1944, with Harry Lumley in the cage. That night Rocket Richard scored five goals after spending the afternoon moving furniture at his home and then complaining to Dick Irvin that he felt tired.

Never before had Sawchuk allowed more than six goals in an NHL match. The Canadiens drilled forty-five shots at him. A charitable local press allowed that had a lesser goalie been in net the score would surely have been much higher. But it was also noted that this wasn't the first time Montreal had fired so many shots Terry's way. In a match the year before, the Habs peppered him with exactly the same number, but that night Detroit left town with a 4-0 victory.

Sawchuk would always look back on the slaughter in Montreal as one of the watershed events of his career. He referred to it often, calling upon the memory to remind himself never to take success for granted, because a goalie's luck can all too quickly change.

Terry fretted through the first extended slump of his career. He couldn't fathom what he might be doing differently from in the past. "I've asked everybody who might know," he said one day after practice. "All of them—Mr. Adams, Tommy and the players—tell me I'm playing just the same as I did last year. Yet the pucks just keep going by.

"Always before," he continued, "in amateur and in the pros, whenever I had a bad streak, it lasted for only one game or two. This one just keeps going on and on."

Typically, Sawchuk insisted on taking full responsibility for Detroit's plunge in the standings. "I'm paid to keep pucks out of the net," he said. "I think I should have been able to fire up the team more. Last year I would come up with the odd save early in the game to prevent a goal, and the team would seem to get a lift from that and pull on out in front. Now that one big save isn't there. The puck goes by me instead."

No one else placed any of the blame for the team's

decline on Terry, at least not publicly. Tommy Ivan and Jack Adams told reporters the problem lay with Detroit's defence, which was going through an uncharacteristic rough patch. Red Kelly wasn't playing up to form; every year veteran Bob Goldham took a little longer to hit his stride; and Benny Woit needed time to adjust to a full-time role in place of the departed Leo Reise.

Proclaimed Adams, "Terry Sawchuk, called a superman and one of the greatest goalies in history last season, is still tops with me."

Detroit's braintrust knew there was nothing to be gained by expressing even the slightest unhappiness with their goaltender's performance. When he was playing well, Terry would strut into the dressing room exuding confidence. But just one or two bad outings could leave him as insecure as the rawest rookie. "Do you really think I was okay?" he would anxiously ask teammates and even reporters after a game.

"You always had to be careful with Terry," says Benny Woit. "He became more sensitive every year. Adams was smart enough to know that his goalie was the team's last line of defence. Sawchuk needed to hear praise to get going again, not that he was letting down the team."

Looking back, some Wings suspect that Adams always had a particular soft spot for Terry. "Even on those rare occasions when Terry let in a bad goal, Adams would always put the blame on someone else," Johnny Wilson recalls. "It was my fault for missing a check or maybe Marcel Pronovost would get the blame for not clearing a rebound. The problem was never with the goaltending. At least that was the way Adams saw it."

In truth, Adams admired *all* modern goaltenders, not just his own. "Today's goalies are about the most wonderful athletes in sport," he said that season. "They see more shots in ten minutes than the old-timers did in an hour. And the shots are coming in screened, deflected, and every other hard way."

Deepening the gloom in the Detroit camp was the death of James Norris from a heart attack on December 4. His twenty-five-year-old daughter, Marguerite, a graduate of exclusive Smith College, took over as team president, becoming the NHL's first female executive. James Norris, Jr., Little Jim, was already in place as president of the Chicago Black Hawks.

As slumps invariably do, this one ended as suddenly as it began for both Sawchuk and his teammates. Overnight Terry recaptured his Vezina-winning form of the season before. By mid-December Detroit stood atop the standings.

Leading the resurgence was hockey's most potent one-two punch, Gordie Howe and Ted Lindsay, who climbed to the top two spots on the league scoring chart and stayed there the rest of the season. They barely seemed to have noticed that Sid Abel was gone or, for that matter, who played centre between them in his place. A succession of pivots received auditions after Reg Sinclair failed to click. The joke making the rounds was that the Production Line should now be called the Doughnut Line, since it was missing a centre.

This was the fifth season of the Howe-Lindsay collaboration. Best friends from the start, they remained inseparable at the rink and in their private lives. When Ted Lindsay married shortly after the 1952 Cup victory, Howe moved in with the newlyweds and stayed for almost a year.

Lindsay had made it a personal project to build up the confidence of his painfully shy friend. To help Howe realize his nearly unlimited potential, Lindsay constantly stroked his ego by telling him that he could outskate and outshoot anyone else; that one day soon Howe would be the greatest player the game had ever seen.

By this point they had developed an uncanny ability to anticipate each other's every movement on the ice. Set-piece plays were honed to perfection during countless hours of experimentation in practice.

One favourite began with Howe carrying the puck into the opposition zone and then cutting sharply toward the goal. Lindsay, meanwhile, raced to a spot just in front of the far side of the net. Without so much as a glance over, Howe would unleash a perfect cross-ice pass that reached Lindsay at the very moment he came into position for a shot at the unguarded side of the cage.

Banking shots off the boards of the Olympia and then gathering in the rebounds as they charged toward the goal was another Howe-Lindsay specialty. Teammates remember them carefully marking their spots in the corners every time the boards were repainted.

The partners retained a childlike passion for the game. Howe, Lindsay and a small circle of close friends that included Metro Prystai, Marty Pavelich and Red Kelly usually stayed on playing shinny long after the regular morning practices had officially ended. Often it took repeated orders from Tommy Ivan, who worried that they were wearing themselves out, to finally get them off the ice.

When asked the secret of his success, Ivan would laugh and inevitably answer, "I open the gate and say, 'Gord and Ted, get on the ice.'"

Ivan was tremendously popular among his players, who appreciated the role he played as a buffer between them and Jack Adams. One day a particularly vitriolic Adams outburst left Metro Prystai in tears. When Adams finally departed the dressing room, Ivan put his arm around Prystai's shoulders. "Don't pay any attention to Jack," he said. "He's nuts."

It didn't appear to bother Ivan that Adams was the one

usually quoted in the newspapers, or that the Red Wings were generally regarded as Jack's team. Though the two didn't always agree, Ivan was quick to acknowledge the large debt he owed his boss. "Jack Adams is just about the best thing that ever happened to me," he said.

When Ivan took over the team at the start of the 1947-48 season, he was the first man in recent memory to be handed such a job without a background as an NHL player. Born in Toronto, Ivan—originally Ivanoff—played amateur hockey in Ontario but, at five-foot-five and 135 pounds, his future was not considered bright. After a head injury forced him to retire as a player, Ivan turned to refereeing and then to coaching junior squads affiliated with the Red Wings.

"I liked the way he handled youngsters and handled himself," recalled Adams, who by the mid-1940s was being pressured by James Norris to step down as Detroit coach and concentrate fully on his front-office duties. When he received his discharge from the Canadian Army in 1945, Ivan, then thirty-four, went to work full-time for the Red Wings as Adams's anointed successor.

He coached one year in Omaha and the next season moved on to Indianapolis. "By that time I was certain Tommy was the right man for the Wings," Adams said. "There hasn't been a minute since that I haven't felt he was the perfect choice."

The Wings finished second in Ivan's rookie season. By the start of the 1952-53 campaign, he had coached Detroit to four successive league championships and two Stanley Cups.

His players remember him as a superb bench tactician who always managed to stay a move ahead of his opponents. And yet, he insisted that hockey was really the simplest of games. "Fundamentally, there are only two basic defence manoeuvres," he said. "Either you knock the puck away from the man or you knock the man away from the puck."

On the attack, Ivan believed in swamping the enemy goalie with shots, on the theory that some of them were bound to go in.

Few coaches knew how to get more out of their personnel. Though he could be tough when necessary, Ivan never used foul language and only under severe provocation berated a player in front of his teammates. He had a knack for giving even a fifth defenceman or a spare forward enough ice time to keep him sharp and to make him feel essential to the success of the team. Unlike Adams, Ivan was convinced that hockey players responded better to encouragement than abuse.

The dapper little coach, who was considered the best-dressed man in the game, even developed a special talent for handling the increasingly high-strung Sawchuk. The darkness that had begun to creep into the goalie's personality the season before put down deep roots during the 1952-53 campaign. Terry started to turn away from all but a handful of his teammates, preferring to keep to himself. It was impossible to know what his mood would be from one day to the next.

One of the best-known Sawchuk stories from around this time has him affably greeting the popular Marty Pavelich in the dressing room before practice every day for more than a week. Then, one morning, nothing. Pavelich said his usual hello and Sawchuk refused to even acknowledge him. Every day, Pavelich tried to initiate a conversation, but Sawchuk wouldn't speak. Pavelich never had any idea why.

Ivan made a point of sitting with Terry before every game in an effort to soothe his nerves and help him prepare mentally. He recalled that Sawchuk would "shake his head unconsciously, a little twitch, over and over. I'd put my hand on his arm, and I'd talk quietly about anything but hockey."

During a television appearance a quarter of a century

later, Ted Lindsay paid a heartfelt tribute to his former coach. "It was not the mode twenty-five years ago for an NHL coach to act like a decent guy," Lindsay said. "They used to whip rather than coax. Tommy was different. He understood players as human beings."

"Why did this have to happen just when the club was going so good?" Sawchuk asked gloomily late that December after an injury forced him to sit out a game for the first time in his NHL career. "Why didn't it happen a few weeks ago when I was playing bad?"

During a shooting drill Alex Delvecchio ripped a shot that caught Sawchuk between his right skate and goal pad. Doctors diagnosed a hairline fracture of a small bone in his instep. He was expected to be out for at least three weeks.

Terry celebrated Christmas, his twenty-third birthday and New Year's Eve with his foot bound in a plaster cast. He spent most of his time-off worrying that his replacement, Glenn Hall, would permanently steal his job. Hall ranked as the top goalie in the Western League, where he had been sent to the Wings' Edmonton farm club after a season in Indianapolis. One day he was certain to star in the NHL. The only question appeared to be whether he would eventually push aside Terry and get his chance in Detroit, or be packaged off in another of Adams's blockbuster deals.

"You remember what happened the last time a Detroit goalie was forced out with injuries," Sawchuk said, referring to his own debut in place of Harry Lumley. "Yes, and Lum was gone from here the next season—maybe that will happen to me now."

Hall did nothing to alleviate Terry's fears during his brief stay. Detroit won four, tied one and lost one with Hall guarding the net. He even helped lower the team goals-against average slightly—from 1.97 to 1.95.

Hall's performance left Trader Jack dizzy from thinking about the future possibilities. "Sometimes it takes a setback like this injury to Sawchuk," he mused, "to realize there is talent in reserve."

Bad luck and ill health dogged Terry the rest of the season. The cast was off his foot less than a month when, during a 5-1 win in Toronto, a drive by Harry Watson smashed into his mouth, breaking three upper teeth. It took twelve stitches to stop the bleeding. Later in the game, Sawchuk returned to the clinic for additional repairs when the stitches started to slip.

Not long after that, he began to complain that he wasn't feeling well. He felt more tired than usual, and his nerves troubled him. The club doctors examined him, but the test results all came back negative.

For the first time, Sawchuk noticed that when he talked about his physical problems some of his teammates would roll their eyes and kid him that his aches and pains were all in his head. "The boys would tease me about making excuses for myself," he remembered. "They said it like they were kidding, but I felt they were making a point."

Sawchuk withdrew into himself even further. He began to wonder if there might be some truth to the suggestion that his problems were largely psychosomatic. As the start of the playoffs drew closer, all he really knew for sure was that he felt rotten.

Though the Wings had clinched their fifth consecutive league championship well before the season entered its final weekend, they were not yet free to relax and conserve their strength for the post-season. With two games still to play—against Chicago and Montreal—Gordie Howe stood just one goal away from equalling Rocket Richard's single-season record of fifty.

"That record meant a lot to all of us," Ted Lindsay said later. The Detroit press, the fans, and every one of Howe's teammates were rooting hard for him to catch and then surpass his arch-rival.

For weeks now as Howe sewed up his third-straight scoring title and approached Richard's mark, all the old comparisons between them had been endlessly rehashed—and new ones introduced that applied to the current situation. Rocket boosters complained that the present seventy-game schedule afforded Howe an unfair advantage over their hero, who had set his record during the fifty-game season of 1944-45. The popular counter-argument was that the league was much weaker during that wartime campaign, when dozens of old-timers and career minor leaguers filled in for regulars serving in the armed forces.

Evidence of how personally the two stars regarded their rivalry was seen in a game late that season in Montreal. "The Rocket had a breakaway," Howe recalled. "At the time, I was closing in on his goal-scoring record, and there was no way I wanted him to score. So I jumped off the bench and checked him. The fans went nuts. All we got was a two-minute penalty for having too many men on the ice."

On Saturday, Howe, who worked double shifts, couldn't click against a much-improved Black Hawk squad. Chicago's 4-3 victory enabled Sid Abel's crew to nail down the final playoff spot, just ahead of the fading Maple Leafs.

And so the stage was set for a climactic final effort by Howe the next night in Detroit against Richard and the Canadiens. The Rocket, who would finish third in the scoring race behind Howe and Lindsay, had already left his imprint on the season. On November 8 against Chicago, he scored the 325th goal of his career to pass Nels Stewart and become hockey's all-time scoring leader.

Richard was fiercely proud of his fifty-goal record. To

help him hold onto it, Dick Irvin assigned left winger Bert "Dirty Bertie" Olmstead the task of shadowing the Red Wing ace.

Just as they had the night before in Chicago, every one of Howe's teammates focused not on winning, or scoring themselves, but only on setting him up for the record-tying goal. But wherever Howe went, Olmstead followed. Only two of Howe's five shots on net could be considered solid scoring chances. Both times Gerry McNeil alertly made the save to preserve Richard's record and a 2-1 Montreal victory.

Before the same fans who had jeered him at the end of the last playoffs, Dick Irvin slid out onto the Olympia ice and raised Richard's arm in the traditional victory salute of a boxer. "The winner and still champion," he gloated later to the press.

Howe's failure to catch the Rocket provided a peculiarly downbeat ending to what had otherwise been another splendid regular season for the Wings. Detroit finished fifteen points ahead of runner-up Montreal and would dominate the post-season honours in their usual fashion.

For the third year running, Howe, Lindsay, Kelly and Sawchuk captured two-thirds of the positions on the NHL's first All-Star team. A fifth teammate, Alex Delvecchio, was named the centre on the second squad. Red Kelly picked up his second Lady Byng Trophy and Gordie Howe, in addition to winning an unprecedented third-consecutive scoring title, collected his second-straight Hart Trophy as league MVP.

Sawchuk bounced back from his early-season slump to easily capture another Vezina Trophy. His personal goals-against average of 1.90 exactly equalled his mark of the season before, and bettered by a wide margin the 2.12 posted by runner-up Gerry McNeil. Despite having missed seven games, Sawchuk led the league with a total of thirty-two wins (including nine shutouts).

Entering the playoffs, the Red Wings appeared so powerful that there was already excited talk in the Detroit press
that they might once again capture the Stanley Cup in the
minimum eight games.

Detroit writers delighted in comparing the local side to
baseball's mighty New York Yankees, who also enjoyed an
as yet unbroken string of league championships (in addition
to consecutive World Series titles) dating back to 1949.
Both franchises featured strong front offices, astute bench
bosses, deep farm systems and offensive power to spare.
The Yankee line-up included sluggers Yogi Berra, Hank
Bauer and a young Mickey Mantle; the Red Wings featured
five of that season's top eight scorers—Howe, Lindsay,
Delvecchio, Prystai and Kelly.

Taking the baseball analogy even further, the writers
often glowingly compared Adams to Branch Rickey, the
famous Mahatma of the summer game, to whom he bore
an uncanny physical resemblance. Like Rickey, who was
then running the Pittsburgh Pirates, Adams had grown
portly and jowly with the advancing years and the two
shared a preference for horn-rimmed glasses and soft
fedoras.

"They are on common ground in imagination, intensity
and, most important, the ability to sense when a superstar or
journeyman athlete is ever so slightly over the hill," Watson
Spoelstra gushed unashamedly in *The Detroit News*.

The Red Wings were barely expected to break a sweat in
their semi-final tune-up against third-place Boston. In the
fourteen games played between the two teams during the
regular schedule, the Wings won ten, lost two and tied two.
Often the scores were embarrassingly lopsided—10-1, 10-
2, 7-1 and 6-1. Detroit, who led the league in scoring with
222 goals, outscored Boston 62-19.

Sure enough, Detroit handed Boston a 7-0 pasting in the

opener. Sawchuk breezed to his third consecutive playoff shutout, and his fifth in his last nine playoff games.

But in the second game, a virtuoso performance by Bruin goaltender Sugar Jim Henry shattered the dream of another playoff sweep. Though Detroit thoroughly dominated the action, Henry, the former Red Wing farm hand, stopped forty-three shots, many of them seemingly certain goals, in leading Boston to a 5-3 upset.

Sawchuk's stretch of playoff perfection—dating back to Elmer Lach's first-period goal in the second game of the 1952 finals—ended at 229 minutes and 19 seconds, when Fleming Mackell lashed a set-up from Johnny Peirson past him at 7:56 of the first period. Terry played poorly, appearing tired and uncertain, especially compared to the razor-sharp Sugar Jim.

Detroit reloaded and once again came out shooting when the series resumed before an overflow Sunday-night crowd of 13,909 at Boston Garden. But it was the Bruins who struck first. Winger Ed Sandford (who would score six goals in the series) beat Sawchuk after grabbing the puck near the Detroit blue line and outskating Red Kelly to the net.

Tony Leswick jammed one under Henry to even the score in the second period. From that point both Sawchuk and Sugar Jim were unbeatable through regulation time and on into extra play. The Wings fired fifteen shots at Henry and rattled a shot off the goal post in the first eleven minutes of overtime. Considering the huge edge enjoyed by Detroit throughout the game, what happened next hardly seemed fair. In the thirteenth minute, Bruin winger John McIntyre dashed in from centre ice, swung around Bob Goldham and backhanded a twenty-five-footer past Sawchuk into the Detroit net for a 2-1 Boston victory.

McIntyre's goal appeared to destroy whatever remained of Terry's confidence. In game four, Henry again outplayed him by a wide margin. The 6-2 Bruin victory pushed the defending Stanley Cup champions to the brink of elimination.

"If they had thrown a football at him it would have gone in," Red Kelly recalled of Sawchuk's performance during the series. "We got so desperate that we would be trying to stop the shots from the blue line from even getting near that goal of his. Mind you, it wasn't that Sawchuk wasn't trying or anything, but rather that he was fighting the puck."

"What we needed," adds Johnny Wilson, "was the same type of performance from Terry that Jim Henry gave Boston. We were looking for just a couple of good games, even one, to get us back on an even keel."

Sawchuk had felt physically weak and jittery before the playoffs began. Now his failure to perform anywhere close to expectations pushed him dangerously close to the point of emotional collapse. "Maybe I was too anxious," he said a few days later. "Maybe being underweight thirty-five or thirty pounds hurt me. I wish I could figure it out."

Adams considered placing an emergency call to Glenn Hall in Edmonton. But he and Ivan decided to stick with the goalie who had, after all, just won his second Vezina, and who had been nearly flawless under the same intense spotlight of the playoffs just the year before.

Besides, Sawchuk wasn't entirely to blame for Detroit's predicament. Boston coach Lynn Patrick was busy accepting congratulations for a move that had helped shackle the league's top two scorers. At the start of the series, Patrick assigned the veteran trio of Milt Schmidt, Woody Dumart and Joe Klukay the task of checking Howe, Lindsay and their current centre, Marty Pavelich.

It took the newly dubbed Blanket Line the opening game to get the hang of its new task. Howe scored once and Lindsay twice in the Detroit victory. But in the three games since, they had managed just one goal apiece. Howe's tally came as the point man on a Detroit power play.

Considered washed-up earlier in the season, the thirty-six-year-old Dumart (a former member of the famous Kraut Line with Schmidt and the now retired Bobby Bauer) drove Howe nearly to distraction with the tenacity of his checking. The inability of hockey's premier line to outskate and outscore a threesome whose aggregate age was 101 years gave rise to the theory that they had entered the playoffs already exhausted from working overtime to get Howe his fiftieth goal. Late in the series, when word leaked out that Howe had become engaged to be married, it was also rudely suggested that he might possibly have his mind on other things.

"Can you imagine that Howe," cracked Dumart after hearing news of the coming nuptials. "He got engaged without even telling me and we've spent so much time together."

The Red Wings' world seemed to make sense again when they struck for three goals in the first four minutes of the crucial fifth game at the Olympia. In the second period, Howe finally broke free of Dumart to score on an unassisted breakaway. Detroit won 6-4 after holding off a late Boston rally.

"We'll take the series now," Red Kelly predicted. Added Tommy Ivan, "We may give the Bruins a few surprises in Boston."

But it was the Wings who were left shocked by the outcome. The Bruins jumped out to an early 2-0 lead at the Garden in game six before Reg Sinclair retaliated for Detroit midway through the second period. Fleming Mackell got that one back for Boston in the third stanza on what had to be the ugliest goal of the playoffs. Mackell skated up the left side and let go a high shot from fifty feet out. It should have been a routine grab for Sawchuk. Instead the puck passed beneath his glove and into the net just under the crossbar.

The pandemonium that rocked the Garden's rafters after Mackell's goal had barely subsided when Ted Lindsay got the Wings back within one. On a set-up from Kelly and Howe, Lindsay slapped a six-footer past Henry. But Bruin rookie Leo Labine nullified Lindsay's effort just over four minutes later, beating Terry for an unassisted goal after stealing the puck from a pile-up in front of the Detroit net. Ivan pulled Sawchuk for an extra attacker with ninety seconds remaining on the clock. But Sugar Jim held firm and Boston emerged with a 4-2 win.

The Wings could scarcely believe they had been booted out of the semi-finals by a third-place team which had beaten them only twice in fourteen regular-season games. Detroit outplayed and outshot the Bruins, forcing Henry to handle 230 saves to Sawchuk's 140. In the finals, Boston would last just five games against the Canadiens, who captured their first Stanley Cup in seven years.

"I wouldn't have believed it if I hadn't seen it myself," said Jack Adams. "We outshot them...but we just couldn't score. I just can't explain it."

Surrounded by reporters in the gloom of the Red Wing dressing room, Sawchuk was disconsolate. Over and over again he was asked to describe his muff of Mackell's shot from outside the blue line. "I thought I had it but it dipped," he said plaintively. Terry accepted full responsibility for Detroit's defeat, describing himself as "a big flop. I've been a big flop in this series. I've been a big flop all year."

Sawchuk pledged to make things right again. "I'll be back next year and I'll be the best goalie in the league."

But where would he be playing? Even before the start of the sixth game, rumours circulated that a disgruntled Jack

Adams was on the verge of trading one or two and maybe even more of Detroit's greatest stars, players who until now even Trader Jack had described as "untouchables."

Ted Lindsay or Red Kelly or possibly even Gordie Howe—the wildest speculation said all three—were reported to be heading to Chicago. Black Hawk president Jim Norris, Jr., now the head of the NHL's most powerful clan, said publicly that he would make a strong effort to obtain at least one of the three before the start of the next season.

A more persistent, and believable, rumour had Sawchuk going to New York, with Glenn Hall moving up from Edmonton to take over the big job in Detroit.

Adams refused to tip his hand to the press. "Nobody can tell what the future holds any more than anyone would have predicted the Bruins beating us," he said. "Sure we'll make some trades. We always do. We have to in order to make room for the good young prospects in our organization."

Heading home to Detroit, a heartbroken Sawchuk felt certain that he had played his last game as a Red Wing.

## Chapter Five

## BACK ON TOP

JACK Adams drew out the suspense until July before finally announcing that Sawchuk would be staying on in Detroit. The trade rumours revolving around him as well as the team's other top stars had persisted ever since the shocking upset loss to Boston in the spring. Kelly, Lindsay and Howe were also told they could unpack their bags.

"No other club has come up with anything," shrugged Adams, who had wisely concluded that a fire sale of his All-Stars was no way to go about reclaiming the Stanley Cup. "Who could you trade off this team? It's a young club. All our star players are in their mid-twenties, most of the good prospects are younger than that, and we have only two players in their thirties, Bob Goldham and Tony Leswick. This could be the best club in the league."

Many close to the team were particularly surprised that Sawchuk was spared the axe. Soon after his disastrous play-off performance, he had angered Adams by at first refusing to participate in yet another attempt to discover the cause of his dramatic weight loss of the past year.

"Terry wanted to take a trip somewhere," Adams said. "So I told him that if he didn't go to the hospital, a lot of things were going to happen to him, a lot of things that weren't so nice."

Still Sawchuk resisted. He fled to Toronto and hid out from Adams for a week. "I just had to get away from it all," Terry explained. He was still brooding over the loss to Boston. He had also had more than his fill of doctors and hospitals.

Rumours circulated that the twenty-three-year-old might even be contemplating an early retirement. Throughout his career—when he was sick or injured or depressed about a slump—Sawchuk would often threaten to quit the game. With just one memorable exception that still lay years ahead, he would inevitably change his mind within a day or two. Then he would deny ever having had the thought in the first place.

"Me quit hockey?" he said when confronted by reporters this time. "That's ridiculous." Like the boy who cried wolf, eventually no one took his threats seriously.

Sawchuk soon realized that there was no future in fighting the boss and returned to Detroit. An even more intensive barrage of medical tests than usual failed to solve the mystery of his weight loss. "All they found," Terry said upon his release from Detroit Osteopathic Hospital, "was that I had a low blood count."

The best news was that, for the first off-season in three years, he would not have to undergo surgery on his right elbow. He still couldn't lift his arm over his head, and there had been some discomfort during the past season. But most days the elbow continued to feel better than it had since he was a kid. Sawchuk could look forward to a summer of golf and baseball and the other pleasures he hadn't always been able to enjoy since before his first operation.

Sadly, it proved to be a short-lived idyll. On June 1, while playing a morning round of golf back home in Winnipeg, Terry felt groggy and was forced to quit the game. He went to his parents' house to lie down.

A few hours later he woke up with a temperature of 102. "In the afternoon he said, 'Mama, I have awful burning pains in my stomach,'" Anne Sawchuk recounted to the press. Rushed to St. Boniface Hospital, he was operated on for acute appendicitis. "It scared us," said his mother, who had already lost two sons. "I couldn't sleep."

An announcement soon came from St. Boniface that the local hero would make a full and speedy recovery. His Winnipeg doctors expressed the opinion that the rapid weight loss of the past year might have been caused by the problem with his appendix. They said it could also account for Terry's nervousness and physical fatigue at the end of the last season.

Lying there in hospital, recuperating from yet another operation, Sawchuk could at least take heart in knowing that his earlier complaints hadn't necessarily been the product of an overly fertile imagination, as some of his teammates had so unkindly suggested—and as even he had feared.

Sawchuk had vowed to make it up to his teammates and the fans for his playoff collapse. But by the time Adams announced his stand-pat policy in July, there was an even more urgent reason for Terry to be grateful for the opportunity to stay on in Detroit. Early that spring, before returning home to Winnipeg, he had met and fallen in love with a local girl.

She was Patricia Ann Morey, a fine-featured, strikingly attractive brunette whose father owned Morey's Golf and Riding Club on Union Lake Road west of Pontiac, a Detroit bedroom community. Pat was working behind the cash register in the clubhouse when Sawchuk asked her for directions to the first tee. By the time he left for Winnipeg about a month later they were already discussing marriage.

After recovering from his appendicitis, Terry returned to Detroit in early July and presented Pat with an engagement ring. The next week a lavish engagement party was held on the lawn of the Moreys' home adjoining the golf course.

Those who knew him best agree that meeting Pat was the best thing that ever happened to Terry. She is inevitably described in almost saintlike terms—loving, patient,

supportive and a wonderful mother to the seven children
they eventually brought into the world.

Sawchuk, it need hardly be said, was not an easy man to
live with. His moodiness grew worse with every passing year
and he often preferred the company of his male friends to
being at home with Pat and the children. Theirs was a stormy
relationship that came close to breaking up on at least one
occasion. But no one among their friends ever doubted how
much Terry loved his wife. He was crazy about Pat from the
start, and stayed that way until the day he died.

On August 6, 1953, they were married at St. Patrick's
Roman Catholic Church in Union Lake Village. The date
had been set far enough in advance of the start of training
camp in September to allow time for a honeymoon in the
Wisconsin Dells, and then a leisurely return home through
Michigan's Upper Peninsula.

Jack Adams was still seething about the loss to Boston
when the Red Wings gathered for the start of another training camp in Sault Ste. Marie. That first night, to drive home
the point that nothing was forgotten or forgiven, all hands
were made to suffer through a complete screening of the
game films of the ill-fated series.

Adams declared loudly and often that the goaltending
job was up for grabs between Sawchuk and Glenn Hall.
After two Vezina wins, three consecutive All-Star selections, and Frank Boucher's famous endorsement, Terry had
to go out and prove himself all over again.

"If Sawchuk continues like this, of course he'll be our
goalie," Adams acknowledged after the incumbent had
looked as sharp as ever in early workouts. "But I wouldn't
hesitate to send Sawchuk to a farm team if Hall does better
than him. We are bound by no rule or precedent."

At first married life appeared to have steadied Terry. "Pat

is a good listener when I talk about my hockey troubles," he said, claiming to have cast aside all his doubts and worries and to have stopped brooding over his failure in the play-offs. Despite the stiff competition provided by Glenn Hall, Pat refused to let her husband even consider the possibility that he might be demoted to the minors. During training camp, she was back in Detroit optimistically readying a three-room apartment for occupancy in October.

The life of a hockey wife, especially one whose husband played for the Red Wings, was never easy. Adams openly resented the distraction that he believed home and hearth presented for his players. He had watched with mounting dismay as first Lindsay, then Delvecchio, Howe and now Sawchuk settled into strength-sapping domesticity.

"We made the greatest record in history with a team that breathed, ate and slept hockey," he would fondly recall of the 1951-52 Stanley Cup squad. "The players, most of them young and unmarried, lived together and lived hockey like a Notre Dame team lives football."

Around his club, wives were regarded with suspicion at best, and sometimes with undisguised hostility. During play-offs when the team was on the road or sequestered in their Toledo redoubt, Adams issued a standing order that hotel switchboards were not to put through calls from players' wives.

"The wives were just nobodies in the grand scheme," recalled Colleen Howe in *After the Applause*. "I remember once when I wanted to reach Gordie during the playoffs, I had to explain to the general manager what I wanted. *Just to talk to my husband*. As far as they were concerned, my only purpose in life was to make sure that Gordie was well fed, well rested, and well taken care of."

A widely held belief in sporting circles at the time was that sexual activity sapped an athlete of his stamina. It was a theory Adams bought into completely and which explains why he tried to keep his players away from their wives and girlfriends before big games. "Don't leave your game between the sheets!" he admonished them with increasing frequency as the playoffs drew near.

One of the reasons Pat and Terry had married after such a short courtship was to observe an unwritten club rule forbidding players to marry during the hockey season. They were so much in love and anxious to get on with their lives together that a wait of several more months seemed intolerable. Lindsay and Howe had also carefully observed this club stricture.

Pat's home-cooking helped Sawchuk gain back some of his lost weight. He reported to camp at 176 pounds, nine pounds more than he weighed at the end of the playoffs, and fourteen pounds more than when he was bedridden during his appendectomy. "I expect to gain more," he said optimistically. "Last year I got a bloated feeling when I ate. That helped keep me from gaining weight. Since the appendectomy I've been eating well.

"I'm better right now than in any game all last season."

Adams and Tommy Ivan were equally convinced that Terry had regained his form. "That boy should have his greatest season this year," predicted Ivan. Once again, future Hall of Famer Glenn Hall was handed a ticket back to the minors.

Sawchuk's pledge to regain his position as the league's top goaltender proved more difficult than anticipated. The competition that year was unusually stiff. At mid-season, for the first time, he wasn't named to either All-Star squad, finishing third in voting behind Chicago's Al Rollins and Harry Lumley of Toronto, who had exchanged teams in a major swap before the start of the previous season.

The All-Star omission came on the heels of a brief

December swoon by both Terry and the Wings. Detroit, en route to a sixth consecutive league title, dropped briefly out of first place behind Montreal. In the meantime, Sawchuk lost a seven-goal lead over Lumley in the Vezina race and at one point fell behind by ten goals. It would take an extraordinary second-half performance for him to close the Vezina gap and earn a spot on the second All-Star team behind Lumley in the final balloting. Of Sawchuk's twelve shutouts that season, six came in a span of just sixteen games shortly after the start of the New Year.

In the end, Al Rollins wasn't so much beaten out by Terry for the second-team spot as he was forsaken by his Chicago teammates. The Black Hawks won just twelve games in tumbling back to the cellar after making the play-offs the season before. For uncommon valour on behalf of an atrocious team, Rollins received the Hart Trophy as the league's most valuable player.

In light of his earlier fulminations, Jack Adams displayed remarkable restraint in introducing just two newcomers— rookie forwards Bill Dineen and Earl "Dutch" Reibel—to a line-up that had hardly changed since the Stanley Cup sweep of 1952. But then, as Adams himself had conceded, "Who could you trade off this team?"

Certainly not Gordie Howe, who won yet another scoring championship (his fourth in a row). Nor blue-chip blue-liner Red Kelly, the recipient of the NHL's newest bauble, the James Norris Memorial Trophy, awarded to the league's top defenceman. Kelly polled 162 of a possible 180 points in the inaugural balloting, more than twice as many as Montreal's Doug Harvey.

For the second time in four years, the Vezina race came down to the final game of the season and once again pitted Sawchuk against a Toronto challenger. In 1951's battle of the rookies, Al Rollins produced a season-ending 1-0 shutout in Boston to edge Sawchuk by a single goal. This time Terry and his adversary, Harry Lumley, would fight it out face-to-face.

Conn Smythe had been Lumley's ardent admirer ever since the 1945 Detroit-Toronto Cup final, when the then eighteen-year-old rookie sparkled in a seven-game losing cause, shutting out the Leafs twice and allowing just nine goals. Despite the success of Rollins in Chicago, Smythe had had no reason to regret the high price (Rollins plus star centre Cal Gardner and defenceman Gus Mortson) he had paid to pry Lumley from the Hawks. Lumley's outstanding work in this, his second season as a Maple Leaf, lifted Toronto back into the playoff picture. Lumley's thirteen shutouts broke Sawchuk's modern mark of twelve.

Most of the pressure was on Lumley, who had never won a Vezina in his ten-year career. Lumley's previous best shot had come in 1948 when he entered the final two games deadlocked with Toronto's Turk Broda. Then, overcome by a bad case of jitters, he allowed a total of ten goals in the two matches.

This time he seemed a lock. As the season entered its final weekend, Lumley held a five-goal edge on Sawchuk. In Toronto on Saturday night, fifth-place New York pounded the Leafs 5-2. Lumley looked awful on at least three of the five Ranger goals. The loss was a serious setback for the Leafs, who were in a dogfight with Montreal for second place.

The same night at the Forum, Sawchuk faced Richard, Geoffrion and the other Habitant snipers without the benefit of three of his regular defencemen: Kelly, Goldham and Pronovost. All three were nursing injuries in anticipation of the start of the playoffs. Though Gordie Howe obligingly worked a regular shift on the blue line, it didn't help as the Wings fell 6-1.

"I don't think Terry Sawchuk belongs to the right clique

on the Detroit team," needled Dick Irvin a few days later. "When Sawchuk was in the thick of his fight with Harry Lumley for the Vezina Trophy his teammates didn't try to protect him.... By this time, Sawchuk must know he's on his own. He can't expect any help from the rest of them."

One year before, the Red Wings had exhausted themselves trying to set up Howe for his fiftieth goal. In Montreal they appeared far less enthused about helping Sawchuk win the Vezina and the $1,000 league bonus that went with it. Or maybe Adams, Ivan and Terry's teammates had simply concluded, like almost everyone else, that Lumley already had it won.

The Leafs still had a shot at second place as they skated out for the season finale at the Olympia Sunday, March 21. Lumley led the Vezina race by a seemingly insurmountable six goals.

Nonetheless the Wings, embarrassed by their performance the night before, went all out in support of Terry's longshot bid. Goldham and Pronovost rushed back to duty, allowing Howe to return to his usual spot at right wing.

Howe opened the scoring early in the first period, firing a shot that appeared to carom into the net off a Leaf skate. Just over four minutes later Bill Dineen made it 2-0 to cut Lumley's Vezina lead to four goals.

Soon after Dineen's score referee Red Storey added controversy to the growing drama by calling back a goal by Detroit's Johnny Wilson. Storey ruled that Wilson deliberately used his arm to knock a passout from Dineen past Lumley into the Toronto net. A fuming Jack Adams and his players saw it differently. "It went in off his chest and was a good goal," roared the boss from his seat behind the Red Wings bench.

Lumley appeared every bit as nervous as in his earlier showdown with Turk Broda. Tony Leswick pared his lead to three goals when he lashed a rebound past him early in the second period.

At the other end, Sawchuk effortlessly turned aside Toronto's few scoring chances. He made just one miscue the entire game—but it was a costly one. Deep into the second period, Leaf defenceman Jim Thomson lifted a high floater toward him from about ten feet outside the Detroit blue line. Instead of skating out to catch the puck, Sawchuk hesitated, then stayed back. The puck plopped about five feet in front of the net and took a high, crazy bounce into the left side of the net. Thomson's freak goal was only his second tally in 209 games. His last one had come just five games before on a similar shot against the Canadiens.

The situation looked slightly more hopeful when Johnny Wilson scored at the 2:09 mark of the third period. Lindsay added another at 11:09, and just under two minutes later he converted a perfect set-up by Howe to raise the score to 6-1 and place Sawchuk within a goal of tying Lumley.

A minute and four seconds remained on the clock. Tommy Ivan pulled his goaltender for an extra attacker. But the Leaf defence rallied around their man and staved off the threat. When the siren sounded, Terry hugged and congratulated an ecstatic Lumley, who had surrendered eleven goals during the weekend.

"I guess the better man won," said Sawchuk, whose goals-against average remained under 2 (1.94 compared to Lumley's winning mark of 1.86) for an unprecedented fourth-straight season. "That blooper by Thomson was a heartbreaker. It took a freak hop and I couldn't reach it. What a way to lose $1,000."

Toronto's twin weekend losses cost them the battle for second place with Montreal. The Maple Leafs stayed on in Detroit to prepare for the start of their semi-final with the league champions two nights later. Montreal drew fourth-place Boston, who had finished comfortably ahead of New York and Chicago.

Even Conn Smythe didn't like his team's chances against Detroit. "They've got too many guns for us," conceded the former artillery commander.

Pavelich fired two goals and Lindsay, Howe and Leswick added singles in Detroit's opening salvo, a dominating 5-0 triumph that saw Sawchuk start the playoffs with a shutout for the third year running. "Remember what happened to you last year after you won that first one from Boston," Adams cautioned his troops.

One writer described the Red Wings who had been ousted by Boston as a "tired, practically worn-out crew that dragged itself through the playoffs." The Leafs saw no evidence of battle fatigue this year. Toronto's only win came in the second game, a 3-1 final that marked the Leafs' first victory at the Olympia in thirteen regular-season and playoff matches. After that Detroit peeled off three straight wins by scores of 3-1, 2-1 and 4-3 to clinch the series in five games.

Sawchuk clearly outplayed Lumley, who only began to regain his regular-season form in the final two games. Then it took a late winning goal by Red Kelly and a double-overtime marker by Ted Lindsay to finish off the Leafs.

"Things are entirely different this year," Terry said during the series. "I'm determined to make up for last year's pitiful performance."

In the other semi-final, Montreal swept aside Boston in the minimum four games to set the stage for one of the most thrilling Stanley Cup finals ever played. Facing off were hockey's two best teams, its two greatest stars, as well as superbly balanced supporting casts that included many, if not most, of the top players in the game. Every one of the league's seven leading scorers that season—Howe, Richard,

Lindsay, Geoffrion, Olmstead, Kelly, Reibel—skated for either the Red Wings or Canadiens.

For three seasons running Detroit and Montreal had finished one-two atop the standings. From the twenty-two points that separated them in 1951-52, Montreal had whittled the spread down to just seven points in the current campaign. Each team had won a Stanley Cup in the interim.

The newest addition to the Montreal arsenal was Jean Béliveau, a long, lean, wondrously gifted twenty-two-year-old centre whose donning of the famous *bleu, blanc et rouge* jersey had been anxiously awaited by Hab fans for more than two years. To finally secure the reluctant Béliveau's signature on a contract, Montreal was forced to buy the entire Quebec Senior League and turn it professional.

Through crippling injuries and suspensions, the defending Stanley Cup champions (who had so easily handled Boston the previous spring after Detroit could not) managed to stay close to the Wings all season. Dickie Moore suited up for just thirteen games after fracturing his jaw. A broken ankle early in the season limited Béliveau's production to thirteen goals in forty-four games. Bernie "Boom Boom" Geoffrion, who was cast in the same fiery mould as his hero, Maurice Richard, impatiently sat out two suspensions for misbehaviour.

Now that Toronto had faded out of the picture as a serious Cup contender, the Detroit-Montreal rivalry reigned supreme. "Detroit was our big rival, there's no doubt about that," Maurice Richard later told author and broadcaster Dick Irvin, Jr. "I remember I used to meet their players in the aisleway of the train. We'd pass by each other and I wouldn't say hello to anybody. I didn't hate too many players, except the guy who played with Gordie Howe. Number seven. Ted Lindsay."

The enmity between Richard and Lindsay dated back to the Red Wing captain's rookie season, when Adams assigned him to check the Canadiens' star. Lindsay, just nineteen, proceeded to hook, gouge and slash his foe with maddening ferocity until Richard had finally had enough. In the bloody fight that followed, the Rocket, to his stunned indignation, came out with no better than a draw. The two had despised each other ever since.

Like Richard, Benny Woit remembers how the long overnight train trips had their effect on the ripening feud between the two hockey clubs. The old six-team NHL often scheduled back-to-back weekend matches between the same opponents. The Habs and Wings would play at the Forum in Montreal on a Saturday night, and then ride the same overnight train to Detroit for the rematch on Sunday. During the playoffs, the back-and-forth shuttling between the two cities kept the players in dangerously close proximity just when tensions were at their highest.

"This happened one year during the playoffs," Woit starts his story. "Dickie Moore and Ted Lindsay had had a big fight in that night's game. Later, as we were boarding the train to go back to Detroit, we had to walk through a compartment full of Canadiens to get to our car. Well, who else but Dickie Moore was standing in the middle of the aisle looking for a seat. I walked by first and then turned to look back. Moore and Lindsay were standing there glaring at one another, their noses nearly touching. All the Canadiens stood up. Everybody on both teams was ready to fight. Finally, Lindsay and Moore turned away and we walked on through. That's the closest I ever saw one of those train trips come to turning really nasty.

"Geez, we hated those guys. There was nothing we liked better than to beat the hell out of the Canadiens."

"We've always played that style. I was brought up under it," Jack Adams once said of the tight-checking, solid positional play that had become the trademark of Detroit teams. At the Olympia in the opening game of the finals, the Red Wings ground out a 3-1 victory in a textbook display of defensive hockey.

Whenever a Canadien made a break for the Detroit zone, a Wing was there to checkmate the move. It took Montreal nine minutes and forty seconds just to break through the Detroit defence for their first shot on Sawchuk, who faced only eighteen the entire game. Lindsay, Reibel and Kelly scored for the Wings. Bernie Geoffrion picked up his own rebound and put a backhander past Sawchuk for Montreal's lone reply.

Maurice Richard had gone scoreless in the semi-final against Boston and then was frustrated again in the opener of the finals. But in the second game the Rocket burst out of his slump, contributing two of the three power-play goals scored by the Canadiens in a 3-1 decision. All three Montreal goals came within a span of fifty-six seconds in the first period. Referee Red Storey first thumbed Howe off the ice for high sticking. Moments later Howe was joined by Tony Leswick, whose sin was slashing. Enjoying a two-man advantage, Montreal's power play put the game away right then and there.

Dickie Moore banked a shot off Geoffrion, who was out front screening Sawchuk, for the first goal. In those days, a penalized player didn't automatically return to the ice after a goal was scored, so Detroit remained two men short. Twenty-one seconds later, Richard took a pass from Moore and ripped a slap shot by Sawchuk. Just before Howe jumped back over the boards, Terry made a spectacular save to rob Richard of another goal. The Wings were still a man short when the Rocket got that one back a few seconds later. On a set-up from Moore, he whipped a backhand shot high into a top corner of the net.

Detroit took back the series' lead with a 5-2 victory in game three. Sawchuk stalled Montreal's momentum in the first period with big saves on Tom Johnson, Eddie Mazur and Richard. At the other end, rookie goaltender Jacques Plante appeared to be fighting the puck. Earlier in the season Plante had taken the number-one job away from Gerry McNeil, who would get his chance later in the series.

His nerves under control and his game restored to its highest level, Sawchuk proceeded to make good on all the promises of the previous spring. "Terry the Pirate more than earned his shutout," reported *The Gazette* after Detroit's 2-0 triumph in game four pushed the Canadiens to the brink of elimination. "Sawchuk was credited with only 28 saves (since Goldham and Woit made so many for him) but some of the stops he handled were incredible. The nimble Detroit goalie kicked aside three straight shots from Johnny McCormack, Bert Olmstead and Floyd Curry in the first period.... He also rose to netminding heights in the second stanza when he handled Beliveau's sizzler neatly."

The tight-checking, hard-hitting contest could easily have gone to the Canadiens, who carried the play throughout most of the game. Sawchuk and his air-tight defence made all the difference. Kelly, Goldham, Pronovost and Woit had rarely played better.

The Cup was within Detroit's grasp when the series resumed at the Olympia for game five. In desperation, Dick Irvin replaced Plante with Gerry McNeil, who hadn't played since February 11 when he injured an ankle in Chicago. Irvin had viewed McNeil suspiciously ever since the netminder had, like Sawchuk, fought a losing battle with his nerves during the playoffs the year before. McNeil had asked to be taken out "for the good of the team" and was replaced by Plante.

Both goalies were unbeatable through regulation time.

McNeil coolly saved the game for Montreal on at least a half-dozen occasions. In the third period, he robbed both Tony Leswick and Johnny Wilson. Sawchuk maintained the scoreless deadlock by stealing goals from Richard and Geoffrion while the Wings played shorthanded.

In the first minute of overtime, the crowd at the Olympia was on its feet and ready to celebrate when Gordie Howe broke in alone on McNeil. The game's greatest player blistered a shot from ten feet out. Sprawling, McNeil somehow managed to kick it out. The stop was so spectacular that the audience momentarily forgot its disappointment and saluted McNeil with a round of applause.

It was Sawchuk who cracked first. Just past the five-minute mark, veteran centreman Kenny Mosdell (a first-team All-Star that year) spun around Bob Goldham and fired a backhander that beat Terry on the far side. "Goldham got a piece of Mosdell," Sawchuk grimly recapped for reporters. "The puck went across in front of me, clipped the goalpost and went into the corner of the net as I grabbed for it."

Dick Irvin believed that two key factors saved the day for Montreal: McNeil's clutch performance and the deployment throughout the game of four lines to Detroit's three. "The fourth line made the difference," Irvin said. "We wore them down with fresh legs."

Relying on the same formula, the Canadiens evened the series with a 4-1 win at the Forum in game six. This was Sawchuk's only weak performance of the playoffs. The opening goal by Bernie Geoffrion—on a wicked slap shot from twenty-five feet out—temporarily unnerved him. The crowd hadn't finished cheering Geoffrion's goal when Floyd Curry beat Sawchuk from close in. Then Curry scored again from almost the same spot a little over a minute later. Rocket Richard completed the damage later on with just his third goal of the playoffs.

Only two games before, the Stanley Cup had been Detroit's for the taking. Now the Wings looked like an exhausted and beaten hockey club. Throughout the sixth game, Tommy Ivan scrambled his lines in a futile attempt to kickstart the offence.

"If we lose Friday night it will take the greatest team in hockey to beat us," crowed Irvin before he boarded the night train back to Detroit for the final showdown of the 1953-54 season.

"Thank gosh for the Harlem Globetrotters," Jack Adams would say when it was all over. The reference was to basketball's famous court jesters, whose long-standing engagement at the Olympia pushed back the start of the seventh game from Thursday to Friday night, giving the leg-weary Red Wings three days instead of the usual two between playoff matches to recuperate.

The additional day off proved a tonic to Sawchuk and his teammates. Detroit outshot Montreal thirty-three to twenty-three in the seventh game and dominated the play for the first two periods.

If not for Gerry McNeil, it would have all been over in the first twenty minutes. Marcel Pronovost, who had excelled throughout the playoffs, tested him in the first minute of play and again later in the period. McNeil also made a tremendous save on Johnny Wilson.

Yet it was the Canadiens who drew first blood. Bert Olmstead stood in front of the net, partially screening Sawchuk, when Floyd Curry shot from forty feet out midway through the first period. Terry got a piece of it, but the puck trickled into the net. Detroit evened the score on a power play late in the second period. Red Kelly fired a low drive that caught a corner of the net behind McNeil.

In the third period, the Red Wings slowed a step while

the Canadiens kept coming on. Several times Sawchuk produced game-saving stops. The best of these came against his former teammate Gaye Stewart, who had been promoted from Buffalo of the American League for the playoffs.

Five times in his NHL career Stewart had scored twenty or more goals. Now he broke through the Detroit defence and fired at a lower corner. "Sawchuk tumbled into it, smothering the puck in his pads," wrote Vince Lunny in *The Hockey News*. "Although he thought for a fleeting moment that he had lost it, he looked into the net and a wide grin broke over his face as he realized the puck was still under him."

For only the second time in NHL history, a seventh game of a Stanley Cup final went into overtime. The previous occasion had also involved Detroit, who defeated the Cinderella New York Rangers on a goal by Pete Babando in 1950.

The end of this epic struggle came suddenly and improbably at 4:29 of extra play. Doug Harvey took possession of the puck behind the Montreal net and fired it around the boards toward the blue line. The puck bounced onto the stick of Tony Leswick as he headed to the Detroit bench at the end of a shift. All Leswick wanted was to get rid of it. From about thirty feet out, he flipped a shot at the Montreal net.

Harvey nonchalantly reached up a gloved hand to knock the floater out of the air. But as the overflow crowd of 15,791 watched in stunned disbelief, the puck deflected off Harvey's thumb and over McNeil into the net.

For a second or two the building remained silent. Then a roar went up and fedoras, rubbers and programs flew through the air and onto the ice. The Wings swarmed Leswick, thumping his back and mussing his jet-black hair. Fans climbed over the boards to join in. A bald-headed man tackled Sawchuk to the ice as he tried to make his way to his teammates.

More than anyone else, the victory belonged to Terry. Throughout the post-season he had been the most valuable Red Wing on the ice. When his exhausted teammates faltered in the third period of the final game, his save on Gaye Stewart carried them into overtime. The goat of the season past was once again a playoff hero.

A photograph taken later that night in the Detroit dressing room shows Sawchuk kneeling in front of the Stanley Cup, the focus of everyone's attention. Lindsay has the goalie's head affectionately cupped in his hands. Tommy Ivan is beaming down at him. Terry has just taken a long sip from the Cup and now jokingly has his tongue out, asking for more.

## Chapter Six

# THE WHAMMY

"I wish there were no summers," Terry groaned a few months after the Stanley Cup victory. "The only summer sunshine I ever seem to see is when I'm looking out of a hospital window."

This time it was an automobile accident that ruined Sawchuk's off-season. On the night of July 11, while driving home with a friend from a suburban golf course, his car skidded off the road and hit a tree. Sawchuk was rushed to hospital and treated for a collapsed lung as well as bruises and cuts on his hands and knees. His golfing companion suffered a fractured hip. Sawchuk's car was demolished.

"Another car was coming toward me, as I remember it, on this gravel road," Terry said from his hospital bed the next day. "Fortunately I wasn't going very fast. When a third car pulled out into my lane coming toward me, I had to leave the road on the right or hit him.

"This won't affect my hockey career in any way. It's only a minor injury. I'll be out in a few days."

By now Terry had developed a macabre fascination with the injury jinx that kayoed him for a fifth straight summer. Like all goalies who played in the days before face masks, he accepted broken teeth and facial cuts as unavoidable hazards of his trade. Even the eye injury in the minors that had almost ended his career and the three operations on his elbow didn't seem all that unusual considering how he made his living. But a burst appendix and a ruptured lung in successive summers on top of the mysterious weight loss and *everything* else that had happened to him? This was getting strange.

Sawchuk turned the evidence of his misfortune into a

most unusual hobby. "I've been collecting all the parts they take out of me," he told a reporter that winter. "I have one bottle for the teeth I've lost, another for the bone chips and another for my appendix. I had them specially pickled to add to the collection.

"I know it sounds odd, but what's the difference between that and collecting stamps or old coins," Terry insisted. "Not many people have the chance to get the collection I have of old pieces of me."

A week after the car wreck Sawchuk was back home with Pat, who was expecting their first child at any moment. Terry's mother, Anne, arrived from Winnipeg to help out during the last days of Pat's pregnancy and after she brought the baby home.

On August 5, Pat delivered a healthy boy they named Gerald Thomas after Terry's fifteen-year-old brother. Sawchuk often told interviewers that his dream was to last long enough in the NHL to one day play alongside his brother, a promising right winger on a juvenile team back home in Winnipeg.

That summer Tommy Ivan announced his departure from the Red Wings to become general manager of the Chicago Black Hawks. Ivan had hoped to one day succeed Adams as the GM in Detroit, but Trader Jack, now fifty-nine years old, gave no indication of voluntarily stepping aside.

Ivan's recruitment by the Hawks was applauded around the league as an important first step in the rejuvenation of an almost moribund franchise. The Hawks had finished in the cellar four of the past five seasons and were losing so much money that owner James Norris, Jr. had threatened to cease operation unless the league helped rebuild them to a competitive level.

The NHL's three strongest teams, Detroit, Montreal and

Toronto, agreed to help stock the Chicago line-up. Toronto contributed forwards Harry Watson, Dave Creighton and Bob Hassard. Montreal pitched in with another trio of attackers, Ed Litzenberger, Dick Gamble and Paul Masnick. In addition to Tommy Ivan, Detroit president Marguerite Norris sent her big brother the versatile Metro Prystai. This last transfer was lustily condemned by Detroit fans, who didn't appreciate the new tilt in the relationship between the Hawks and Wings. When James Norris, Sr. had been alive, they knew that the best interests of their own team always came first.

The surprise choice to succeed Ivan was thirty-seven-year-old Jimmy Skinner, a rotund little man in whom many saw an uncanny physical resemblance to Jack Adams. Skinner had most recently been the coach of the Wings' Junior A club in Hamilton. Before that he handled the junior Spitfires in Windsor. A career minor leaguer in his playing days, Skinner's closest prior brush with the NHL came in 1944, when he was the last man cut at the Red Wings' training camp. After that he had turned to coaching.

It was generally assumed that Ivan's old job would go to Bud Poile, the boss of the Wings' top farm club, the Edmonton Flyers. But Adams chose Skinner for two important reasons: he was familiar with several members of the varsity squad from having coached them as juniors (including Sawchuk during his two-week stay in Windsor); and because he would do exactly what Adams told him to do.

"He was a door-opener, a yes-man for Adams," Ted Lindsay recalled of Skinner. Unlike Tommy Ivan, who had acted as a buffer between Adams and the players, Skinner held the old man in awe. From his nearby seat in the stands, Adams would scream instructions at his coach. Ivan had tuned him out and carried on with his own game plan. But Skinner would get rattled and lose his concentration trying to please Adams.

In Ivan, the Red Wings lost a friend and their staunchest advocate. While many of the players liked Skinner, who was outgoing and personable, not many of them thought he was an adequate replacement for Ivan as coach.

At the start of the 1954-55 season, Detroit no longer necessarily ranked as the NHL's best team. All that had separated them from Montreal in the Stanley Cup final the previous spring was the superlative goaltending of Terry Sawchuk and a fluke goal by Tony Leswick. The Canadiens possessed a better balanced and more explosive attack.

"I don't even rate Detroit as the team to beat," Toronto coach King Clancy said. "The Canadiens look tougher to me."

The Red Wings dropped five of their first seven matches against Montreal. At the New Year, for the first time since 1948, Detroit did not stand atop the standings. The Canadiens led the second-place Wings by four points. Geoffrion, Béliveau and Richard led the league in scoring.

But it was not yet time to write Detroit's epitaph. The Wings needed time to adjust to the shock of losing Tommy Ivan and to their new coach. It also didn't help that injuries and slumps hampered both Gordie Howe and Ted Lindsay throughout the season. Because Detroit didn't enjoy the same surplus of talent as Montreal, a slowdown by any of the Big Four—Howe, Lindsay, Kelly and Sawchuk—was bound to show in the standings.

In early November, a shoulder injury forced Howe out of the line-up for the first time in 382 consecutive regular-season matches, an Iron Man run dating back to January of 1949. Howe missed six games and then struggled to regain his scoring touch. In one span of seventeen games, he netted just four goals.

Lindsay, whom the Wings counted on in so many ways, suffered through an even tougher season than his partner.

The captain was still trying to shake off an early slump when injuries coupled with league suspensions for bad behaviour put him out of action for a total of twenty-one games. When he did play, Lindsay looked so ineffective at times that old enemy Dick Irvin uncharitably pronounced: "You don't have to bother putting a check on Ted Lindsay any more. He's faded away to nothing."

Just when Detroit fans were ready to give up on a seventh-straight league championship, the Red Wings went on a mid-season tear that saw them win fourteen of twenty games (with four ties) and temporarily seize first place from the Habs. By mid-January Sawchuk led the league with nine shutouts and had closed the Vezina lead built up earlier by Toronto's Harry Lumley.

Terry and his defence provided the backbone through this stretch. Providing the spark in Lindsay's absence was Marcel Bonin, a brawny twenty-three-year-old French-Canadian winger who had been riding the pine before Terrible Ted went out with injuries. In the manner of Eddie "The Entertainer" Shack, who came along a few years later and whose manic skating style has been likened to a deflating balloon, Bonin could lift a crowd to its feet without his once ever having actually touched the puck.

At first Jimmy Skinner tried him in Lindsay's spot alongside Howe and Delvecchio. But Bonin proved too distracting there. He finally clicked on a new line with centre Dutch Reibel and right winger Bill Dineen. In the fourteen games Lindsay sat out during this period, the trio figured in twenty of the thirty-nine Detroit goals.

A wire-service photo from that season shows a shirtless Bonin flexing his extravagant muscles in a classic muscle-man pose. He was willing to do almost anything on a dare or for a laugh. A stunt Bonin routinely performed for his astonished teammates was to bite chunks out of an ordinary water glass and then slowly chew the shards into slivers. A stern warning from Jack Adams finally put an end to that particular bit of fun.

But Bonin, who was traded before the next season and eventually became a fan favourite with Montreal, is best remembered today as the hockey player who once wrestled a bear. The bout took place when as a stripling of seventeen he visited a touring carnival that featured a fighting bear. A prize of $1,000 was offered to anyone who could pin the beast for ten seconds. The legendary boxer Joe Louis acted as referee.

"As a gag, I gave it a try," Bonin remembered. Though the bear was declawed and had no teeth, it remained a larger, tougher and smellier opponent than anyone he ever fought on a hockey rink. "I got knocked around for about ten minutes and realized there was no $1,000 for me and that was that."

In late January, the Wings suddenly stopped winning. They dropped out of first place and fell five points behind the Canadiens. On February 5, Boston hammered Detroit 8-4, the most goals Sawchuk had allowed since the 9-0 nightmare in Montreal two years before.

Four days later Jack Adams announced that for the first time in Terry's five-year NHL career, he was being benched for a reason other than injuries. "They were scoring goals on him that ordinarily he'd put in his hip pocket," Adams explained. Glenn Hall was summoned from Edmonton and told he would be starting the next three games.

"I've known Terry since he was a youngster," Adams continued. "I could see the strain was starting to tell. We figured this move was both for the best interests of the team and the best interests of Sawchuk. It is in no way a disciplinary move.

"Actually it can have benefits in several ways. Terry can take some needed rest and come back much sharper. We will get another look at Hall, who has been playing well. And while Terry is out, some of the other players on the club may appreciate his efforts more than they have part of this season."

Sawchuk was stunned by the news, which he only found out about after Adams made his announcement to the press. "I really don't think I need a rest," he said, "but I guess they think I do."

It was no secret to reporters covering the team that during the past few weeks Terry had been even more short-tempered and gloomier than usual. His moods always acted as a barometer of how well both he and the team were playing. At the best of times, reporters approached the goalie warily, hoping to be lucky enough to catch him on one of his good days.

"You'd see him sitting there, lost in his thoughts, and some nights you'd lose your nerve," wrote Joe Falls of the *Detroit Free Press*. "You'd say to yourself, oh, well, you'll get him another time; let's see what Gordie and Alex and Sid are saying."

"His style was to listen placidly to a question, then look the reporter in the eye and snarl, 'get lost,' or words to that effect," Jim Proudfoot of *The Toronto Star* remembered. "A simple question, sensible in his case, such as 'how do you feel?' would elicit this response: 'With my hands dummy.' To a query about some incident—'you saw the game, didn't you.'"

Like many players, Sawchuk had learned that he couldn't always trust reporters to keep confidences or to get their facts straight. He was angered that December by a Boston newspaper report that had him on the verge of quitting the game because of a problem with his vision. As already noted, during his long career Sawchuk often threatened to retire. But not this time, and he definitely wasn't having any trouble with his eyesight.

John Walter of *The Detroit News* did some checking and discovered that the rumour had started with an acquaintance of Terry's, who talked to him after a game in New York. Terry told him that his stomach was upset. The acquaintance repeated the story to referee Red Storey, who mentioned it to referee-in-chief Carl Voss, who repeated it to Boston Bruin president Walter Brown. By the time Brown passed it on to veteran Boston reporter Bill Grimes, Sawchuk's complaint had escalated from a mildly upset stomach to career-threatening eye trouble. Grimes wrote the story, which was picked up by the wire services and announced as fact by radio stations in every NHL city.

"What really used to steam Terry was how a reporter might act like his friend one day, and then turn around and write something negative about him the next—like maybe how he was slipping and about to be traded," says Benny Woit. "Terry really didn't want the attention of the press. He just wanted everyone to leave him alone."

Woit, Marcel Pronovost and other friends believe that Sawchuk's moodiness with reporters and many of his teammates was his way of protecting his privacy and staying focused on his job. "Fame and fortune never sat well with him and he had a tough time accepting criticism or accolades," Pronovost told author Howard Berger. "He cherished his privacy and looked upon all the public focus as an intrusion. Being rude and abrupt was his defense mechanism...it was not the *real* Terry Sawchuk."

None of his close friends deny that Terry could be difficult and often impossible to figure out. One of the things that most annoyed teammates was his nonchalant attitude toward practices. Sawchuk had never been an enthusiastic practice goalie. After all, a fellow could get injured just as easily in a workout as in a game. But the days when he showed up and did the absolute minimum became more frequent with the passing years. Often he was in a foul temper, hung-over from the night before.

"If you shot a puck that hit him anywhere other than the pads, he'd glare at you," a former Wing remembers. "If you shot a high one, he said, 'Don't do that again!' Then, if you fired a second high one, he'd throw that stick at you. Have you ever seen a goalie stick flying at you? That's scary.

"Terry figured all that counted was how he performed in the actual games. Which was true, but that didn't help the rest of us sharpen our shooting skills. I know his attitude pissed off some of the guys." Most of the Wings would end up down at the other end of the rink, peppering shots at practice goalie and trainer Lefty Wilson.

"There's no doubt that Terry was a moody bugger," agrees Lefty Wilson. "You never knew whether he was going to talk to you or kick your ass."

Pronovost, who roomed with Sawchuk for years on the road, has often recalled how, when they first awoke in the morning, he would say good morning to his friend in both French and English. "If he answered, I knew we would talk at least a little that day. But if he didn't reply, which was most days, we didn't speak the entire day."

And yet, with only a few exceptions, most of Terry's Detroit teammates remember him fondly. "We all just learned to live with him, to accept his moods," Johnny Wilson says. "Number one, he was a great goaltender. We felt lucky to have Terry for our teammate. Sure, he often didn't take practices seriously—but he was always ready to play the games."

Wilson says that at least part of Sawchuk's grouchiness was put on for the benefit of his teammates. "He was a

kibitzer. Sometimes he'd act like he was mad about something, but he was really just kidding around, playing on his
reputation as a miserable SOB. You could see it in his eyes.
When you got to know him, you realized what a terrific
sense of humour Terry had. There were a few guys on the
team who didn't understand that. But none of us, even the
ones who weren't all that crazy about Terry, would have
traded him for any other goalie in hockey."

Almost as soon as Adams announced Sawchuk's benching,
rumours began circulating that he was about to be the central figure in a major trade. Terry felt angry enough at
Adams right then that he half convinced himself that this
time a deal might be for the best. At least he put on a brave
front for the press.

"A year ago the reports had me going to Chicago or New
York," Sawchuk said. "I was really upset. Now they've got
me on the trading block again. This time I don't care. It
doesn't bother me a bit. If I'm traded, I'm traded."

Glenn Hall looked as capable as ever in backstopping
Detroit to a 2-1 victory in Toronto on Saturday night. The
following evening in Chicago, the Red Wings trounced the
Hawks 5-1.

Hall never did get his promised third start. He was hur-
riedly called back to Edmonton, where his wife was sick in
hospital. So Sawchuk filled in for the man who had been
filling in for him. His strong performance and a late goal by
Dutch Reibel lifted Detroit to a 2-2 tie with Chicago in his
return.

After just two games away, Sawchuk's abilities appeared
fully restored. Had the enforced holiday refreshed him?
Had his nerves suddenly stopped jumping? As usual, Jack
Adams felt certain he knew the answer.

"Terry is back using his famous submarine crouch,"

Adams said. "I told him shortly before taking him out of the line-up he had forgotten the one thing all young goalies try to copy from him—his crouch."

One day a young though not entirely innocent Gordie Howe picked up Black Jack Stewart's hockey stick and was amazed by its great weight. "Jack, how the hell do you shoot with a stick like this?" asked Howe. "It's not for shooting," replied Stewart, "it's for breaking arms."

Even judged by the standards of the old six-team NHL, 1954-55 stands apart as a season unmatched for its violence and controversy. Several times that year the mayhem spilled into the stands. During a game at the Olympia in mid-November, Ted Lindsay climbed into the seats after a heckler. Other Red Wings loyally followed their captain, including Sawchuk, who, goal pads and all, managed to clamber up and over a seven-foot fence to get into the fray.

When he wasn't injured or suspended, Lindsay simmered on full boil, fighting foes and fans alike. On January 22 in Toronto, two nights after coming back from the injuries that gave bear-fighting Marcel Bonin his chance, Lindsay whacked a spectator with his stick after the fan lunged over the boards at Gordie Howe.

In the past, NHL president Clarence Campbell had been content to levy fines against Lindsay and the league's other violent offenders. But he had finally decided that the growing lawlessness must be contained. Over the predictable protestations of Jack Adams, Campbell suspended Lindsay for ten days, which meant he would have to sit out four games.

Though not everyone was paying attention, a clear message had been sent forth from the president's office in Montreal. Before the season was through, Campbell's crackdown on violence would play a key role in deciding the outcome of the scoring and Vezina races, the final standings and the winner of the Stanley Cup.

Maurice Richard led the league in scoring, two points in front of teammate Bernie Geoffrion, when the Canadiens faced off against the Bruins on March 13. Hockey's all-time scoring leader had his heart set on winning the scoring title that had mysteriously eluded him his entire career. Montreal stood two points ahead of Detroit in the battle for first place.

An eruption of the famous Richard temper that night in Boston formed the next link in the fateful chain that had started with Lindsay's suspension. When a high stick from Bruin Hal Laycoe cut Richard on the top of his head, he responded by viciously hacking Laycoe across the shoulder and face with his stick. Twice the officials intervened and took away his lumber. Both times Richard broke free, picked up another stick from the ice, and went back at Laycoe. Finally, he turned on linesman Cliff Thompson, punching him hard twice in the face.

It was only one of several times that season that Richard had attacked an opponent with his stick. He had also struck another linesman, George Hayes, with an empty glove. That time Campbell had let Richard off with just a $250 fine.

But now the league president was determined to make an example of Richard, who through the years had been issued countless warnings and fines but never seemed to learn his lesson. Did the Rocket, who was worshipped by hockey fans throughout Quebec, think himself above the laws that governed lesser players? After weighing the evidence, Campbell suspended Richard for the final three games of the season and the entire playoffs.

Outside of *la belle province*, the decision handed down by Campbell was largely applauded as righteous and long overdue. Boston captain Ed Sandford summed up the general feeling when he said, "Too bad for the rest of the Montreal team, but he had it coming to him."

The Red Wings, the team with potentially the most to gain by Richard's absence from the Montreal line-up, rejoiced. First place was still up for grabs, and another Stanley Cup suddenly seemed in the bag. The strong feeling was that no team, not even one as deep in talent as the Canadiens, could possibly withstand such a devastating loss.

"I had thought Richard might be suspended until January 1 next season," said Jack Adams, conveniently forgetting his earlier complaint about the harshness of Lindsay's four-game suspension. "Not enough," echoed Jimmy Skinner.

But the most hypocritical reaction of all came from Richard's nemesis, Terrible Ted Lindsay, the outlaw who twice that season had fought with the paying customers. Lindsay managed to keep a straight face when he told reporters that Richard should have been suspended for life.

In Montreal and throughout Quebec, there was stunned disbelief at the severity of Campbell's judgement. In light of Lindsay's earlier suspension, fans had expected their hero to be suspended for the remaining three games of the regular schedule. But not the playoffs, never that.

Disbelief quickly turned to rage. Campbell was accused of selling out to the owners of the league's other five teams, who wanted Richard cut down to size once and for all. Some French-Canadians even suggested that Campbell's decision was the result of an anti-French bias.

On Wednesday, March 16, the day Campbell announced Richard's suspension, the Red Wings beat the Bruins 5-4 to move into a tie with the idle Canadiens for first place. Detroit had been the hottest team in hockey for more than a month now, losing only once in their past fifteen starts. The Wings had two games remaining, in Montreal the next night, and a rematch with the Habs Sunday at the Olympia.

Montreal also played a home game Saturday night against the Rangers.

Campbell's habit was to attend most games at the Forum. But since the announcement of Richard's suspension, his office had received dozens of threatening calls. Montreal police urged him to stay away from Thursday night's game.

Campbell refused to be intimidated. Accompanied by his fiancée, who was also his secretary, Campbell entered the building shortly after the start of the game and, though greeted by a storm of verbal abuse, stoically took his usual seat.

By the end of the first period, the mood of the Forum crowd had turned ugly. The Canadiens trailed 4-1 and had looked dispirited and bewildered. "Without Richard, the team had lost its soul," Montreal's general manager Frank Selke recalled in his memoirs. "Our boys were certain that, in one fell stroke, they had lost both the league championship and the Stanley Cup."

The crowd started shouting, "*On veut Richard—à bas Campbell!*" ("We want Richard—down with Campbell!") and pressed toward the box where Campbell sat. They pelted Campbell and his fiancée with peanuts and programs. A young tough in a leather jacket threw a punch at the league president. Then a tear-gas bomb exploded and smoke slowly filled the arena. People began hustling for the corridors and the exits. Campbell and his fiancée sought shelter in a passageway.

The Red Wings waited out the tumult in their dressing room, not certain at first what was going on in the stadium around them. They found out about the gas bomb when the team doctor burst in, tears streaming down his face. Several players hurried to place wet towels under the door to stop the gas from seeping in. A short while later someone reported that people were breaking windows and looting stores in the streets outside the Forum.

Through it all the players tried to stay focused on the game which, as far as they knew, would resume once the arena cleared of smoke. After about an hour, word finally came that Campbell had declared the game forfeited to Detroit.

"Quiet, quiet everybody," a sweating Jack Adams stood up and roared. "Listen, you guys, I want you to pay attention to this. We're going out of here together. I want everybody to remain in the group, and nobody, nobody do you hear, is to stop to talk to anyone. We'll keep moving along quickly to the bus waiting at the end of the hall, and get the heck out of this place."

Much later, when the team bus had finally made its way through the confusion of the downtown streets to the train station in Westmount, Adams took a parting shot at the hockey player who had triggered what immediately became known as the Richard Riot—and at the fans who had made such a tragedy possible.

"In my thirty-eight years of hockey I've never seen anything so disgraceful," Adams said. "If they hadn't pampered Maurice Richard, built him up as a hero until he felt he was bigger than hockey itself, this wouldn't have happened."

The rioting continued through the night. The next day the situation remained so volatile that Richard made a public appeal for calm. Speaking in French and English, Richard firmly told his fans that the violence must stop— "so that no further harm will be done. I will take my punishment and come back next year."

Following the forfeit in Montreal, Detroit led the Canadiens by two points. Just as tight was the battle between Sawchuk and Harry Lumley for the Vezina. Lumley held a slim two-goal advantage with two games still to play for the Maple Leafs, who were fighting Boston for third spot.

The Toronto press complained that Sawchuk had received two "terrific breaks" in the past few days—the first when Richard, who had scored eight goals against him in twelve games, drew his suspension; the second when Terry only had to play one period against the Canadiens before the riot broke out Thursday night. Prior to Thursday, the Habs had averaged better than three goals a game against him.

More than two hundred police patrolled the Forum when Montreal beat New York 4-2 on Saturday night to pull back into a tie for first place. Because they had outscored Detroit by thirty goals to that point in the season, Montreal could take the title with a win or a tie in Detroit. Nothing less than a victory would do it for the Wings.

The same evening in Toronto, Lumley blanked Chicago 5-0, a win that clinched third place for the Leafs and put even more pressure on Sawchuk to come up big against the Canadiens.

Police searched everyone who entered the Olympia on Sunday for tear-gas canisters and other articles of mischief. After warnings of a possible riot by radical Montreal die-hards, dozens of officers were strategically placed through-out the arena. The surreal backdrop seemed to further unnerve the Canadiens and to bring out the best in the red-hot Red Wings.

Ted Lindsay, who had missed the last three games with injuries, checked himself out of the hospital to personally spearhead Detroit's drive to a seventh-consecutive league title. His opening goal as well as scores by Reibel and Leswick put the Wings up 3-0 by early in the second period, when it was announced that Toronto had lost in New York by a score of 3-2. If Sawchuk could hold the shutout, he would win the Vezina by a one-goal margin.

Lindsay scored twice more for the hat-trick and Del-vecchio added a single to complete a 6-0 rout that one

Montreal writer called "the most painful hockey slaughter ever suffered by the Montreal Canadiens."

"With three seconds to go I knew I was in," Terry said after being carried off the ice by his teammates. "I bet I hit the ceiling of the Olympia when I jumped."

In winning his third Vezina in five years, Sawchuk produced a league-leading twelve shutouts and once again kept his goals-against average under 2 (1.96). Harry Lumley, who had won the prize by the same one-goal margin the season before, admitted to being miffed by Montreal's poor performance in the season finale. "You'd hardly credit a team with Canadiens' power getting blanked in the final game with the league title at stake."

The defeat was probably hardest on the Canadien who couldn't play. Rocket Richard lost the scoring title to Bernie Geoffrion by a single point. Richard never again came close to winning the Art Ross Trophy he coveted so much.

Red Burnett of *The Toronto Star* voiced the prevailing opinion when he wrote that the third-place Maple Leafs had about as much chance "as a snowball parked on the equator" in their semi-final against Detroit.

The Wings whipped Toronto in four straight, by scores of 7-4, 2-1, 2-1 and 3-0. It was a case of too much firepower and too much Sawchuk.

"I've never seen Terry Sawchuk look sharper," praised Adams. "He made two and three game-saving stops a night in the last three games of the Toronto series. That's the difference between a great goalie and the average netminder."

Without Maurice Richard in the Montreal line-up, many analysts expected the Habs to struggle at least a little in their series with fourth-place Boston. But the Canadiens pulled themselves together to beat the Bruins in five games and reach the Stanley Cup finals for the fifth-straight year.

It had been wrong to think that Montreal would be unable to recover from the loss of the Rocket. The Canadiens had too much pride and too much talent to roll over and die in the finals. Also sustaining them was their searing hatred of the Red Wings.

Detroit won the opener at the Olympia—but just barely. It took Marty Pavelich's shorthanded goal late in the third period to finally decide the outcome. The score was 2-2 when Pavelich intercepted a Doug Harvey pass and beat a lunging Jacques Plante. At 19:42 Lindsay added an empty netter to put away the game 4-2.

Sawchuk turned in another outstanding performance. Yet no matter how well he played, or how much reassuring praise he received from Jack Adams, he continued to be the focus of persistent trade rumours. A new one that surfaced on the opening day of the finals had Terry heading to Chicago along with Benny Woit and Alex Delvecchio in exchange for Eddie Litzenberger and two unnamed players.

The word around the league was that no matter what he did in the playoffs, Sawchuk was as good as gone from Detroit.

A few hours before the start of the second game, Dink Carroll of *The Gazette* visited the Detroit hotel room shared by Bernie Geoffrion and Jean Béliveau. "You want a scoop?" asked Geoffrion, his faced covered with shaving lather, while Béliveau stretched out on his bed. "If Glenn Hall's wife doesn't get sick he would be tending goal for the Red Wings in this series. Terry Sawchuk knows it. He won't be playing for Detroit next year....

"You want another scoop? Detroit was going to trade Ted Lindsay to Boston for Ed Sandford a few months ago. I predict Sawchuk will be sold or traded to Boston.

"What a life—hockey," shrugged Geoffrion, who was

himself feeling a little jaded with the game. At the start of the semi-final with Boston, Geoffrion had been booed by the fans at the Forum for beating their beloved Richard in the scoring race.

The Howe-Lindsay-Reibel line dominated the play in the second game, combining for twelve points in a 7-1 blowout. Lindsay scored four times and appeared to be having the time of his life. Terrible Ted was at his most provocative and infuriating in the third period, when he goaded old foe Dickie Moore into a major penalty.

When Moore dropped his gloves to fight, Lindsay turned away laughing and repeatedly pointed up at the score, which stood at 7-0 at the time. Moore, who had already been issued a minor penalty, began to pound furiously on the wire screen that separated him from the penalty timekeeper. When referee Red Storey upped his sentence to a game misconduct, Moore went berserk. He charged across the ice to the Detroit bench and again challenged Lindsay to fight. Lindsay just grinned and once again pointed up at the score. Then Moore and Gordie Howe jousted briefly with their sticks. Moore was finally dragged back to the Montreal bench, where he attacked a heckling fan before making his way to the dressing room.

Both Lindsay and Howe, who had a goal and three assists, were determined to atone for subpar performances during the regular season. Howe had finished an unaccustomed fifth in the scoring race and, for the first time in recent memory, neither player would be named to either of the post-season All-Star squads.

Bernie Geoffrion got the fans back on his side with three goals in a 4-2 Canadiens' triumph when the series resumed in Montreal. The loss was Detroit's first in fifteen games. Montreal won the next one 5-3 to square the series.

The home-ice advantage proved to be a crucial factor throughout the finals. Back in Detroit for game five, Gordie Howe turned the hat-trick in a 5-1 final that placed the Wings just one win away from their seventh Stanley Cup. Howe's playoff total of eight goals and eleven assists set a new record, breaking the old mark of eighteen established by Toe Blake of the Canadiens in 1943-44.

Sawchuk came down with a slight case of the flu before the game. But his defence provided ample protection and he had to face only twenty-one shots. Doctors ordered him to stay in bed during the return trip to Montreal.

Once again home ice proved a charm in game six. Geoffrion's second goal of the night, which boosted the score to 4-2 in Montreal's favour, enraged a still-feverish Sawchuk. He argued that Geoffrion had kicked the puck in. When referee Red Storey refused to listen to reason, Sawchuk had to be pulled off him by the linesman and his teammates. The final score in this one was 6-3.

Interviewed in Winnipeg a few weeks later, Terry described the series so far. "After we win the first two at home, we figure we'll fool them when we get to Montreal," he said. "They'll be looking for us to play it close so we go out to throw it at them. Boom!—it backfires and we lose. We get another lead at home and go back to Montreal and we figure we'll really jolt them this time. Just go all out, that's all. Boom!—another backfire. What a crazy series."

Happily for the Red Wings, they had finished in first place, which meant the seventh game was played at the Olympia. Detroit hadn't lost at home since these same Habitants had beaten them way back on December 19.

Sawchuk robbed Kenny Mosdell in the opening minute of play and came up with at least four more crucial stops before Alex Delvecchio opened the scoring at 7:12 of the second period. Delvecchio whirled around defenceman Butch Bouchard and unleashed a fifteen-foot, ankle-high backhander past Plante into the far corner.

Howe scored what proved to be the winner later that period when he deflected a Marcel Pronovost shot into the Montreal net. At the start of the third period, the Canadiens went full out on the attack. But the strategy backfired when defencemen Tom Johnson and Butch Bouchard were caught up the ice, allowing Delvecchio to slip through for a break-away. Delvecchio fooled Plante with a perfect deke to score his second goal of the night and pad the lead to 3-0.

Montreal finally got one back when Floyd Curry batted Geoffrion's rebound past Terry. Then, with just over five minutes remaining on the clock, the Wings closed ranks and patiently waited out the final buzzer.

It was the mighty Red Wings' second Stanley Cup in as many years, their third in the past four seasons, and their fourth in the past six years.

By the start of the next season, fully half of the 1954-55 Stanley Cup line-up would be inexplicably traded away by Jack Adams, leaving in ruins the dynasty he had built. Among the missing, as so often predicted, was Terry Sawchuk.

The Red Wings' victory party was still going strong at 3:15 the next morning when Ted Lindsay made his way to the microphone in the ballroom of Detroit's Sheraton-Cadillac Hotel.

"Ladies and gentlemen!" Lindsay said, cutting through the drunken chatter and the playing of the orchestra. "Ladies and gentlemen! Attention, please! Let us observe a few moments of silence out of respect to Dick Irvin and the Montreal Canadiens, whose train is pulling out!"

As the laughter swelled, Lindsay paused a moment, a

wicked grin creasing his face. "My friend Dick—he's the one who faded away tonight."

Under the direction of a new coach, Toe Blake, Montreal would win the Stanley Cup for the next five years.

TERRY, Pat and young Gerry vacationed in Winnipeg that spring. Sawchuk's homecomings were always big events in the old neighbourhood, compared by one family friend to the return of a conquering hero. Most days Terry, his nine-month-old son cradled in his arms, took leisurely strolls down Bowman Avenue, frequently stopping to chat with old neighbours and proudly show off the new addition.

Despite the trade rumours that had dogged him for the past three years, Sawchuk was genuinely shocked when, on Friday, June 2, word came that he was the centrepiece of a massive nine-player deal with the Boston Bruins. Desperate for a quality goaltender, Boston parted with forwards Ed Sandford, Real Chevrefils and Norm Corcoran, defenceman Warren Godfrey, and rookie goalie Gilles Boisvert in return for the three-time Vezina winner and forwards Marcel Bonin, Vic Stasiuk and Lorne Davis.

"I first heard the rumour over the radio Thursday," a shaken Sawchuk told the reporters who gathered outside the family home. "Then Boston phoned me today to tell me they were my new owners."

It was the Red Wings' second major trade in less than a week. Five days before, Jack Adams had dealt Glen Skov, Tony Leswick, Johnny Wilson and Benny Woit to Chicago. There were now just ten survivors from the squad that had won the Stanley Cup less than two months before.

"We let Sawchuk go because we found ourselves with two top goalies," Adams said the night of the deal. "Hall is more advanced now than Sawchuk when he joined us and all the players insist Glenn has been NHL material for the past year.... It was a case of trading one of them and

Sawchuk is the established player. Consequently, he brought a better offer."

Terry tried his best to maintain a brave front for the press, saying that he was "a bit sorry" about the trade. "It's still an honour to be playing in the NHL, especially under a coach like Milt Schmidt."

But those who spent time with Sawchuk in the days immediately following the deal remember how completely devastated he was by the news. Naïvely, considering all the warning signs, Terry had convinced himself that this day would never come. It seemed unthinkable that he was being forced to leave the organization that for so long had been his second home.

The trade further eroded Sawchuk's always shaky confidence. Soon afterwards Trent Frayne visited Terry and Pat at the four-bedroom ranch-style house they had recently built on her father's golf course in Union Lake. Frayne recalled a steamy summer night spent drinking beer with the distraught goalie at the golf-course clubhouse.

"Does it mean I'm washed up?" Terry repeatedly asked Frayne of the trade. He couldn't understand why Adams had chosen Glenn Hall over him. What had he done to deserve to be traded? What did it all mean?

Adams's *official* explanation for his summertime house-cleaning was that he did it all in response to telltale signs of deterioration he (though no one else in hockey) had first spotted in the Wings midway through the past season. The subsequent Stanley Cup victory deterred him not in the least. As Adams often said, he had made the mistake of standing pat with an aging championship squad once, and that was never going to happen again. Room had to be made on the roster for such young minor league stars as Hall, Johnny Bucyk, Norm Ullman and Bronco Horvath.

That the trades substantially reduced the club's payroll

was an unspoken, though no doubt equally persuasive, consideration for Adams. Detroit's incoming rookies would naturally earn far less than the outgoing veterans they were replacing. Sawchuk's annual salary by that point was approximately $16,000, the highest of any goalie in the league.

Salary considerations had often played a part in Red Wing trades. Bill Quackenbush and Black Jack Stewart numbered among the team's top earners—and the NHL's outstanding performers—when Adams had dealt them away.

"When you're with Detroit and that salary goes up too high, you can figure you'll be going because they have somebody right behind you all of the time," Sawchuk said later.

There were also whispers that Adams and others in the Detroit hierarchy had grown weary of Sawchuk's temperamental nature. Terry often rudely brushed off fans who asked for autographs. He also hated and usually tried to avoid making speeches to youth groups and other organizations on what was known as the rubber-chicken circuit. These were cardinal sins in an organization that paid more attention to customer goodwill than any other in professional sport.

Looking back it's plain to see that the deals made by Trader Jack that summer destroyed the Detroit dynasty. Of the five players sent to the Red Wings in the Sawchuk trade, only Warren Godfrey still held a place on the squad by the end of the next season. Adams was fleeced just as badly by his old protégé Tommy Ivan in the swap with Chicago. Only one of the four players received, defenceman Bucky Hollingworth, stuck with the team for a full season.

Some say now that Adams was never the brilliant judge of hockey talent he was always made out to be, especially by the sycophantic Detroit press. The revisionist viewpoint is that much of the credit for the Wings' success should rightly go to the team's two top scouts, Carson Cooper and Fred Pinckney, who for years kept the organization stocked with a deep stream of prize talent.

Adams talked of the promise of Horvath, Bucyk and Ullman. But soon Horvath and Bucyk would also be traded away, only to become stars with another team. Adams dealt Sawchuk to Boston for nothing of real value. Yet the Canadiens, who weren't yet convinced of the abilities of Jacques Plante, had been willing to offer a package for Terry that included young defenceman Tom Johnson, a future Norris Trophy winner. It was even rumoured that Montreal might be willing to deal the great Doug Harvey.

"If we had got Harvey we would have won seven or eight Cups," Ted Lindsay recalled bitterly to *The Globe and Mail*'s David Shoalts. "Adams didn't make the deal because he didn't want to make Montreal stronger. Geez, they won the next five Cups, so how much stronger could you have made them."

Lindsay didn't object to the *idea* of trading Sawchuk. Adams was right that Glenn Hall was fully capable of replacing him in net for the Wings. Today, Hall calls his predecessor "the greatest goalie I ever saw." But there are knowledgeable hockey fans who would argue that the man known by the moniker Mr. Goalie eventually became just as good and maybe even better.

No, what Lindsay and many others resented was that Adams had gotten so little in return for the goalie then widely regarded as the best in the game.

Boston general manager Lynn Patrick could hardly believe his good fortune in having landed Sawchuk. "Oh, we'd been negotiating a trade with Detroit, all right," Patrick said, "but we'd been talking about several players, only one of them a goaltender. No goaler's name had been mentioned, however, and we thought we were talking about Glenn Hall…. In our wildest dreams we didn't think we could pry loose a guy of Sawchuk's status. When we found out that the mysterious goaltender of our negotiations was Terry, we were flabbergasted."

Patrick readily acknowledged that his team needed good goaltending "in the worst way." The now-retired Sugar Jim Henry had suddenly lost his magic the season before. Youngster Johnny Henderson also saw some action, but he too was found wanting.

"Last year we had twenty-one tie games and I believe if we'd had Sawchuk we might have won ten or eleven of them," said Patrick, the eldest son of hockey patriarch Lester Patrick and a former All-Star left winger in his own right. "Sawchuk will transform the Bruins from a club fighting desperately for a playoff position the last few years into a title contender. In my book he is one of the three great all-time goaltenders along with Frankie Brimsek and Bill Durnan."

Equally thrilled with the acquisition were Sawchuk's new teammates. "Goaltending is 75 per cent of a team," declared veteran defenceman Hal Laycoe. "And the Bruins now have the best in the league."

In fact, the Sawchuk deal appeared so heavily loaded in the Bruins' favour that many people quickly concluded that the goalie must be damaged goods, otherwise Adams would never have let him go so cheaply. The old gossip about Sawchuk's supposedly failing vision resurfaced. Even Lynn Patrick began to worry that he'd been hoodwinked by Adams. Finally, to squelch the rumour once and for all, Terry took a well-publicized eye test. His vision was perfect.

Sawchuk never really did get over the shock of the trade

that sent him to Boston. In his heart, he would be a Red Wing until the day he died. But suddenly that summer the idea of tending goal for the Bruins seemed vastly more appealing than at least one alternative. In August, Terry received his third notice from the United States draft board.

He had ignored the previous two notices believing it was all a mistake. As a Canadian, he assumed he was exempt from the draft. Now he discovered that anyone who spent more than six months out of the year in the U.S. was eligible.

"The letter itself was mostly a questionnaire," Terry explained of the latest notice. "But I don't know what to expect next. Two years in the army would sure mess up my career."

In September, he left the Bruins' training camp in Hershey, Pennsylvania, to report for a pre-induction physical examination. The medics took one look at the scars running up his perpetually swollen right elbow and immediately rejected him for service due to a "physical deficiency."

But the whole experience had started Terry thinking about the future. His wife was an American and his son had been born there. He liked the United States, especially Detroit and Union Lake, which he and Pat planned to make their permanent home. His future was there now. That winter he applied to become a United States citizen. He got his papers in 1959.

"I can't say enough about Terry's attitude during our training period at Hershey," said Boston coach Milt Schmidt, the former Bruin great who had succeeded Patrick behind the bench. "To say the least it has been wonderful.

"Sometimes fellows convince themselves that they're being pushed around when they're traded from a team which has been on top to another, but not Sawchuk. We

weren't at Hershey more than a couple of days before he
told me how badly he wanted to do well in Boston. 'Milt,'
he said, 'I'm looking forward to having the best years of my
career with the Bruins.' Don't think that didn't make me feel
good."

Welcome-back signs and long ovations greeted Sawchuk
during his triumphal return to the Olympia for the annual
pre-season All-Star game. He told friends that he got all
choked up when most of the 13,187 fans stood and cheered
as he skated out to take over for Harry Lumley midway
through the second period.

An interesting sidelight to the match, which the Stanley
Cup champions won 3-1, was that all three goalies who saw
action had been developed and introduced to the NHL by
the Red Wings. Terry's successor, Glenn Hall, played
impressively throughout the game, but later confessed he
was so nervous "I thought my pads would shake off."
Terry's predecessor, Lumley, allowed all three of the
Detroit goals. After he had shut out the Wings during his
stint, Terry received a generous last round of applause from
his old fans.

Boston's saviour had come—or so it seemed. Sawchuk
allowed only fourteen goals in the nine games the Bruins
played during October, an average of just 1.55 goals per
outing. He recorded three shutouts—against Toronto, New
York, and in his first appearance of the regular season in
Detroit, when he and Hall battled to a scoreless draw.

With the Wings, Terry had often been overshadowed by
Howe, Lindsay and Kelly. Now he was the main attraction
on a team which, mostly because of him, was being touted
as a potential league champion in the early-season polls.
Patrick and Schmidt had built a fast and gritty squad led up
front by veteran centres Fleming Mackell and Cal Gardner,
and highly regarded youngsters Don McKenney and

Leo Labine. A quartet of veterans—Fern Flaman, Bob Armstrong, Bill Quackenbush and Hal Laycoe—guarded the blue line.

Fans in Boston talked of Terry as a superstar in the same league as such established local heroes as Ted Williams of the Red Sox and the Celtics' Bob Cousy. Early that season the Bruins drew some of their biggest crowds since the heyday of the old Kraut Line. A total of 78,387 spectators eagerly pushed through the turnstiles the first seven home games, an increase of more than 21,000 from the season before.

Sawchuk, who had never wanted or enjoyed the spotlight, now found it impossible to avoid. There were more autograph seekers than ever to oblige—or, as was more often the case, to rudely ignore or push aside after games. The Bruin front office urged him to help promote the team at one function or another on the hated banquet circuit. Win or lose, Terry was almost always the first Bruin approached by the Boston press, who hadn't yet learned to leave him alone.

Sawchuk's public wanted to know everything about him, no matter how trivial. "Doris Day and Bing Crosby," Terry obliged a woman reporter who asked him to identify his favourite vocalists, among other enthusiasms, for a column entitled "Inside Stuff." Readers also learned that he enjoyed the orchestral stylings of Guy Lombardo and his Royal Canadians; "From Here To Eternity" was his pick for best movie; he preferred steak for his pre-game meal; and his greatest thrill so far in hockey was playing in his first NHL game.

Even when a slump that started in mid-November dropped the Bruins to the bottom of the standings, where they lingered on past the New Year, no fingers pointed at the goalie, often the scapegoat in such situations. "We still

have the greatest goaltender in hockey in Terry Sawchuk,"
insisted Bruin president Walter Brown, "and I don't care
how many goals they've been scoring on him. He's still the
greatest."

Sawchuk appreciated the vote of confidence. "Everybody in Boston has been wonderful to me—the management, the players and the fans. There have been nights
when the fans could have been rough on me, but they
haven't been. I'll always give them my best."

Someone asked how he felt about the prospect of missing out on the bonuses he'd grown accustomed to as a
member of the Red Wings—$1,000 for a Vezina win;
$1,000 for making the first All-Star team ($500 for the second team); $1,000 for finishing first in the team standings;
$1,000 for winning the Stanley Cup.

"I can shrug them off," he answered testily. "Like all the
other guys on this team, I'm thinking about making the
playoffs, not about the bonuses I won't be getting."

"You know, it's a funny thing about those bonuses," he
later joked. "When I was making out my tax returns, they
were an awful lot of trouble to figure. That's one job I
won't have to tackle this year."

Sawchuk's friends say that his show of enthusiasm for
life as a Boston Bruin was just that, a good show. "Terry
never wanted to play anywhere but in Detroit," says Benny
Woit, who had been traded to Chicago in the first of
Adams's big summertime deals. "Whenever I saw him that
season he told me how much he hated it in Boston. Not that
he wasn't playing just as well as ever. With Terry, you knew
he'd always try his best no matter what the situation. But,
boy, he missed Detroit and the old gang."

Johnny Wilson, who had also gone to the Hawks, agrees
with Woit. "Terry just didn't like anything about Boston. He
didn't like the city or even the arena. Terry was developed

in a winning organization. And then suddenly he was with a team struggling to make the playoffs. I don't think he appreciated that."

There are reports that even this early in his stay with the Bruins Sawchuk actively lobbied to rejoin the Red Wings. "Terry just wasn't happy in Boston," Lynn Patrick recalled. "When he'd see Jimmy Skinner, he'd call to him, 'When are you going to get me back?'" Several times the following summer, when he was back home in Union Lake, Sawchuk dropped in to see Jack Adams at the Olympia, ostensibly just to say hello.

Some wondered if maybe Terry was lonely for Pat, who was pregnant again and stayed behind in Union Lake. He shared a house that season and the next with several of his teammates.

Any lingering insecurities Terry may have had about the trade that wrenched him away from Detroit could only have been exacerbated by Glenn Hall's performance in his place. When the Wings won only three of their first seventeen games, there were howls at the Olympia that Hall wasn't up to the job. But by mid-season the Wings had risen to third spot and Hall was well on his way toward winning the Calder Trophy as top rookie, just as Sawchuk had before him. Jimmy Skinner later commented that he saw Hall play only one bad game that entire season.

Boston endured a season-long injury epidemic that put fifteen different players out of action, some for as long as a month at a time. Finally, in mid-January, the Bruins once again began to display signs of their early promise.

The catalyst for the turnaround was the return to action of several of the wounded—and another trade with the Red Wings. This time Boston received forwards Jerry Toppazzini and Real Chevrefils, both ex-Bruins, in return for forwards

Murray Costello and Lorne Ferguson, two more of Adams's acquisitions who would not last long in Detroit.

Boston won three of four games immediately following the trade, and between them Chevrefils and Toppazzini scored six of the thirteen Bruin goals. Another key contributor was rugged winger Vic Stasiuk, yet another former Wing. Finally getting the chance to play regularly after years of riding the Detroit bench, Stasiuk scored nineteen goals that season and led the team with thirty-seven points.

The Bruins stood dead last on January 20, ten points behind fourth-place Toronto with Chicago wedged in between. But in March, Boston caught and passed Toronto, and then dropped just behind in a race for the last playoff spot that would go down to the final weekend of the season. "The fiery fellow," as one member of the Boston press described Sawchuk, played sensationally during the stretch drive. In one span of seventeen games, he produced two shutouts and eight one-goal efforts. He held the Canadiens, the league's highest scoring squad, to just one goal during back-to-back Boston victories in early March.

In the end, the Bruins fell short of Toronto by two points, stumbling home with a record of 4-5-1 in their last ten games. Toe Blake's Canadiens finished atop the standings, a whopping twenty-four points in front of the runner-up Red Wings, whose string of consecutive league titles ended at seven. A surprising New York squad, led by youngsters Andy Bathgate, Harry Howell and goalie Gump Worsley, held down third spot.

Once again Montreal and Detroit met in the Stanley Cup finals. This time the Canadiens clobbered the Wings in five games.

Earlier Sawchuk had joked about how simple preparing his income tax return would be without having to include the usual bonuses. For the first time in his NHL career, he wasn't named to either All-Star squad. Top honours went to Jacques Plante, who also captured the Vezina and whose abilities Montreal's management no longer doubted. Glenn Hall got the nod for the second team.

It was all a big adjustment. One season after leading the NHL in victories, Sawchuk now led the loop in defeats, with thirty-three. His goals-against average, which in five seasons with Detroit had never climbed above 1.99, ballooned to 2.66. His shutout total dropped down to nine from twelve the season before.

But he was still a hero in Beantown. Thanks largely to his star power, the Bruins attracted more than 360,000 fans to the Garden, their best attendance since the winter of 1949-50. Local hockey writers and broadcasters voted Sawchuk the outstanding Bruin in home games. About his or anyone else's performance on the road they couldn't fairly comment, since they rarely travelled with the team.

"He kept us in contention most of the games," recalled Lynn Patrick. One match in particular stood out in the general manager's memory, a night in New York when Boston edged the Rangers 1-0. "Sawchuk must have made thirty-five or forty saves and almost every one of them was miraculous."

Terry had done everything everyone had expected of him—except lead the club to post-season glory. And no one was placing the blame on him for that. Patrick said that only one thing had surprised him about his famous goalkeeper. "Terry always needed reassurance about his work," he said. "He got down on himself a lot when the team was going bad. Milt Schmidt and I always used to pat him on the back and tell him what a fine job he was doing."

At one point during the darkest days of the team's first-half slump, Terry had talked of quitting. Patrick had laughed off the goalie's comments. He knew all about how

Terry had often brooded about quitting in the past only to quickly change his mind. Nobody in hockey took Terry's threats seriously any more.

"Goalies have capitulated to broken bones, allergies and shattered nerves, but Terry Sawchuk of the Bruins is probably the first to leave the lineup because his white corpuscles are not behaving," Harold Kaese wrote in *The Boston Globe* the following December.

"You knew, without looking, that Terry Sawchuk would be the goalie who had mononucleosis," noted *The Toronto Star*'s Milt Dunnell. "Everything else happens to the Manitoba iron man."

The injury whammy that had long been the bane of Terry's existence unerringly struck him down just when life in Boston was finally becoming tolerable. He and the Bruins had picked up where they left off the season before, when they looked like potential champions during most of a late-season run at the final playoff spot. By the fourteen-game mark Boston stood alone in first place, a position they would maintain past Christmas.

Sawchuk led the Vezina race and was playing so well that people were already talking him up as a potential candidate for the Hart Trophy as league MVP. The 1956-57 season was shaping up as one of his best yet.

In the past, the whammy had rarely given any advance warning. This time it came on slowly and sleepily. At first he hardly noticed its effects. But by late November Terry found he was constantly tired and his nerves more ragged than ever. "I thought I was lazy because I wanted to lie down all the time," he recalled. "I thought maybe I'd become too complacent mentally too." Winning no longer seemed as important as it had; in truth, he didn't seem to care much about anything at all.

"But we were winning and in first place and I kept getting by even though I could hardly wait for each game to end because my legs were so tired."

Ever since some of his Detroit teammates had ribbed him about being a hypochondriac, Terry had been careful not to complain too loudly about his injuries. Nobody on the Bruins, not even the five players he shared a house with in the Boston suburb of Newton, had any idea of how poorly he was feeling until he missed a practice. The next day Terry explained to the team doctor, Edward R. Browne, that he had felt too miserable to even get out of bed.

Infectious mononucleosis is a disease of the blood stream which affects the glands and causes loss of strength and a general feeling of lassitude. Terry exhibited all the classic symptoms, including enlargement of the lymph nodes in his neck, armpits and groin. On the evening of Wednesday, December 12, he entered Boston's Carney Hospital.

"It was like being hit between the eyes," said Milt Schmidt after he received the physician's report. Sawchuk might be out anywhere from two weeks to two months and maybe even longer. The standard treatment for mono then, as it still is today, was to encourage patients to get plenty of rest and relaxation, and to try to forget about their worries.

"It feels like the red and white blood corpuscles have chosen up sides and are playing a game of hockey in your veins," Terry joked about his affliction. While in the hospital he received visits from his coach, general manager and most of his teammates. Soon so many people were dropping by to see him that a "no visitors" policy had to be introduced to enable him to get some peace. More than one thousand get-well cards arrived from his fans. Sawchuk later thanked them all during a hockey broadcast seen across Canada.

When he was admitted, he felt so weak that nurses pushed him in a wheelchair whenever he had to leave his room. But mono can be a deceptive illness. A few good days can mislead a patient into believing that he is almost back to normal when, in truth, the disease may take several more weeks to run its course.

This was the trap that Terry and Dr. Browne fell into. Within days of the initial diagnosis, Terry felt so much better that he began to lobby for a return to active duty. He watched with mounting frustration as the Bruins, with minor-leaguer Norman Delefice tending goal, struggled to a record of three wins and a tie in the first six games of his absence.

Only a few days before, Dr. Browne had publicly estimated that Terry's recovery would likely take two months. Now he announced that the goalkeeper would return to action in a game against Detroit December 27 at the Boston Garden—just fifteen days after Terry had first entered Carney Hospital.

Sawchuk's insistence that he was ready to come back was both laudable and understandable. Always a dedicated team player, Terry knew that without him the Bruins could not possibly hold onto first place. And once begun, a freefall in the standings might prove impossible to stop.

It is worth repeating here that Sawchuk was anxious to play. "I want to make it clear," he said later, "that no pressure was put on me by the Boston club to return to the game…. I wanted to get back in there."

But what became increasingly clear during the controversy-filled weeks that followed was that, no matter what he wanted, Sawchuk should never have been allowed to rejoin the team so quickly. Two weeks of recuperation from mononucleosis might sometimes be sufficient for a man in a normal occupation. But it was nowhere near enough time for an NHL goalie, who every game carried thirty-five pounds of soaking wet equipment and endured an unnaturally heightened level of physical and emotional stress.

Dr. Browne, the team physician of the Boston Bruins, should have known this. The suspicion quickly grew that the Bruins, desperate to secure a playoff berth, callously decided to roll the dice on Sawchuk's health and take their chances.

TERRY checked out of the hospital on December 24 and on Christmas night watched the tail-end Black Hawks thump the Bruins 4-2 at Boston Garden. The loss cut Boston's lead over second-place Detroit to a single point.

During the course of Sawchuk's by now seven-game absence, it had become obvious to everyone that his replacement, twenty-three-year-old Norman Delefice, was not up to the job. But in the time-honoured tradition of veteran goalies, Terry stoutly defended the rookie's performance, which he had watched with interest from a perch in the radio broadcast booth. "He would have caught me flat-footed on it too," he said of a power-play goal by Harry Watson that beat Delefice on the short side. "I'd have taken him to go for the far corner and would have been moving."

After just one practice, which Dr. Browne assured him would be more than enough to get back into game shape, Sawchuk made his return to the line-up Thursday December 27 as scheduled. The combination of his much-heralded comeback and the excitement of a showdown with the visiting Red Wings for first place drew a capacity crowd of 13,909 to the Garden.

Through two periods Sawchuk looked much like his old self. But he visibly tired in the final twenty minutes when the Wings scored three goals to complete a 5-3 victory and take possession of first place. "In the third period, I knew what to do but couldn't do it," Terry said. Jack Adams had ordered his men to shoot at every opportunity, believing that Sawchuk would be rusty after his layoff. All three of Detroit's third-period goals came on long shots that Sawchuk would normally have handled with ease.

He sounded confident enough after the game. To a glum-looking Lynn Patrick, who had been sounding off all week that Detroit was at best a third- or fourth-place team, he called out across the dressing room, "I'll be all right. I never missed goals like that before in my life, and I won't again."

Terry was as good as his word in the Bruins' next outing, a rematch with the Wings that Sunday night at the Olympia. He made twelve saves in the third period, many of them described in game reports as "brilliant," while leading the Bruins to a 4-2 victory that placed them back on top of the standings. And once again he helped to fill the house; the crowd of 15,130 was Detroit's largest to that point in the season.

Though he had played well against the Wings, Terry already knew that he had come back too quickly. "After returning to the team from the hospital in Boston, I tried to adjust myself to continue playing with the Bruins, but I wasn't in the right frame of mind," he said later.

When he had first contracted mononucleosis, all he wanted to do was sleep, which is a typical symptom of the disease. Now the problem was insomnia. Night after night he lay in bed staring at the ceiling and smoking cigarettes. "I'd lost my appetite, my nerves were shot and I was edgy all the time." Sawchuk also began to lose weight, something his skinny frame could hardly afford.

In his first five games back, the Bruins won two, lost two and tied one. He allowed seventeen goals and often looked bad even on easy shots. His timing was clearly off. The Bruins, whose offence had mysteriously deserted them, quickly slid down the standings into third place behind Detroit and Montreal.

Depression is often a side-effect of mono, especially among sufferers who, like Sawchuk, don't get the rest and relaxation they need to start to feel better again. Forgetting that he had been eager to return to the line-up, Terry began to blame Lynn Patrick for rushing him back too soon. After one miserable performance, he angrily told the general manager, "You shouldn't have played me."

Better than anyone, Patrick knew how limited the Bruins' goaltending options were. No one else in the minor-league system was any better than Delefice. Sawchuk showed enough flashes of excellence that Patrick kept hoping he would work his way back to his old form.

Patrick based his optimism on the type of performance Terry gave in Boston's 2-1 victory at the Olympia on January 10. During the first period alone, he stopped seventeen shots. Twice he robbed Gordie Howe and he made outstanding saves on rookies Billy McNeill and Billy Dea. The win enabled the Bruins to climb back into a second-place tie with the Wings, one point back of Montreal.

What Patrick didn't know was that the effort Sawchuk expended in that game and all the others since he'd come back had pushed him to the edge of his endurance. Terry, who had received permission from Milt Schmidt to stay overnight in Detroit, drove home to Union Lake with Pat after the game. "When we arrived home I was too weak to get out of the car and had to sit for fifteen minutes before I could move," he remembered. Once inside the house, his knees buckled beneath him. "I went into the den and broke down and cried. Pat tried to settle me down but I was scared. 'I'm through,' I told her. 'I don't know what's the matter with me and I'm through.'"

Still he continued to play, not wanting to let the team down. He wasn't sure what the reaction of Patrick and Schmidt might be if he told them he wanted to rest for a few days, that he needed time to pull himself together. He knew the Bruins didn't have anyone else and he was afraid that everyone on the team would think he was a hypochondriac and, even worse, a quitter.

Though no one incident can be looked back upon as the trigger, Sawchuk reached his breaking point during back-to-back weekend losses to Montreal on January 12 and 13. He and Dickie Moore exchanged angry words late in the 4-1 defeat at the Forum on Saturday night. But that was nothing new. Sawchuk had always had a short fuse and he and Moore were old foes. The next night he starred in a 3-1 loss at home. "The one model of consistency was Terry Sawchuk," noted *The Boston Globe*. "Sharp and efficient the goalie blocked some beauties in a total of 31 saves."

Sometime between the end of Sunday night's match and the following Tuesday morning, Terry came to what this time, after all the false alarms of the past, he believed was an irrevocable decision to retire from the game. "I took a long look at myself and at my situation, took into consideration my responsibilities to my family, my teammates and the Boston club, and came to the decision that I just had to call it quits."

On Tuesday morning the Bruins were scheduled to practise at a suburban arena. Instead, Sawchuk paid a visit to Walter Brown, the Bruins' president, at his office in the Boston Garden. Brown was sorting through his mail when Terry came in and told him he was leaving the team.

"I was surprised, to put it mildly," Brown recounted to the press. "In fact, I was stunned. He told me, 'The pressure is getting to me. I'm not doing a good job. I'm letting the team down—and I want to quit.'"

Ironically, at approximately the same time that Sawchuk handed in his notice, NHL headquarters in Montreal announced the All-Star squads for the first half of the season. On the strength of his sensational work before he became sick, Terry out-polled all other goalies in the voting to earn a place on the first team.

Before he talked to the Bruins' president, Terry had apparently told only Pat about his intention to quit. Even the five teammates with whom he shared the house—Allan Stanley, Don McKenney, Jack Caffery, Jack Bionda and Bob Armstrong—were surprised to discover how serious the situation had become. According to Stanley, a veteran defenceman who had been purchased from New York a week before the start of the season, Terry never once mentioned to any of them that he was thinking about quitting. They all knew he was feeling tired, and that he wasn't happy with the way he'd been playing. Terry had also been a little more aloof and moodier than usual. But none of them had even guessed that he might be close to making such a decision.

All that afternoon Milt Schmidt, who had stayed home from the morning practice with the flu, tried unsuccessfully to contact his errant goaltender. At the house in Newton, Terry barricaded himself in his room, refusing all calls.

Finally, early that evening, Stanley and Terry's other housemates convinced him to talk to Schmidt on the telephone. Terry reportedly told the coach that he was "fed up," and that he was planning to go home to Detroit. He said that in his last eight games he had played only two good ones. From that he had concluded that he was washed up.

After spending hours just trying to get Sawchuk to talk to him, Schmidt was himself more than a little fed up. "I told him, 'You'll have a pretty black name all over the country, and you'll never be able to escape it,'" he recounted for the *Toronto Telegram* the next day. "'And your family, your wife and kids, will pay for the name you give them.

"'You're not sick, your nerves are not shot. You're just quitting, walking out on the team and your name. Well, you're the one who is going to suffer the consequences. As far as I'm concerned, a quitter is the lowest animal.'"

During what was obviously a heated exchange, Schmidt, who was well liked by most of his players, urged Sawchuk to see the team doctor for another examination. But Terry no longer had faith in Dr. Browne. It was Browne, albeit at Terry's insistence, who had declared him fit to play. He refused to even consider Schmidt's suggestion.

Sawchuk was still determined to quit when the conversation ended. Schmidt asked him to at least sleep on his decision. However, if Terry didn't show up for practice the next day, Schmidt said he could consider himself suspended.

By now word had gotten out that the league's All-Star netminder had tendered his resignation—and this time chances looked good that he wouldn't change his mind. The Boston press as well as representatives from the wire services descended on the big house in Newton. All to no avail. Terry stayed in his room.

Schmidt cooled off a little between the time of his conversation with Sawchuk and the point two or three hours later when he made a cautious statement to the press. He still hoped that his goalie would change his mind by morning. "Terry told me that he has decided to quit the club, but I will have no official statement to make until after tomorrow's practice," Schmidt said.

Sawchuk's walk-out quickly became the biggest hockey story since the Richard Riot; front-page news in most NHL cities the next day. "Emotionally Upset Sawchuk Quits Bruins; Club Stunned" headlined *The Boston Globe*. Most of New England's 106 daily newspapers featured front-page updates on the story every day for the following week.

On Wednesday morning when Sawchuk didn't show up for practice or contact Dr. Browne for an appointment, Schmidt angrily made good on his threat of the night before. He announced that Terry's salary had been cut off and that he was being "suspended for life."

"I think we've gone far enough with him," he said. "Now he has only one out—if he is really mentally sick. If he is sick, we'd send him home for a few weeks to rest. But how do we know if he's sick if he won't see us?

"I'd be the first to apologize to him if he is sick but I wish to goodness he'd let us know. I know this much, though, the players are going to play all the harder to prove that one fellow is not the whole team."

Lynn Patrick cut short a scouting trip through Western Canada to fly back and deal with the crisis. The GM, who as a member of the famous Patrick family was considered hockey royalty, appeared to regard Terry's resignation as little short of sacrilege, saying "the game is bigger than Sawchuk." Patrick completely endorsed the actions taken by Schmidt.

Like his coach, Patrick enjoyed a reputation as a likeable and fair man among the majority of his players. But it should be remembered that these were still the dark ages in player-management relations and that Patrick was very much a product of his time. The next month in New York, Ted Lindsay and several other players would announce the formation of a players' association. Patrick's response when he heard the news was typical of the arrogance displayed by the owners and managers of a league that made millions but shared precious little of it with the players. "They [the players] don't need any kind of protective association," he said. "They have been treated as well as, if not better than, any group of professional athletes, and I can't see what they stand to gain by this type of association."

Neither Schmidt nor Patrick appeared capable of grasping what should have been obvious: Terry Sawchuk was an emotionally troubled and physically sick young man who deserved to be cut some slack. In his eagerness to help his team, Terry had damaged his health first by coming out of the hospital too soon, and then by continuing to play to the point of breakdown—all because he didn't want to disappoint his general manager, coach and teammates.

Immediate and strong exception was taken to the militant stance of the Bruin braintrust. Medical experts interviewed by the press unanimously agreed that Sawchuk had been rushed back into service too quickly. "Don't quote me," a Toronto doctor said, "but if Sawchuk's mononucleosis was correctly diagnosed, it sounds to me as if they put him back on the ice far too soon."

"If Terry had this in December and went back in goal after a couple of weeks, he went back far too soon," offered a doctor interviewed by the Canadian Press. "This can take six weeks to six months to overcome. If there's any mental reaction, it's simply a result of extreme depression that goes with the disease—it often causes a 'don't give a darn' feeling. Patients just feel rotten, but they're not running enough fever to justify feeling that bad, so they can't understand what's wrong with them."

Even league president Clarence Campbell, usually management's most enthusiastic cheerleader, expressed doubts about the good intentions of the Boston Bruins. "I believe it unlikely that Sawchuk was hounded to play when physically unfit, but I do not dismiss the possibility," Campbell said.

The notoriously fickle Boston press (which for years had carried on a love-hate relationship with baseball great Ted Williams, who in any other city would have been deified) seemed about evenly divided on the question of whether Terry was a lily-livered "quitter" or a martyred hero who deserved their compassion.

"It was pretty bad," Sawchuk complained later of some of the stories written about him. "Those reporters called me everything in the book...including a quitter. I guess those guys have to make a living, too—but they sure said a lot of things about me that weren't true."

No matter where their sympathies lay, almost all reporters sought to play up the most sensational angles of Sawchuk's resignation. One unfairly compared his case to that of Jimmy Piersall, the Red Sox outfielder who had been institutionalized after suffering a mental breakdown. Colourful stories published in Boston and every other NHL city linked Sawchuk to a long line of goaltenders who had succumbed, as Jim Gillooly expressed it in the *Boston Record*, "to puck-shot, an occupational malady long dreaded by goalers."

Among the cases most often cited was that of Toronto's Frank McCool, whose jittery nerves and sensitive stomach inspired the nickname "Ulcers." By the seventh game of the 1945 finals against Detroit, McCool was in such bad shape that midway through the third period, the score tied 1-1, he called time and retreated to the dressing room to drink his stomach medicine and summon his strength. McCool, though doubled over in agony, returned to action and held off the Red Wings until the Maple Leafs finally won the game and the Stanley Cup.

After seven brilliant seasons with the Canadiens, Bill Durnan, who had won six Vezina trophies, quit suddenly in the middle of the 1950 Stanley Cup playoffs. "My nerves are shot and I know it," Durnan said. "I didn't realize how wearing the pressure was until I blew up at the dinner table one day and plastered a steak on the wall, missing my wife with it."

A combination of nerves and injuries knocked Durnan's successor, Gerry McNeil, out of the Montreal line-up in the spring of 1953. McNeil's departure opened the door for rookie Jacques Plante. Then, when Plante faltered in the playoffs a year later, McNeil went back in and played superbly until Leswick's fluke goal in overtime won the Stanley Cup for the Red Wings. After reliving Leswick's goal over and over again all summer, McNeil announced his retirement the next fall—although he did later try a comeback.

Terry's own successor in Detroit, Glenn Hall, was a famously nervous type. Teammates called him "Pukey" for his habit of throwing up before every game and sometimes during intermissions. "I often look at those guys who can whistle and laugh before a game and shake my head," Hall once said. "Me? I'm plain miserable."

Today, goalies are so well protected by the latest face masks and other modern equipment that there is very little risk of them sustaining really serious injuries. But in the old bare-faced era a netminder literally put his life on the line every time he took his place in front of the cage. Puck-shot, rubberitis, goalie jitters—the malady had many names and, sooner or later, most goalies fell victim to it.

Within the goaltending fraternity, Sawchuk's resignation was regarded as perfectly understandable. "Goalies get whacky from stopping pucks," said Turk Broda. "Sawchuk probably didn't mind it when the team was winning. Hockey's like that. When you are winning, playing goal is a breeze. But when the team starts to skid, fans get on the goalie and the job becomes almost a torture. The pressure is tremendous. You just can't relax."

"I know just how Sawchuk feels," Gerry McNeil sympathized. "It's pretty hard to explain to anyone who has never been in the nets. Usually it starts with a bad goal, one that bounced by you or deflected in off the goalpost. First thing you know they mount up…. Don't be too hard on Terry, or any other goalie. Nobody knows what it's like who hasn't tried it."

Harry Lumley, who by now toiled for Buffalo of the

American League, said he could appreciate why Sawchuk quit, but that he was a little surprised by the timing. "He's riding the top of the crest," Lumley said. "His team is winning and he's just been picked All-Star. Mind you, the pressure can get pretty serious.... Even after the season is over, your nerves are bad—for a longer period each year. The summer was half over before I got straightened away last year."

Hockey's most thoughtful observers reflected that perhaps it was time to platoon goalies, thus easing their individual burden, as the Leafs had done so successfully with the tandem of Al Rollins and Turk Broda in 1950-51.

"Maybe the incidence of cage fever among goalies points up the outdated working conditions of the trade," wrote Milt Dunnell. "If a centre or a right-winger spends two minutes and 30 seconds on the firing line, the coach throws in relief. But the man who carries the heaviest load of any on the club is expected to play 60 minutes of 70 games."

One day, though not for almost another decade, Sawchuk himself would play a leading role in ushering in the platoon system. But for the time being, Montreal coach Toe Blake delivered the best line on the debate. "If my kid ever takes up goalkeeping, I am going to do one thing," he said. "I am going to hit him on the head with the stick."

By late Wednesday afternoon Lynn Patrick and Milt Schmidt began to have second thoughts about the hard line they had so far taken with Sawchuk. His permanent absence would not only cripple the team's morale and all but kill Boston's chances of winning the Stanley Cup, it would also cost the hockey club a considerable sum of money. If the Bruins continued to slip in the standings, as seemed likely, the loss in box-office receipts could be as high as $100,000 for the remainder of the season.

Perhaps as a first step in rebuilding the relationship with Terry, Schmidt flatly denied having called him a "quitter" in his interview with the *Toronto Telegram*. He said the reporter got everything else right, but "I was misquoted the length of the ice on that one."

Sawchuk prepared to return to Detroit the next day by train. On Friday night he and his family were to appear on CBC television's "Graphic," a fifteen-minute program which interviewed celebrities in their homes. He and Pat had made the commitment months before.

Before Terry left for home, Schmidt hoped to talk to him again—preferably face to face. But every time he called, Sawchuk refused to come to the phone. The coach finally asked Allan Stanley to act as a go-between.

"I was happy to do anything I could to help," Stanley says. "You know, I really liked Terry. I considered him a good friend. When I had moved in after I joined the Bruins, he had insisted on giving me his room, which was larger than the one I was supposed to get. There was really no reason for him to do something like that. He just wanted to give it to me."

Stanley persuaded Sawchuk to meet with Schmidt at the house that night. During a private two-hour conversation, the coach left open the possibility of a return to the Bruins once Terry finally felt better. The next day Schmidt told reporters that Terry now seemed a little less determined to quit the game for good. "I guess I was a little hasty in saying that," he quoted Sawchuk as telling him. "The real reason that I'm quitting is that I have been awfully nervous and shaky."

Schmidt and Patrick both began talking optimistically about how they expected Sawchuk to return to the club in about a month's time, after he had had a good long rest. Patrick, however, made it clear that Terry would have to eat a little humble pie first. "If he comes back and says he's sorry, that he made a mistake," Patrick said, "I'll be glad to talk to him. But he'll have to come to see me. The thing to remember is that he's human and so are we."

Hidden away in the house in Newton, Sawchuk hadn't yet fully grasped the furor his resignation had caused. He was stunned to see more than a dozen reporters and photographers waiting to greet him when he arrived at South Station early the next afternoon to board the overnight train to Detroit.

"I'm not talking," he insisted at first. When the newsmen continued to badger him for a quote, Sawchuk stopped in the middle of the platform. "I've quit," he said tersely. "I'm mad. And I've got news for you. I'm going to sue four Boston papers for what they said about me after I get home."

Even during the train ride there was no peace. Early Friday morning as the high-speed Wolverine Flyer sped across southern Ontario toward Detroit, two enterprising young reporters from Windsor staked him out, hoping for an exclusive on board interview. They had gotten on the train in St. Thomas after taking the night bus from Windsor.

But the closest they came to their quarry was the outer door of his private compartment, where they waited in vain for hours. "I don't want to talk to anyone," Sawchuk told the conductor to tell them when they pushed a pleading note under his doorway.

About twenty more newsmen, including a television crew, lay in wait when the train pulled into Detroit shortly after 7 a.m. Sawchuk spotted them and dashed through two Pullman cars in an attempt to escape. Scrambling in pursuit, the reporters caught up to him soon after he stepped down onto the platform.

"I've got nothing to say," he said angrily. "Leave me alone. I'm not talking so quit bothering me."

"Swinging his small handbag Terry walked rapidly for freedom," Marshall Dann of the *Detroit Free Press* described the scene. "Newsmen panted at his side, yelling questions and getting angry replies. Photographers leap-frogged ahead to flash pictures of the chase."

"Can't a guy quit a game?" Sawchuk asked plaintively. "Just don't bother me. Get out of here and leave me alone.

"All you'll get is a punch in the nose," he threatened a particularly tenacious reporter from a Toronto daily.

Other passengers stopped and stared as the scrum made its way along the platform. Finally worn down, Terry agreed to talk to them over a cup of coffee in the station coffee shop.

"I was treated real good there, maybe too good," he answered an opening question about his treatment in Boston. "I never got chewed out there once in two years and I deserved it a number of times. In fact, I never heard anybody get bawled out."

More than one dispatch noted that Sawchuk seemed to tense up whenever anyone mentioned Milt Schmidt's name, although he refused to comment specifically about the Bruin coach. In fact, he brushed aside almost all their questions.

"Give me a couple of days and I'll give you a story," Sawchuk told them as he got up to go. He invited them all to a press conference at his home Monday at noon. Until then, he would have "nothing more to say."

The story continued to build through the weekend. On Friday afternoon a reporter reached Anne Sawchuk in Winnipeg. She traced her son's troubles back to the crash diet Jack Adams had put him on in the autumn of 1951, saying that he "has never been the same since." Other than that, she couldn't shed any light on the current situation. "Terry doesn't tell me too much in the letters he writes and the phone calls he makes. He doesn't want to worry me."

Terry's father, Louis, added that they expected to hear from their son "momentarily." Louis had been planning a trip to Detroit but now felt that the situation there was under control.

That evening, thousands of hockey fans across Canada and the northern United States tuned in as CBC television took them live inside the Sawchuk home at Union Lake. Earlier, when the crew was busy laying cables and positioning the lighting, writers and photographers gathered outside the house had tried to talk their way inside. Pat had politely but firmly barred them at the door.

When the cameras rolled, Terry spoke of his hockey-playing days as being behind him, and repeated that he would tell the whole story at Monday's press conference. "I know it isn't fair to the people in hockey," he said of his unexpected retirement. "But this is the way it has to be."

He went on to say that he would still recommend hockey as a career to any youngster. As for how he would earn his living in the future, Sawchuk mentioned the possibility of a full-time position with a local tool-and-die firm owned by a friend of his. He had previously done some off-season promotion and sales work for the firm.

By Saturday, probably at Pat's urging, Terry had agreed to consult a physician about his troubles. Dr. E. Clarkson Long was a trusted friend of several of the Red Wing players. After examining Terry that weekend, he declared him to be exhausted and on the brink of a nervous breakdown. Dr. Long estimated that it would take about thirty days for the goalie to recover.

Maybe it was Terry's relief in knowing that at least one doctor believed him when he said he was sick, or perhaps the future didn't look quite so bleak now that he was back home with Pat. Whatever the reason, during the course of that weekend he began to seriously re-examine his decision to quit the game.

In Toronto, where the Bruins lost 4-1 to the Leafs on Saturday night, Lynn Patrick did his best to encourage Sawchuk's positive outlook. The Bruin GM continued to talk optimistically about how he expected Sawchuk to rejoin the team in about a month's time. And now there was no mention of Terry having to apologize before he would be welcomed back.

"He is the greatest goaltender I've ever seen," said Patrick, who knew how desperately Terry, always so insecure about his talent, must have needed to hear such reassurance right then. "That's what I thought of him when I worked out a five-player deal for him two years ago and that's what I still think of him."

"Anyone care to trade places," Terry joked nervously at the start of his promised press conference on Monday morning. The hockey public's still-burgeoning fascination with the unfolding drama had forced a change in venue from the Sawchuk living room to the Presidential Suite of Detroit's Hotel Statler. More than thirty-five representatives of the media were on hand—from all three Detroit dailies, two Toronto newspapers, at least three national magazines, and the AP, CP, UP and INS news services (but no one, curiously, from any of the Boston papers). A dozen photographers focused on Sawchuk who, dressed in a well-tailored brown suit, looked tired and pale as he stood behind a desk equipped with four microphones. He blinked once or twice from the glare of the television floodlights and then slowly began to read a prepared 350-word statement....

"Since my illness in December, when I spent twelve days in Carney Hospital in Boston for infectious mononucleosis, I certainly have not felt in the right frame of mind, though I have tried to adjust myself to continue playing for the Bruins.

"My nerves are shattered. I couldn't sleep and I lost my appetite. I took everything into consideration before making my decision—the Boston organization, my teammates, myself and my family, and I decided that I was not in condition to continue at this time…."

There was more, none of it earthshaking. The biggest news was Sawchuk's confirmation that he was at least willing to consider a comeback with the Bruins should he start to feel better in a few weeks' time. "I promised Milt that if I felt better later on, I'd discuss my future with the club," he said, adding unconvincingly that there had never been any conflict between himself and Schmidt or Lynn Patrick.

On Friday at the train station, Terry had promised to give the press "a story," hinting that he would have something of interest to say about Milt Schmidt, who had allegedly called him a "quitter." But over the weekend, again no doubt due to the soothing influence of Pat, he had obviously decided that there was nothing to be gained by badmouthing his former—and possibly future—employers. Reporters left the Presidential Suite disappointed, and the story quickly faded from the front pages.

Without Sawchuk, Boston continued to struggle along in third place, losing twice and tying one in the first three games of his absence. The goaltending situation appeared so suspect with Norman Delefice in the cage that thirty-six-year-old Sugar Jim Henry called from his home town of Winnipeg, where he operated a service station, and offered to pitch in as an emergency replacement.

Lynn Patrick had something a little more promising in mind. One week after Terry's walk-out, he closed a deal with the American League's Springfield Indians for twenty-five-year-old netminder Don Simmons. "In my opinion, he's faster than Sawchuk, much better with his hands, and he can do everything you would expect of a major leaguer," former Bruin great Eddie Shore, Springfield's owner, said of Simmons.

Patrick revealed that he had first tried to land Simmons when Sawchuk was stricken with mono in December, and that he had been following the progress of the Springfield goalie for more than two years. "When we decided a year ago last spring that we had to get a goaltender, Sawchuk was our first choice but Simmons was our second. If we hadn't gotten Sawchuk from Detroit, Don would have been with us a year ago."

Simmons, a lean, dark-haired 160-pounder who worked from a modified crouch, almost singlehandedly reversed Boston's sinking fortunes. Following a loss to the Rangers in his NHL debut, Simmons provided spectacular goaltending as the Bruins went undefeated in their next eight games.

The more Patrick saw of his new goalie, the less he talked about Sawchuk's eventual return to the line-up. Just two games into Simmons's tenure, a Boston paper printed a report that should Terry come back, he and the rookie would share the position. Patrick refuted the story, calling Simmons the team's "full-time goaltender."

"As long as I'm manager of the Bruins, we'll never platoon goaltenders," Patrick said. "I don't believe in it."

The Bruin GM quickly returned to the hard line he had angrily expressed after Terry first went missing, when he had said "the game is bigger than Sawchuk." Now he seemed determined to prove it. "I can't remember when I last talked with the man but it was before I went out to the West Coast the first week in January," Patrick said coldly of Terry in early February. "I haven't seen or talked with him since and I don't have any plans to do either at the present time."

Meanwhile, in Union Lake, Terry slowly regained his health and contemplated his future. "No, I haven't made up my mind," he said about the possibility of a comeback. "What's the sense in trying to do that until I've got all my health back again?"

He said that he had gained nine pounds and felt better than he had in years. The moment he left the team the Bruins had cut off his salary. To help pick up the slack, he was working part-time for his friend at the tool-and-die firm. "It's nothing steady," he said. "In fact, the doctor lets me work only three days a week now anyway."

Simmons continued to shine as the Bruins chased the Red Wings and Canadiens in a tight race down the stretch. At the end, only eight points separated third-place Boston from Detroit, who won the league title for the eighth time in nine years. Hobbled by injuries for most of the season, Montreal fell back into second, two points in front of the Bruins. New York held down the final playoff spot.

In the semi-finals, the Bruins, who managed to contain Howe and Lindsay just as they had in the playoff of 1953, upset the Wings in five games. But Boston proved no match for the now healthy Canadiens in the final. Montreal needed just five games to capture their second straight Stanley Cup.

With Don Simmons having proven beyond any reasonable doubt that he was a big-time goaltender, Lynn Patrick finally felt free to vent his true feelings about Sawchuk. Patrick said openly that he would love to keep Terry on permanent suspension, leaving him no option other than to stay retired. "We, and I'm sure I'm speaking for Milt and the players, don't want him back on our club," said Patrick.

Sawchuk's old housemate, Allan Stanley, takes exception to the notion that he and the rest of the Bruin players wouldn't have welcomed Terry's return. "I never heard anybody talk Terry down," he says. "If anything, I think the players would have been happy to get him back. Terry Sawchuk was a hell of a goalie."

At any rate, Patrick couldn't afford the luxury of maintaining Sawchuk's suspension. Tarnished reputation and all, Terry remained a valuable property. Patrick, as pragmatic as any general manager, was anxious to recover the team's investment.

He let it be known that the Bruins were open to offers. Serious bidders would be free to talk to Sawchuk themselves to determine whether he was ready to start afresh somewhere else. The first to call was Chicago's Tommy Ivan. "Despite Terry's illness and his surprising walk-out he has so much talent that it's ridiculous to write him off," said his former coach. "I'll go all out to try and get him."

Then a surprise bidder entered the auction. Even though Glenn Hall had been named that season's All-Star goalie, Jack Adams had, for reasons peculiarly his own, found him wanting. Disgusted by his team's early exit from the playoffs, Trader Jack was ready to deal.

And his first order of business was to bring Terry Sawchuk back home to the Red Wings where he belonged.

A teenaged Sawchuk suits up for stardom.

ABOVE: Sawchuk in semi-final action against Toronto in 1954. Leaf Ron Stewart hovers in the background.

OPPOSITE PAGE, TOP: With a little help from Gordie Howe, Sawchuk puts the brakes on Montreal's Floyd Curry in the opening game of the 1952 Cup final. BOTTOM: Sawchuk congratulates Harry Lumley after narrowly losing out to the Toronto goalie in the 1953–54 Vezina race.

IMPERIAL OIL-TUROFSKY COLLECTION/HOCKEY HALL OF FAME

ABOVE, TOP: Mercurial Detroit boss Jack Adams gives Sawchuk an appreciative hug after his Vezina triumph in 1955. Weeks later, Adams would trade his All-Star goalie to Boston in one of the biggest deals of the decade.

BOTTOM: Sawchuk never felt comfortable in Boston. He missed his family in Detroit and lobbied for a return to the Red Wings.

OPPOSITE PAGE, TOP: A thirsty Sawchuk and friends relish their narrow victory over Montreal in 1954's seven-game Cup final.

BOTTOM: Two reasons to celebrate: Sawchuk has just clinched his third Vezina, and the Red Wings win their seventh consecutive league championship in the final game of the 1954–55 regular season.

AP WIREPHOTO

UNITED PRESS TELEPHOTO

ABOVE: During his second stint as a Red Wing, Sawchuk was named a second-team All-Star in 1958–59 and again in 1962–63.

OPPOSITE PAGE, TOP: Attended to by a student nurse, Sawchuk convalesces in a Boston hospital in December of 1956 after contracting mononucleosis. His premature return to the line-up had unforeseen repercussions. BOTTOM: Amid a swirl of controversy, Sawchuk boards a Detroit-bound train after walking out on the Bruins in January of 1957.

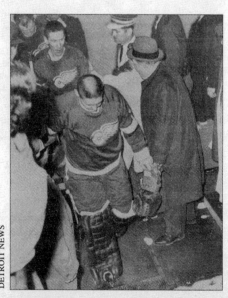

ABOVE: Donning the face mask gave Sawchuk renewed confidence and helped return his game to its highest level.

OPPOSITE PAGE, TOP: Sawchuk, always the most volatile of goalies, heatedly makes his point to a goal judge at Maple Leaf Gardens.
BOTTOM: A weary Sawchuk heads for the dressing room after handing Chicago a 2–1 defeat in game four of the 1961 Cup final.

ABOVE: An exhausted Stanley Cup hero savours the Toronto victory over Montreal in the 1967 finals.

OPPOSITE PAGE, TOP: Toronto platoon partners Sawchuk and Johnny Bower accept the Vezina for 1964–65 from local politician Fred Gardiner. BOTTOM: Sawchuk receives the congratulations of his Toronto teammates following his 100th career shutout in 1967.

First pick in the expansion draft of 1967, Sawchuk proved a
bust during his one season as a Los Angeles King.

Detroit coach Bill Gadsby and Sawchuk in 1968 during the goalie's farewell stint with his beloved Red Wings.

Sawchuk in action with the New York Rangers during the 1969–70 season, the final stop in an unparalleled career.

## Chapter Nine

# THE HOMECOMING

**BY** April an elated Sawchuk was telling his neighbours in Union Lake that at any moment a deal would be made returning him to the Red Wings. Terry had readily agreed to a request by Jack Adams that he undergo a complete physical examination by team physicians. The results showed him in excellent condition, without a lingering trace of mononucleosis. "I've still got to make a deal with Patrick," Adams cautioned the press. "He may want too much for him."

The fact that Adams wanted Sawchuk back at all surprised almost everyone. After all, Detroit appeared set in goal with Glenn Hall. During his two seasons with the Wings, Hall had been voted the league's top rookie, played the full seventy-game schedule both years, and was elected to the second All-Star team as a freshman and to the first team in the season just past.

Perhaps Adams had been spoiled by Sawchuk's reign of excellence during the recent glory years. The old man was less than pleased when Hall's GAA rose to 2.24 (from 2.11) in his sophomore season, and his shutout total dipped from twelve to four. Then, in the playoffs against Boston, Adams questioned Hall's courage when the netminder couldn't bounce back after taking a puck in the mouth for twenty-three stitches. Adams blamed Hall for the upset loss to the Bruins, publicly deriding him as "puck shy."

"I didn't think I played that badly," Hall said later in his own defence. "Adams was looking for an excuse. Jack picked on me, but all I can do is thank him because he put me in a real high class. The year before he blamed Gordie Howe for our losses."

More than anything, Adams was upset by Hall's refusal to treat him with the deference he had come to expect from his "boys." When Ted Lindsay had announced the formation of the players' association, Adams ordered Hall to have nothing to do with either Lindsay or the association. Hall, a strong-willed farm boy from Alberta, responded by telling his boss to "Fuck off." Hall later recounted, "I wasn't prepared to say, 'Yes, you are right, Mr. Adams, the great and glorious Adams.' I didn't say that. But that got you into trouble, everybody knew that."

The story of how Adams and the league's other executives ruthlessly broke the players' association has been superbly chronicled by David Cruise and Alison Griffiths in *Net Worth*. At first, ownership refused to even meet with Lindsay and the other organizers. Instead, they decided to trade, demote or otherwise humiliate most of the ringleaders. Adams, who felt betrayed by Lindsay and outraged and embarrassed that the revolt had taken root under his own roof, released inflated salary figures designed to convince the public that the players were both greedy and ungrateful.

In fact, NHL players were little better than indentured servants, owned by their masters from their early teens to retirement and underpaid by any standard. Younger players made as little as $2,700 a year (the NHL's average salary was $8,000). From that, they had to pay their own moving expenses in the event that they were traded or demoted to the minors. Though the owners made sizeable profits from the televising of NHL games, they refused to consider sharing even a penny of it with the players.

At the height of the conflict, Adams denounced his players for their lack of loyalty during an impassioned locker-room address. "Are you for this? Are you for this?" he angrily demanded of each one in turn. The players stared down at the floor, refusing to answer. Only Ted

Lindsay met his gaze. "Time will take care of him," Adams sneered before turning away.

That spring Adams put Lindsay and Glenn Hall on the trading block. Trader Jack felt confident he could land Sawchuk to take the place of Hall. Lindsay, who was coming off a brilliant season in which he had finished as runner-up to Gordie Howe in the scoring race, would prove much more difficult to replace.

Terry waited impatiently for more than two months while Adams worked out the details of his return. When he wasn't working at his part-time job, he played as many as twenty-seven holes of golf a day. Pat, who loved the game, would sometimes leave the kids with a babysitter and join him for a round on her father's course. "When she and Terry could manage to slip off late in the evening they liked to spend an hour or so at her father's lounge, wearing informal clothes, sipping beer, and talking with the hockey fans who recognized the Red Wing goaltender," wrote Trent Frayne, who observed the couple during this period. "At those sessions Terry would talk earnestly and in an excited flow of words, shifting repeatedly in his chair."

Lynn Patrick and Adams finally worked out a deal during the NHL's annual meeting in Montreal early that June. Detroit secured Sawchuk's homecoming in return for twenty-two-year-old left winger Johnny Bucyk and an undisclosed sum of cash.

"We should have got more," said an unhappy Patrick, who had been in an unenviable bargaining position. Only one other team, Chicago, had expressed an interest in Terry. But Hawk GM Tommy Ivan had since let Adams know that he preferred Glenn Hall. Ivan figured that Hall was just as good as Terry and a lot less trouble. Patrick had no choice other than to deal with Trader Jack.

Besides, as pundits around the league quickly pointed

out, the deal was almost as big a crap shoot for Detroit as it was for the Bruins. There were no guarantees that Terry would be able to regain his old form or that in some future crisis he wouldn't walk out on the team, as he had so often threatened to do during his first stint with the Red Wings.

Adams knew the risks involved. But he believed that he and Terry had always enjoyed a special relationship; that he knew how to handle the temperamental goalkeeper as no one else could. Adams also counted on Terry being so grateful and happy to be back home with his family in Detroit that, for a while at least, he would make every effort to be a model employee.

"Hall is a fine goalie," Adams stated. "But, as I've often said, when Terry Sawchuk is on his game, he's the best goalie in the world. That's why I dealt with Boston to get him back."

Sawchuk for Bucyk has generally come to be regarded as yet another of the many disastrous deals made by Jack Adams that sucked the life out of the Detroit franchise. With Boston, Bucyk quickly blossomed into stardom after being teamed with two other former Red Wings and fellow Ukrainian Canadians, Vic Stasiuk and Bronco Horvath, on what became famous as the Uke Line. Bucyk went on to score 545 goals for the Bruins over the next twenty-one seasons.

Adams had no idea of the talent he possessed in Bucyk, who had netted just ten goals the past year as a Wing. Both he and Jimmy Skinner dismissed the youngster as lazy and a poor checker. They chose to part with him even though Lynn Patrick, who admitted he felt cheated in the deal, would likely have accepted any one of several other more prominent but ultimately less valuable players from the Detroit roster.

In the short term, Adams had no trouble justifying the

trade. Sawchuk, after all, provided Detroit with often spectacular goaltending for the next seven seasons. During that time, Terry undeniably proved more valuable to the Wings than did Bucyk to the Bruins, who finished out of the playoffs five times.

In July, Ted Lindsay and Glenn Hall departed for Chicago in return for a package of four players that included former Wing Johnny Wilson and goalie Hank Bassen. The players' association led by Lindsay bowed to the unrelenting harassment of the owners and disbanded seven months later. Another twelve years would pass before the players finally succeeded in forming an effective association, this time under the leadership of Toronto lawyer Alan Eagleson.

Despite his banishment, Terrible Ted would forever remain a die-hard Red Wing. "It didn't matter that they traded me," Lindsay said years later. "I have a Red Wing on my forehead and on my behind and on my heart. That will never change."

Sawchuk, who like Lindsay had a winged wheel tattooed on his soul, felt overjoyed to be back in the fold. He could never quite figure out what he would have done if Adams hadn't come calling. "I had decided I didn't want to play for any club, unless it might be the Red Wings," he said soon after his return. Just a few months later, Sawchuk had changed his tune. "When I heard I'd been traded back to Detroit I won't deny I was glad to be playing at home, but I still would have gone back to the Bruins if they hadn't traded me."

Terry rejoined a Detroit squad that was a pallid shadow of the champions he had left behind in 1955. Only a handful of the last Stanley Cup squad—Howe, Delvecchio, Kelly and Pronovost—were still around and functioning at peak efficiency. Norm Ullman, a talented young centreman, had joined the team the year after Sawchuk left. After that the talent was spread awfully thin. Adams tagged this a year for rebuilding and tried to work as many as eight rookies into the line-up. Most of them were complete wash-outs.

Accustomed to more flattering descriptions, Terry found he now entered enemy rinks branded as a quitter and a man unsteadily walking the thin edge of sanity. Before the Wings' first appearance of the season in New York, a local paper ran a story quoting veteran Ranger rearguard Bill Gadsby as saying, "If he sees too much rubber, Terry might go 'Tweet, tweet, tweet' again in mid-season."

Sawchuk exacted his revenge by turning the Rangers aside with a 4-0 shutout, his best game by far of the young season. Then he vented his loathing for all reporters on the New York scribes who trooped into the Detroit dressing room after the game. "When you win a game these guys start coming around," he sneered. "I had enough of you guys last year. Why don't you leave me alone?"

His much ballyhooed return to Boston proved an ordeal he would not soon forget. Many Beantowners initially took his side against Bruin management when he had fled the team. But all that changed with the reports of his unabashed joy at having rejoined the Red Wings. Fans in Boston could sympathize with him wanting to quit the game. What they couldn't abide was his obvious distaste for their beloved Bruins.

It was said that even the despised Rocket Richard had never heard the level of invective that rained down on Sawchuk that night at Boston Garden. Starting in the pre-game warm-up, the crowd of more than 14,000 jeered his every move. They greeted the announcement of his name over the public-address system with a deafening chorus of boos. Many of the fans risked ejection from the building by hurling an array of objects—including eggs, programs, popcorn boxes and men's overshoes—at the fallen hero who not long before was the town's biggest box-office draw since the heyday of Eddie Shore.

At least that hadn't changed. "People paid to see him when he was with us, and it looks as though they're paying to see him against us, too," Lynn Patrick remarked happily after the Bruins' 4-0 victory.

Sawchuk said later that some of the Bruin players laughed in his face. From that day forward he dreaded the Red Wings' visits to Boston, where the fans never forgave him. In the years ahead, whenever he found himself in a platoon situation with another goaltender, he often deliberately sat out games at the Garden.

Warned by friends about what to expect, Sawchuk endured the abuse in Boston with uncharacteristic calm. But a few nights later he took out all his pent-up frustration during a wild brawl in Chicago. Players were paired off over most of the ice surface when Sawchuk suddenly, and for no apparent reason, darted from the safety of his goal crease and sucker-punched Eric Nesterenko, who already had his hands full with the usually mild-tempered Red Kelly. This prompted the intervention of Elmer "Moose" Vasko, who landed a rapid series of solid punches that left Sawchuk reeling before they were finally pulled apart.

Terry had returned from his brief retirement angrier and more unforgiving than ever. That season he collected thirty-nine minutes in penalties, a new record for goaltenders. By comparison, he accumulated a penalty total of only nine minutes in his first three NHL seasons.

Detroit writers covering the team, perhaps fearful of getting back in Sawchuk's doghouse, wrote lavish tributes to his undiminished artistry throughout the 1957-58 campaign. The Wings stood fifth at the midway point, but no one blamed Terry. "The way the club has been going, I feel sorry for him, but his play has been terrific, at times unbelievable," said Jimmy Skinner. "I wouldn't trade him for any goalie in the league."

Complaining of migraine headaches and other physical complaints brought on by the stress of the job, Skinner voluntarily stepped aside as coach the first week in January. Sid Abel, who had been working as a colour man on radio and television broadcasts of Detroit home games, stepped in. "It's just like coming home after a long, long trip," said a wistful Abel, another old employee with an indelible Red Wing tattoo.

It could have been the accumulated strain of all that Pat and Terry had been through the past few months. Or possibly Pat had become fed up with her husband's bad temper and constant skirt chasing. Terry professed not to know what caused Pat to suddenly file for divorce early that February.

News of her suit in Pontiac Circuit Court became public just before the Wings took the ice at the Olympia for a match against the Canadiens. "Leave me alone," Sawchuk shouted when reporters pressed him for a quote. "I don't know anything about it. Ask my wife."

Pat wasn't talking either. But she gave a hint of what life with her volatile husband was like in an interview a few months later. "I never say a word to him on the day he's playing," she said. "He's like an old bear. He blows up fast, but he gets over it just as fast. The kids used to bother him but, you know, Terry left home so early that he didn't know what home life was like. It made him too independent."

Even Sawchuk's most loyal friends were frequently appalled by the way he treated his wife. "He ruined that whole thing with Pat, who was just a wonderful woman," says one. "I always used to tell him to lay off with the women, that he was going to wreck his marriage. But he never listened."

Despite her announced intention to end the marriage, Pat and Terry continued to live together in the house at Union Lake with their three children—Gerry, three, Jo Ann, eighteen months, and a new addition, Katherine, who had been born just three months before. Also temporarily occupying their home were Terry's parents and brother and sister, who had recently arrived from Winnipeg to settle permanently in the Detroit area.

Terry played well that night in a 1-1 tie with Montreal. But he was so distraught that Jack Adams barred all visitors from the dressing room after the game. Adams revealed later that Sawchuk broke down and sobbed uncontrollably when he tried to talk to him about the situation.

Somehow Terry managed to patch over the rift with his wife. Two days later she accompanied him to the Olympia and watched him play in a 5-2 loss to New York. Smiling brightly for the press, Pat said that she had dropped her divorce suit. "We've got everything straightened out," her husband added, refusing to comment further.

Sid Abel had always been able to light a fire under his teammates when he was the Red Wing captain. Now he performed an even larger miracle in his first half-season as their coach, guiding Detroit to a 16-12-5 mark and bringing them home in third place. The Wings lost only twice in their final thirteen starts.

Then, as it had so often in the past, reality intruded in the menacing form of Maurice Richard. The thirty-seven-year-old Rocket personally outscored the entire Detroit team, seven goals to six, in an embarrassingly easy Montreal semi-final sweep.

"He beat me in 1951 when I was a rookie and he did it again this year," said Sawchuk, who actually played a decent series. "It may seem strange, considering the scores, to mention that Terry Sawchuk was as good as any man in a Detroit uniform," wrote Marshall Dann in the *Detroit Free Press* after Detroit had been walloped 8-1 and 5-1 in the first two games.

Jack Adams took the defeat hard, acknowledging for the first time exactly how far his team had fallen since the last Stanley Cup victory just three seasons before. "After nine years of great success we must face the fact that our once powerful team has disintegrated," he said. "Now we're going to start building all over again and we'll wish for the same kind of luck."

Detroit would hit bottom the next season, finishing dead last in the standings for the first time in the club's history. The Wings still possessed that central core of outstanding players; Sawchuk, Howe, Pronovost and Delvecchio all made the second All-Star team. Terry almost single-handedly kept the Wings near the top of the standings for the first two months of the season before the inevitable collapse. But Adams once again had trouble filling out the line-up around his handful of stars.

The highlight of the Red Wing season, if one of the bloodiest fights in hockey history can properly be called that, was the classic confrontation on February 1 between heavyweights Gordie Howe and Lou Fontinato at Madison Square Garden. The two went at it for a full minute behind the Detroit net while their teammates and the officials watched in awe, unwilling to risk coming between the combatants.

"Howe began smashing him with lefts and rights, and then fired an upper-cut that smashed Lou's nose," recounted referee Art Skov. "I just stood back and said, 'No way I'm going to break up this one.' Howe cleaned Fontinato like you've never seen." When the two finally separated, Fontinato's nose was smeared halfway across his face.

"I never saw a fight like that since I've been in hockey," marvelled Sawchuk, who had a ringside seat. "They just stood there slugging each other for all they had."

Terry got off to another hot start in 1959-60. "How can we help leading when we get goaltending like that?" Sid Abel asked after the Wings went undefeated in their first five games. Detroit was comfortably cruising along in second place when, on the morning of the American Thanksgiving, Terry complained of shooting pains in his legs and was rushed by ambulance to Detroit Osteopathic Hospital. Doctors said vaguely that he had come down with some sort of virus. He sat out three games before returning to the line-up.

In early February, the problem recurred, but this time the diagnosis was more precise: Sawchuk suffered from neuritis, a painful inflammation of the nerves, in this case, controlling the lower part of the legs from the knees to the ankles.

Intimates say that the news sent Terry reeling. His doctors reportedly told him that there was a slim chance he could end up in a wheelchair in five or six years' time. They wouldn't even try to predict how much longer he might be able to play hockey. A pessimist both by nature and from years of hard-won experience, Terry feared the worst. The whammy had struck again.

A few years later, during an interview with sportswriter Andy O'Brien, Pat discussed the litany of physical ailments that plagued her husband through the early 1960s. There were two herniated discs in Sawchuk's lower back, which would later require surgery and may have contributed to his neuritis. His upper back was swayed, caused by a condition called lordosis, the result of back muscles that had been shortened by years of crouching in goal. Because of this, when he walked on the street he gave the impression of falling forward. Terry also suffered from insomnia, caused by the constant throbbing pain in his back and legs, and persistent migraine headaches.

"Maybe a wife remembers too many things," Pat told O'Brien quietly. "When it came time to waken him I often had to help him out of bed and, later, into the car for the trip to the rink. Then he'd take a pain-killer pill, timing it so he would unstiffen by the time the buzzer sounded to skate out onto the ice. I gave up pleading with him to retire when I realized how much hockey meant to him."

Pat didn't even think to mention her husband's chronically swollen right elbow, which prevented him from performing even such a simple task as tying his own ties. "It's no problem," Terry once said. "I buy two ties, one for grey and brown suits and another for blue and black threads. My wife ties them the first time I wear them and I never remove the knots, just loosen them enough to slip the tie over my head."

Minor-league netminder Dennis Riggin filled in while Sawchuk's neuritis forced him to sit out nine games in February. During his absence, Jack Adams made yet another ultimately disastrous trade based not on common sense, but solely on the heated emotions of the moment. "More and more that was becoming his way," remembers Lefty Wilson. "With Jack Adams, everything was personal. He'd get so bloody mad that he'd trade a player just so he wouldn't have to look at him any more—and to show everyone else who was the boss."

What set Adams off this time was a Toronto magazine article that quoted Red Kelly as saying the Red Wings had forced him to play with a broken bone in his foot the previous season. Though the story was essentially true (if Adams hadn't actually "forced" Kelly, he had certainly strongly urged him to play), Adams was incensed that Kelly, long one of his favourites, made the fact known to the public. Within forty-eight hours, he swapped Kelly and forward Billy McNeill to New York for Bill Gadsby and Eddie Shack.

Kelly, however, refused to report to New York and announced he was quitting the game, effectively cancelling the deal. But Toronto's Punch Imlach soon sweet-talked him out of retirement and worked out a straight-up exchange with Adams that sent defenceman Marc Reaume to Detroit.

Converted into a full-time centreman by Imlach, Kelly played a leading role in the four Stanley Cups won by the Maple Leafs in the next seven years. And here at least was one old Red Wing ready to surrender his heart and soul to a new team. "I was finally where I always wanted to be," Kelly, the son of a southern Ontario tobacco farmer, recalled of his first game in Toronto blue. "When the people stood up and clapped and cheered me, I felt so tight I nearly burst."

Marc Reaume would never develop into anything more than what he had always been, a fringe player. Spectators at Maple Leaf Gardens razzed Jack Adams so unmercifully about the deal that for the next year or so he usually stayed behind when the Wings travelled to Toronto.

Sawchuk's return to the line-up in late February of 1960 came just in time for him to help Detroit narrowly edge out Boston for the final playoff berth. Punch Imlach's rapidly improving and heavily favoured Maple Leafs opposed them in the semi-final.

Before the start of the series, there were the by now standard snickers about Detroit's reduced circumstances. Len "Comet" Haley, a twenty-eight-year-old rookie, was regarded as a symbol of the Wings' sad decline. Haley toiled over nine seasons in the minors before finally getting the call to the big club that January. Sid Abel placed him with other long-time minor leaguers Jerry Melnyk and Val Fonteyne on what a wag cruelly dubbed the Nothing Line.

But the laughter abruptly stopped when Haley scored the winning goal in Detroit's surprise 2-1 opening-game victory. Toronto bounced back to take the next two games before the Nothing Line struck again in the fourth match. Melnyk slapped home Fonteyne's rebound in the first period of overtime for another 2-1 win that evened the series.

Sawchuk's counterpart from the 1950 Calder Cup, Johnny Bower, stood tall for Toronto throughout the series, but especially during the first four games, when the Wings outshot the Leafs 158 to 114. Bower probably saved the series for Toronto with his work in game three, which lasted into a third overtime session before Frank Mahovlich deflected a blast by Red Kelly (who had scored two previous goals to make the overtime possible) past Sawchuk to finally put it away. Bower made a total of sixty-two saves in the game and came up with unbelievable overtime stops on both Howe and Pronovost.

Toronto's superior depth turned the tide in the final two games, when the Wings ran out of steam and lost by scores of 5-4 and 4-2. Though Bower was undeniably the star of the series, Sawchuk had also acquitted himself with distinction. Certainly he had earned the admiration of Punch Imlach, who would one day team Sawchuk and Bower together in hockey's most famous goaltending platoon. "Every time I looked, Terry Sawchuk was robbing one of our guys on a breakaway," Imlach said. "If Bower was great, so was Sawchuk."

In time Terry would welcome sharing his duties with another goaltender. But at age thirty, he still regarded himself as an everyday player. He was affronted the next fall in training camp to learn that Sid Abel intended to keep two goalies on the roster. The new man was twenty-eight-year-old Hank Bassen, who the year before had been the Western League's most valuable player. Bassen had already played thirty-three games in the NHL with Chicago.

"We don't want to take a chance on being caught short again," Abel said, noting that Sawchuk had missed twelve games the year before.

When Terry struggled early in the season, Abel increasingly sat him down in favour of Bassen. By the start of December, the Wings held first place and Bassen, a wandering netminder in the style made popular by Jacques Plante, had apparently taken over the top job. "I don't know if it's a case of a 'hot hand' or what," Abel said of Bassen, "but he's been doing a tremendous job and has lifted the whole team."

Sawchuk watched and brooded. Finally, during a televised interview in Montreal, he announced that he either wanted to play full-time or be traded. Terry felt he needed to work regularly to stay sharp. If that meant going to another team, well, then he was prepared to move on.

He must have known that there was little chance the Red Wings would—or could—trade him. Jacques Plante, Glenn Hall, Johnny Bower and Gump Worsley, every one a future Hall of Famer, guarded the nets of four of the league's five other teams. Only the Bruins were shopping for a new goalkeeper. After making his early splash, the injury-prone Don Simmons proved a disappointment. But, for Sawchuk, a return to Boston was obviously out of the question.

At any rate, Terry's televised blast had its intended effect. Abel started giving him more work and by the end of the season he and Bassen had virtually split the workload. Bassen, though, clearly enjoyed the better season for the fourth-place Wings, posting a 2.86 GAA compared to Saw-chuk's 3.05.

"He really had only three great games all year," Abel said of Terry. "If it wasn't for Hank's play through the season we wouldn't even have made the playoffs."

Nevertheless, Abel named Terry to start the semi-final opener against, once again, the Toronto Maple Leafs. Abel based his decision on Sawchuk's long playoff experience and the fact that one of his three "great" games had come as recently as the regular-season finale against Montreal.

Though the Canadiens had won 2-0 to clinch first place over the Leafs, Terry turned back thirty-six shots and in the process foiled Bernie Geoffrion's bid to break Rocket Richard's record of fifty goals in a single season. Late in the third period, Geoffrion, who entered the game tied for the record, took aim from point-blank range. Terry sprawled and just managed to deflect the puck away. "Sawchuk was hot," said a dejected Boom Boom, "but still I'm satisfied that I was able to tie the record."

"I really didn't know how we'd do in the playoffs until the last game of the season," Abel said. "Then, in that one game, our defence jelled and Terry had the hot hand. I figured then that we'd be tough."

The Wings had improved themselves by trading with Boston to reacquire Vic Stasiuk. Abel put him on the first line with Howe and Delvecchio after his arrival in January. Another key mid-season addition was Howie Young, a rambunctious twenty-three-year-old regarded as the most colourful defenceman to enter the league since Lou Fontinato. Chants of "We Want Howie" filled the Olympia during the stretch drive. In the twenty-nine games since his promotion from the minors, hockey's newest bad boy had compiled 108 minutes in penalties.

Late in February, Young had barrelled into Johnny

Bower after he left his crease to clear the puck, a hit that continued to pay dividends in the semi-final against Toronto. Bower, nursing the leg he had damaged in the collision, missed the opener and performed below his Vezina-winning standard for the remainder of the series as Detroit upset the Leafs in five games.

For Terry, the clock suddenly seemed to have turned back ten years. "The key to our success has been Sawchuk," said Gordie Howe after Detroit had pushed the Leafs to the brink of elimination. "He's killing Toronto with the kind of goalkeeping that old Johnny Bower used to eliminate us last spring. Terry is the Terry of old, playing like he did when we were winning Stanley Cups and he was the greatest."

Sawchuk held the highest-scoring team to that point in Toronto history to just eight goals in the five games. Each night he was named one of the game's three stars. Even Howe, who led all scorers and, as one reporter noted, "did everything but clean the ice," was only selected in four.

"It's nice to have things go right for a change," said Terry. "I'll tell you something, though. If we keep on playing this kind of hockey, anything can happen."

Sawchuk spoke too soon about his luck having changed. In the first period of the Cup final against Chicago, he left his net to field a loose puck and was rammed by Hawk Murray Balfour. Terry toppled to the ice and lay in agony for several minutes, clutching a left shoulder already black and blue from a previous injury. He should have left the game. But he gamely insisted on playing and the Hawks blasted three goals past him in under four minutes. Hank Bassen took over at the start of the second period and finished out the remainder of a 3-2 Chicago victory.

Tommy Ivan's Hawks, after finishing third, had earned their place in the final by eliminating Montreal in six games, a major upset that ended the Habs' five-year reign as Stanley Cup champions.

Chicago's line-up featured four of the game's most exciting talents—centre Stan Mikita, veteran defenceman Pierre Pilote, goaltender Glenn Hall, and left winger Bobby Hull, a twenty-two-year-old blond Adonis whose rink-length rushes and Howitzer-like slap shots pulled the patrons out of their seats unlike anyone since the prime of Rocket Richard. "I've never been afraid of what I do," said Bassen, "but when Bobby blasts one, he puts the fear of God in you. You see that thing coming at you like a bullet and your life flashes before your eyes."

The entire NHL had pitched in to help rebuild a failing franchise that won its last Stanley Cup in 1938. Of the eighteen players on Chicago's playoff roster, thirteen were purchased from other squads.

To have even a chance of beating such a talented and well balanced line-up, the undermanned Red Wings desperately needed the Terry Sawchuk who had suddenly reappeared in the Toronto series, the goalie who had once had no peer. Sadly, that Sawchuk had departed in the collision with Balfour. Terry nursed the pinched nerves in his shoulder and watched his teammates split the next two games. He played well in his return in game four when Detroit won 2-1 to even the series. But then, in the pivotal fifth game, he fanned on a shot by Mikita and looked shaky on at least two other goals in a 6-3 Chicago triumph. Bassen was back in net when the Hawks won the sixth game 5-1 to capture their first Stanley Cup in twenty-three mostly lean years.

Terry became the frequent target of boos and catcalls at the Olympia the next season. Many fans blamed him for a disappointing campaign that saw Detroit struggle to a fifth-place finish. In forty-three appearances, Terry's goals-against average rose to 3.33, the worst mark of his entire career. There were loud rumblings around the league that he was nearing the end of the line.

That April, Red Wing president Bruce Norris, who had succeeded his sister Marguerite in 1955, summoned Jack Adams to his office and relieved him of his duties as general manager. Trader Jack's dismissal came several years too late for the good of the club, but far too soon to suit the sixty-seven-year-old who had guided the Wings' fortunes for the past thirty-five years. Leaning for support on the arm of Jimmy Skinner, Adams left the Olympia with tears of disappointment streaming down his face.

Jack Adams's life in hockey, it should be noted, did not end there. A few months later he was named the first president of the Central Professional Hockey League, an NHL-endorsed development circuit based in the United States. The little general who had guided the Wings to seven Stanley Cups and twelve first-place finishes died in 1968.

Adams's dismissal held special significance for Sawchuk. It was Adams who had revived his career by bringing him back home to Detroit and who, in the years since, had steadfastly maintained that Terry was still the game's best goalie. With Sid Abel now assuming the dual role of GM-coach, Terry stood on far less certain ground. Abel had chosen to sit him down in favour of Hank Bassen for the majority of the most crucial games of the past season, those near the end when Detroit still had a chance of overtaking New York for the final playoff spot.

With Jack Adams gone, Sawchuk couldn't help but wonder if his own leave-taking would be far behind.

## Chapter Ten

# THE MASK

"I won't go back in without the mask," Jacques Plante had stubbornly insisted back on November 1, 1959, after suffering an ugly seven-stitch gash under his nose in a game against New York.

With that historic ultimatum to Montreal coach Toe Blake, who considered the mask a sissified affectation and had previously forbidden Plante to wear it in league play, an enlightened new era of full facial protection for goaltenders was ushered in. But like most new ideas, this one took a while to catch on. Since Plante had made his stand, among NHL goalies only Boston's Don Simmons had followed his example and covered up.

In 1960, after testing a fibreglass mask designed by Lefty Wilson, Sawchuk complained that it restricted his vision and quickly abandoned the experiment. Now, two years later, he reported to training camp and had Wilson dig out the discarded face gear from the bottom of an equipment trunk. Following the worst season of his career, Terry was willing to try anything that might provide the edge he needed to hold onto his job. Sid Abel had announced that only one full-time goalie would be kept on the roster for 1962-63 and declared the competition wide open between Sawchuk, Hank Bassen and Dennis Riggin.

Terry could no longer afford to indulge himself in the old fantasies about retiring from the game. In the years since his return to the Red Wings, he had invested in two businesses, a garbage-disposal service in Union Lake and a Detroit tavern, both of them resounding failures. Sawchuk knew he had to continue playing hockey to recoup his losses and provide for a family that now included five children (four girls and a boy) ranging in age from one to eight. Two final additions, both boys, would arrive within the next three years.

This time the mask was a fit. "It has helped my game tremendously," Sawchuk enthused at the end of camp, after having easily outclassed Bassen and Riggin to win the top job. "I wouldn't be a bit surprised if it added a few more years to my career."

He found he no longer worried about being cut in the face by a stick or a skate when he dove into pile-ups. There had always been a few players in the league who enjoyed shooting at his head, trying to scare him. They didn't bother him any more either. And though he acknowledged that the mask did slightly limit his vision, especially when pucks were at his feet, he now chose to regard this as a positive thing. "I think the mask keeps you more alert," he said. "That may sound funny. But I think the fact that you know you're losing a little keeps you that way."

With Sawchuk consistently providing the big saves, the Wings jumped off to their fastest start ever, remaining unbeaten through the season's first ten games. He sparkled even in Detroit's few early-season defeats. After stopping forty-four shots during a 3-2 loss in Toronto, Terry was named the number one star of the game. He joked that even the goalposts were working for him. "Last year they looked just like skinny pipes. This year they look like trees."

Everyone was amazed by the difference in Sawchuk's play; how the simple act of putting on the mask had apparently rejuvenated him. "He's getting back on his feet right away after going down to make a save," Abel noted. Added Toe Blake, "The last couple of years it seemed like once a team scored a couple of goals on Sawchuk, he let up a little. But it isn't that way now."

The mask, which in combination with his closely

cropped hair gave Terry a startling resemblance to the Frankenstein monster, not only restored his old confidence, but provided him with a satisfying new hobby—counting the stitches he might have had. "I got hit in the forehead in practice one day," he said early in the season. "It would have been a cut. And twice in games, once on the cheek and once on the chin, I've stopped—or rather the mask stopped them." Before donning the mask, Sawchuk's face, which from up close resembled a crazy quiltwork of old scars, had been cut for more than 350 stitches.

The club many expected to once again miss the playoffs managed to hold onto first place until December 2. At mid-season, Terry finished two points ahead of Stan Mikita in voting for the Hart Trophy as league MVP, and he tied with Glenn Hall for the lead in All-Star balloting.

So far he had performed spectacularly through a painful shoulder injury, a bruised instep and a mysterious stomach ailment that doctors finally diagnosed as a blocked intes-tine. "I thought I had ulcers," said Sawchuk, who spent his thirty-third birthday receiving treatment in the hospital between starts. "My stomach was so sore that I couldn't breathe—I thought I was going to choke."

Finally, and what by now can only seem inevitably, another freak injury interrupted the storybook comeback that had captured the imagination of the hockey public. On January 12 in Toronto, Leaf Bob Pulford accidentally stepped on the back of Sawchuk's glove hand, slashing his tendons. "It looked like a little cut at first," Terry recounted. "Then it opened up and I could see the knuckle bones. Funny thing, it hurt very little. I tried to open my hand as I was going off the ice. But the fingers snapped right under."

He was in the operating room at Toronto East General Hospital for about two hours. "I asked the doctor how many stitches he took, but he said he stopped counting after fifty."

They wrapped Sawchuk's forearm and hand in a plaster cast and said he could expect to be out of the line-up anywhere from six to eight weeks.

There went his chance of winning the Hart Trophy, the sport's most coveted award, and almost certainly of beating out Glenn Hall for All-Star honours. While his teammates spent the next few weeks heavily engaged in the first four-team race for first place in NHL history, Terry found that time hung heavily on his hands.

"When it happened, I thought at least I'd be able to sleep in in the mornings for a while," he told an interviewer two weeks into his convalescence. "But I still wake up at 7 o'clock with the kids. Then I read the paper through, do the crossword and word game and read the paper again a couple more times."

Terry said he couldn't button his shirts or even bathe himself. "But I'm coming along—I can tie my shoes now."

He was less forthcoming with another reporter, Pete Waldmeir of *The Detroit News*, who ran into him around this time when Sawchuk visited the Olympia to ride the stationary bicycle in the training room.

"How's the hand, Uke?" Waldmeir asked affably. "You asked me that yesterday," Terry snarled, and turned away.

He rushed back to the line-up earlier than expected, on February 23 in Chicago, after missing seventeen games and working out in just four practice sessions. After two periods, Sawchuk tired and came out of the game. But the next night he went the distance in a 3-2 Detroit victory over New York and then played out the balance of the season as Detroit fought to a fourth-place finish. A spread of only five points separated the Wings from front-running Toronto, leaving Sid Abel to lament, "If we'd had Terry more this year, we probably would have finished much higher in the season standings."

Sawchuk's goals-against average of 2.48 (his best mark in six seasons) led all goaltenders, but during his absence the team's GAA had risen and the Vezina went to Glenn Hall. Terry finished on the second team, behind Hall, in All-Star balloting, his seventh appearance on the post-season honour roll.

For the first time in recent memory, the Wings bore a passing resemblance to legitimate Stanley Cup contenders. The defence had been dramatically improved by the addition of talented rookie Doug Barkley. Following an injury-plagued 1961-62 campaign, Marcel Pronovost was back in full stride. Another key defender, wily old Bill Gadsby, had been acquired from New York the year before. The Wings had been after the thirty-six-year-old ever since the aborted Red Kelly deal.

That season Howie Young, the crowd-pleasing renegade of the Detroit rearguard, amassed an NHL record 273 penalty minutes, far outdistancing Lou Fontinato's old mark of 202. One writer compared his impact on the outcome of a match to buckshot—"sometimes on target, sometimes not." Inevitably, there came a point in every game when Young appeared to have completely lost control; when he had no choice but to explode. "You can tell how mad Howie is getting by the colour of his face," observed *The Globe and Mail*'s Scott Young. "He starts the game with a lily-white complexion but by the third period his face is fiery red."

Not surprisingly, Detroit topped the league in penalties. But it hardly mattered, thanks to a superb penalty-killing unit led by forwards Bruce MacGregor and Val Fonteyne. Opponents scored just eleven goals while Young served his time in the penalty box.

Still, the bad-boy act was starting to wear thin. Alcohol would soon destroy what should have been a brilliant career. After a game in Chicago on January 1, Young disappeared from the team and went on a four-day New Year's bender. Not even his wife could track him down. Though the Wings provided Young with professional counselling, his misbehaviour both on and off the ice continued. Abel, fearful that his antics might jeopardize the team's chances, used him sparingly for the duration of the playoffs.

Gordie Howe jokingly referred to Detroit's wide-open offensive style as the "Play It By Ear" attack. In his seventeenth season, Number 9 still averaged forty to forty-five minutes of ice time per game and took a hand in more than 40 per cent of the club's goals. Howe won the sixth scoring title of his career and, also for the sixth time, captured the Hart Trophy as MVP, the honour that might have been Sawchuk's but for Bob Pulford's errant skate blade.

Hard-checking and swift-skating, the Red Wings scored an even two hundred goals on the attack, sixteen better than the season before and the team's high-water mark since the last Stanley Cup year. Parker MacDonald, who had been trying to establish himself as a big-leaguer since 1953, blossomed overnight into a thirty-three-goal sniper. Norm Ullman scored twenty-six and Alex Delvecchio (the centreman for Howe and MacDonald on the league's top scoring line) tallied twenty along with forty-four assists.

The Wings entered their semi-final against the second-place Black Hawks as underdogs. But they weren't, at least, the same old *longshot* underdogs. The physical status of Hawk star Bobby Hull, who was nursing a separated right shoulder, shortened the odds even further in their favour.

Even wounded, the Golden Jet smoked two wrist shots past Sawchuk in the first period of the opener to pace Chicago to a 5-4 triumph. Then, in game two, Hull's nose was reduced to a bloody, pulpy mess when he tried to slip past a spinning Bruce MacGregor and got caught by a high stick. Hull could barely breathe, let alone continue to play. The Hawks won 5-2, but the playing field had been levelled.

Three nights later, Gordie Howe celebrated his thirty-fifth birthday with a goal and two assists in a crucial 4-2 Detroit victory. Hull sat that one out and was assumed to be through for the series. His eyes were blackened, his face swollen and his nostrils propped up with splints to keep his nose from collapsing. But the heroic Hull shocked the Wings by donning a special face mask and skating out for the fourth game in Detroit.

By this point, the Wings had figured out how to contain the explosive Chicago offence—with or without Hull. They closed off the neutral zone, thumped the Hawks at the blue line, and outskated them throughout a dominating 4-1 win. Hull scored Chicago's lone goal.

Detroit outshot Chicago ninety-three to thirty-eight in their twin victories. The Wings went on to wrap up the series with astonishingly easy 4-2 and 7-4 decisions in games five and six. Bobby Hull ended his season by scoring three of Chicago's four goals in the final match and assisting on the other tally by Eric Nesterenko.

Despite his infirmities, Hull beat Sawchuk eight times in the series. "The only thing you can do with Hull," sighed Terry, "is just hope you're in the line of the puck and that it hits you."

Encouraged by how they had taken charge of the series against Chicago, the Wings envisioned pulling off an even bigger upset over their opponents in the Cup final, the Toronto Maple Leafs, who had needed just five games to eliminate Montreal.

In truth, Detroit stood little chance against the reigning Stanley Cup champions. Punch Imlach's crew was far and away the best club in hockey during the post-season. In the preliminary round against the Canadiens, Johnny Bower and his stalwart defence of Tim Horton, Bob Baun, Carl Brewer, Allan Stanley and Kent Douglas held the league's highest-scoring club to just six goals. Eight different players scored for Toronto, a good indication of the team's overall balance. Though their line-up included only three players who netted twenty or more goals (Frank Mahovlich, Red Kelly and Dave Keon), the Leafs had finished second in team scoring with 221 goals, just four back of Montreal.

Imlach said later that he counted the series as good as won when Dick Duff beat Sawchuk with two nearly identical hip-high shots in the first minute and eight seconds of the opening game. Terry stood like a statue when Duff let rip. If Sawchuk was off his game, Imlach knew, then the Wings were dead.

Terry looked just as bad on a solo effort by Bob Nevin later that period. After carrying the play to Toronto most of the evening, the Wings came out on the losing end of a 4-2 final score.

In what proved to be another five-game victory for Toronto, Bower almost always delivered the big save when the Leafs needed it; Sawchuk, favouring a sore elbow injured in a fall to the ice, most often could not. At one point, Abel considered sitting Terry down, but in the end he stayed with the man who for most of the past winter had been the league's top goaltender.

Anyway, Abel could see that the Wings were in over their heads. Toronto's relentless forechecking frustrated and wore his men down. Even when playing shorthanded the Leafs posed a constant threat, scoring three times.

Sawchuk looked sharp enough in Detroit's only victory, a 3-2 final in game three at the Olympia. But his best

performance came in the last game, when the Leafs sealed
their second-straight Stanley Cup championship with a 3-1
decision at Maple Leaf Gardens. Toronto led 2-1 late in the
third period when Sawchuk kept Detroit in the game with
saves on Duff and Eddie Shack. After Abel pulled Terry for
an extra attacker, Dave Keon scored into the empty net with
five seconds left on the clock.

"Hockey's New Mr. Zero" trumpeted *Sport Magazine* in
1952, after Sawchuk recorded eleven shutouts as a rookie.
By the end of 1954-55, when he reluctantly departed for
Boston, Terry had whitewashed the opposition a remarkable
fifty-seven times and already passed such illustrious names
as Bill Durnan, Frankie Brimsek and Davey Kerr on the list
of all-time shutout leaders.

Slowly and steadily, while averaging just over four
shutouts per season in the intervening eight years, he had
moved up the ladder past Turk Broda, Roy Worters, Harry
Lumley, Lorne Chabot, Alex Connell and Tiny Thompson.
By the start of the 1963-64 season, Sawchuk had ninety-one
shutouts to his credit and stood just three shy of the all-time
leader, his childhood hero George Hainsworth, who set his
mark while toiling for the Canadiens and Maple Leafs
between 1926 and 1937.

Ordinarily, Sawchuk's pursuit of Hainsworth would have
received extensive coverage in the sports pages of NHL
cities. But that autumn an even more illustrious Red Wing
was chasing an even bigger prize. Gordie Howe started the
season needing only five more goals to pass Rocket
Richard's career mark of 544 and become the all-time leading goal-scorer.

So while an attending army of reporters, photographers
and TV cameramen built Howe's impending achievement
into the most publicized milestone event to that point in

hockey history, Sawchuk went virtually ignored—which was probably just the way he wanted it.

"I don't think it bothered Terry that Howe was getting all the attention," says Lefty Wilson. "That just wasn't his nature. Terry would have hated to have all those reporters chasing him and not Gordie. The press did him a big favour by ignoring him."

Both Detroit record-chasers jumped off to strong starts. Howe beat Glenn Hall twice in a 5-3 win over the Black Hawks in the season opener, and added another goal in the second game when Sawchuk blanked the Bruins 3-0 for his ninety-second shutout. On October 27, Howe tied Richard with a goal against the Canadiens at the Olympia. Sawchuk drew within one of Hainsworth in Detroit on November 7, shading the Rangers 1-0 with the help of a third-period goal by Parker MacDonald. In the game's dying moments, Howe, who had been under almost unbearable pressure since tying the record, hit the post on a sixty-foot try at an empty net.

Three nights later they were packed as much as six deep in the Olympia's standing-room areas, with hundreds more turned away at the gates for the Red Wings versus the Canadiens. Expectation ran high that, in front of the home-town fans who had worshipped him for almost two decades, Howe would end his drought of five scoreless games and break the record against Richard's former teammates.

The drama built until late in the second period when Howe jumped over the boards to help kill a penalty. Wing forward Billy McNeill raced down the ice after taking a pass from Howe deep in Detroit territory. Once inside the Montreal blue line, McNeill passed the puck back to Howe, who snapped a wrist shot toward netminder Charlie Hodge from twenty-five feet out. Hodge tried to hug the goalpost to his left, then banged his stick in frustration when he realized the puck was behind him.

For ten minutes, the 15,027 faithful stood and cheered themselves hoarse. "I feel ten pounds lighter," Howe said while waiting for the maintenance men to finish clearing the ice of tributes.

Sawchuk played magnificently, turning aside thirty-nine Montreal shots in a 3-0 Detroit victory. The shutout, his second in as many games and the ninety-fourth of his career, tied him with Hainsworth. But the evening belonged to only one man. After the game, while Sawchuk sat ignored in his seat by the dressing-room door, Howe patiently posed for pictures and recounted the scoring of number 545. "I knew it was in when I let it go," he said. "I'm glad it's over. Now I can start enjoying life again."

Sid Abel tried his best to deflect some of the attention Terry's way. "It's great that Gordie finally got it," Abel said, "but don't forget the goaltender. He had a tremendous game."

A solitary reporter finally approached to ask if Sawchuk felt slighted by all the attention Howe was getting. "Not a bit," Terry smiled brightly. "As long as Gordie can score and we can win like that, I'll take it every night."

The history-making win over Montreal moved Detroit into a tie with Toronto for third place. But a twin blight of injuries and slumps soon dropped the Wings into fourth spot. Howe's record-tying and record-breaking goals were the only two he scored in seven weeks. With his defence crippled and the Wing forwards neither scoring nor often bothering to backcheck, the level of Sawchuk's own game also plunged dramatically. Detroit had won just one of its past nine games when, in late November, a wrenched back sidelined Terry.

In the recent past, both Hank Bassen and Dennis Riggin had tried unsuccessfully to wrest away the first-string goaltending job. Now Sawchuk's most serious rival since the emergence of Glenn Hall was summoned from Jack Adams's Central Professional Hockey League.

"He could be the find of the century. He could be great," Abel raved of Roger Crozier, twenty-one, who had been acquired from Chicago the previous June in a trade for Howie Young. "It looks like he will be in the Detroit hockey picture for years and years."

Overnight Sawchuk, just a few weeks shy of his thirty-fourth birthday, appeared to have been painted out of the Red Wings' future. Abel handed Crozier the top job after he had played in just a single NHL game, a 1-1 tie with Toronto in which he had soldiered on and given a remarkable performance even after having his cheekbone shattered by a Frank Mahovlich drive. Though the rookie was expected to be out of action for at least ten days, Abel made a point of stressing that "regardless of how well Terry is playing," Crozier would take over upon his return.

"I think he's the only one who can lead us out of this slump," Abel said. "They played better with Roger in goal than anyone else we've had. We've been getting a lot of goals scored against us, so that's an obvious change. It's not because of Terry's sore back, either, because I'd make the switch even if both he and Crozier were healthy."

Not everyone felt as certain as Abel that the new kid had a future in the big league. "Crozier sprawls and goes down too much," pronounced King Clancy, Toronto's assistant general manager. One writer compared Crozier's playing style to "a frenzied acrobat plagued with itch. He bends low in the crouch of a catcher. He falls to his knees. Sometimes, swift and agile, he doubles over in the fashion of an inverted U."

The most popular criticism was that Crozier, at five foot seven and 145 pounds, was too small to long withstand the rigours of NHL play. "He's nothing but a Singer midget," sniffed Clancy. Jacques Plante, who by now tended goal for the New York Rangers, agreed with the others about Crozier's lack of size, and had trouble understanding why the Wings felt they needed a change. "No matter how good he plays," Plante said, "he won't be as good as Sawchuk."

Possibly no goalie before or since has been as good as Sawchuk at his best. But Crozier more than justified Abel's confidence when he returned to the line-up two weeks later. The Wings won twice and played to three ties in his first five games. Abel planned to keep on giving Crozier the majority of the starts, with Sawchuk occasionally coming in as relief.

"Terry is still a fine NHL goaltender," said Abel, who was feeling more magnanimous now that the Wings were back on track. "But he's getting older and needs more rest. I think I'll probably play Roger in stretches of eight to ten games and if it appears he's wearing down because of his size, Terry will go in for five or six games."

This time there was no "play me or trade me" ultimatum issued by Sawchuk. He at last seemed willing to accept that given his age and his many infirmities—the bad back, the migraine headaches, the shooting pains in his legs—it no longer made sense for him to try to play every game. But that didn't mean that Terry had conceded the number one ranking to Crozier. Or that he felt the end of his career was necessarily at hand.

That season Sawchuk set a new record for career games played by an NHL goaltender, surpassing Harry Lumley's old mark of 804. And yet, despite his longevity, Terry was only slightly above the average age of the league's six regular goalies—33.8 years.

In his line of work, Sawchuk felt certain that age had its advantages. "I think experience means a great deal as far as goaltenders are concerned," he said. "Knowing the players, knowing the moves they generally make when they come down the ice with the puck. Knowing whether they're a right-hand or left-hand shot all helps a goalie to defence a player. From year to year there aren't a great many changes in the NHL rosters. So you can store up a fund of information that is valuable to you, gives you confidence when you face them."

Just as he had so often in the past, Sawchuk rose to meet the threat posed by his newest challenger. He soon looked so sharp that Abel had no choice but to give him more of the work. What might have been his best game that season was also certainly his biggest. On January 18 in Montreal, after fifteen games and nearly two months of trying, he beat Montreal 2-0 for the record-breaking ninety-fifth shutout of his career.

According to one game report, many of Sawchuk's stops "bordered on sheer thievery." Ralph Backstrom, J.C. Tremblay and Jean Béliveau were all turned away by brilliant stops in the second period. He foiled John Ferguson on a breakaway and made twelve more saves in a wide-open final frame. The shutout was his first at the Forum since October 27, 1956, back when he wore a Boston uniform.

No happier than usual to see the press after the game, Terry answered, "I didn't give a darn," when asked if he'd been thinking about the record. "The win was more important."

Urged on by the reporters, he reflected on his accomplishment. "Certainly I'm proud of it and feel it means something," he said. "After all, for a shutout you're not allowed one mistake." Gordie Howe's recent milestone had received more publicity, but Terry had no doubt that his was the greater feat. "It's much harder to get. The big scorers can make a dozen mistakes and still get a goal towards a record. A goaler makes a single goof and he has to wait until the next game to start all over. You've got to play sixty minutes to get my record."

Someone told him that he had handled thirty-six shots in the game. "That many? I didn't think there were that many."

By now he was relaxed and having fun. "Hey, do you know I stopped one of those shots with the butt end of my stick?" Terry said, pulling off his jersey. "No kidding."

That winter Sawchuk talked about the changes he had seen in the fourteen years that had passed since his first NHL shutout. "The game is much faster than when I first broke in," he began. "There are more gang attacks today. They throw the puck in and the defencemen move up to the blue line. When they get a crossfire going, with the players on either point slapping the puck at you, it really is murderous.

"They're shooting harder, too. When I started in the NHL there were very few slap shots.... Now more players are using slap shots and they're more accurate with them— Gordie Howe, Bernie Geoffrion, Andy Bathgate, Frank Mahovlich, Bobby Hull, Stan Mikita. When we played Toronto the first two games this season, five of the eight goals were scored on slap shots by defencemen."

Another big difference, and one of Sawchuk's pet peeves, was the all-out effort opponents put on screening and otherwise unnerving enemy goaltenders. "They bang at your feet with their sticks. It isn't that they're deliberately trying to hurt you. They're just trying to detract [sic] your attention.

"Sure the crease is supposed to be inviolate. But how many times do you hear a referee call interference because an opposing player is in the crease? If you take a swing at them, you're the one who gets caught and penalized more often than not."

During a scramble for the puck in a game against New York that February, Ranger winger Vic Hadfield barged into the goal crease and sent Sawchuk sprawling.

"You okay, Terry?" Hadfield asked anxiously.

"Sure, I'm fine," answered Terry.

"Hadfield smacked me five times like that," Sawchuk said in disgust after the game. "And yet he wants to know how I feel."

By early February, Sawchuk had won back the top job from Crozier and was working even more than he would have liked. The full playing load fell on his shoulders when Abel reluctantly dispatched Crozier, who still looked like a budding star, to the Pittsburgh farm club, which desperately needed a goaltender after Hank Bassen went down with a leg injury.

"Help!" Terry joked wearily after playing four games in five days, concluding with a big 4-2 decision over the Rangers. The victory boosted Detroit's lead to five points in the battle with New York for the final playoff spot.

"I'm tired," Terry smiled. "Bring back Roger. I'm not used to playing this many games."

Strengthened by the addition of promising young forwards Paul Henderson, Pit Martin, Eddie Joyal and Larry Jeffrey, none of whom were older than twenty-three, the Wings ended the season with a flourish. In the final six weeks they won thirteen games, tied two and lost just four. Their fourth-place finish was deceiving. Detroit entered the playoffs as the NHL's hottest team.

"Everyone laughs at us when we talk about winning the Cup," Abel said. "But the experts forget that we played with injuries all year long, that we had six regulars hurt at one time…. It's just lately that we've had all our varsity together."

Once again Chicago opposed Detroit in the semi-finals. And just like the year before, the Wings dropped the opener in Chicago, this time by a score of 4-1. Game two was less than five minutes old when Sawchuk was forced out of action with a pinched nerve in his left shoulder. "I went to smother a puck and the pain in the shoulder hit me like an electric shock," he said. The injury was similar to the one he had suffered in the opener of the 1961 Cup final. That untimely mishap had all but killed the Wings' chances against these same Hawks.

Detroit managed to squeeze out a 5-4 victory with stand-by Bob Champoux finishing the game in goal. The twenty-one-year-old, who had spent most of the season with Cincinnati of the CPHL, filled in only because Roger Crozier's services were still urgently required by Pittsburgh.

When the Wings returned home, Sawchuk checked immediately into Detroit Osteopathic Hospital. For four hours he received intermittent traction. Then he was placed in a traction harness attached to a fifteen-pound weight to provide tension. After a couple hours of that, Terry went back for more of the intermittent traction.

It was a horribly gruelling and painful routine that would be repeated time and again during the next several days. What made it even tougher was that Pat couldn't be there to comfort him. Just before the start of the playoffs, Terry had rushed his wife to Pontiac General Hospital for an emergency appendectomy. She was still there recovering.

In one of the grittiest performances of his entire career, Sawchuk, granted a six-hour leave from the hospital, blanked the Hawks 3-0 in the third game. "Writhing, moaning, grimacing behind his face mask, leaning against his goal at every opportunity, Sawchuk tended the nets masterfully," wrote Jim Proudfoot, who covered the series for *The Toronto Star*. Despite stopping twenty-six shots,

Terry was left unimpressed by the eleventh playoff shutout of his career (two shy of Turk Broda's all-time record). "I didn't have that much work to do," he said.

Sawchuk went back in again for the fourth game. This time the effort proved too great, and he was forced to leave after two minutes of play in the second period. Crozier, run ragged commuting between Pittsburgh and the big club, performed strongly in a 3-2 losing cause that evened the series at two wins apiece. Sawchuk was still in too much pain to play in game five, which the Hawks won by another 3-2 score.

"We knew what it was costing him in pain to be there, so we put out for him," defenceman Doug Barkley had said after Sawchuk's shutout in game three. "You wouldn't be much of a guy if you didn't knock yourself out for a fellow who puts himself through what Sawchuk did."

His teammates rallied around him again when Terry returned to action for the crucial sixth match at the Olympia. By now they were so solicitous of his welfare that during every break in play one or more would skate over to ask if he was feeling all right. Sawchuk, growing annoyed, finally told them to leave him alone, that he would finish the game. He stopped twenty-six shots in a 7-2 victory that sent the series back to Chicago Stadium for a seventh game.

Only three months before, Abel had unceremoniously handed Crozier Sawchuk's job. Now, no matter how badly Terry was hurting, Abel counted on him to save Detroit's season. "I don't know what it is Terry has against Chicago," Abel said, "but it looks like he's hot right now…and I want him in the nets tomorrow night. That's the big one; the only one right now."

The Red Wings built a 3-1 lead on goals by Floyd Smith, Gordie Howe and Alex Delvecchio, and were controlling the play in the second period of the finale when Hawk enforcer Reggie Fleming rammed Sawchuk into the boards.

behind the net. For a minute or two, Terry lay unconscious on the ice. Dizzy and seeing double when play resumed, he surrendered a goal to Bobby Hull before taking himself out of the game at the next intermission. Parker MacDonald scored an insurance goal and Crozier held on for a 4-2 victory that put Detroit into the Stanley Cup finals for the third time in the past four years.

Afterwards, when Chicago coach Billy Reay visited the packed and noisy Detroit dressing room to offer his congratulations, a livid Sawchuk stopped him short.

"Tell that meathead Fleming to stay away from me or I'll take his head off with my stick," Terry screamed. When Reay started to deny that Fleming had deliberately charged him, Sawchuk cut him off with a stream of expletives.

Embarrassed, Reay turned to leave. At that point Terry was heard to mumble, "I'm through with hockey. I've taken enough injuries in this game...it's not worth it."

The dozen or more reporters in the room pressed him to declare whether this was an official announcement of his retirement. Earlier in the series he had also said he was quitting—but then had backed down, saying, "I was fooling."

The answer was still the same. "No," he said quietly, "I was just fooling."

Only a maddeningly frustrating, bloop goal scored by a broken-legged defenceman came between the Red Wings and a Stanley Cup championship that spring.

In another replay of the year before, Detroit met the defending champion Maple Leafs, who had overcome the Canadiens in a gruelling seven-game semi-final. Second-place Toronto had beaten Detroit eight times, tied three and lost three during the regular schedule. But, in a thrilling final that would go the maximum seven games, there was little to choose between them.

After Detroit and Toronto split the first four matches, Sawchuk's towering performance in game five at Maple Leaf Gardens brought the Wings closer to sipping champagne from the Cup than at any time in the past nine years. Terry, who had played so poorly against the Leafs the year before, made thirty-three often incredible saves in Detroit's 2-1 victory. "I never saw anything like it," wailed Toronto's King Clancy, an NHL fixture since 1921. "I'm sure he didn't see at least four of those shots but the puck ended up under his legs as he sprawled on the ice. He was the difference."

A loud cheer from his teammates greeted Sawchuk when he returned to the dressing room after appearing on TV as the game's top star. "It was like having a Sandy Koufax going for you," Bill Gadsby said. "He did to the Leafs what Koufax did to the Yankees in the World Series. I don't think they'll recover from that one."

Toronto did, but just barely. Two nights later, Detroit was dominating the play with the score knotted at 3-3 in third-period action at the Olympia. What happened next has become one of the most oft-repeated tales in hockey lore. Hit just above the ankle by a slap shot, Leaf defenceman Bobby Baun was carried to the infirmary. The team doctor felt certain the leg had been broken. But Baun refused to leave the game. "Freeze it," he ordered.

Play continued into overtime. Just before the two-minute mark, Baun picked up a pass at the blue line and released a feeble, bouncing shot that deflected off the stick of Bill Gadsby and flipped over Sawchuk's shoulder into the net. "I got the stick out of the way too late," said a weeping Gadsby who, in an eighteen-year career, had yet to play on a Cup winner.

Terry tried his best to take the loss philosophically. "That's how it goes in this game," he shrugged. "I had a good line on that lousy bouncer by Baun. Then at the last minute it hit the shaft of Bill Gadsby's stick and shot to the top corner. I never had a chance."

Sid Abel made the usual noises about how his boys would bounce back and win it all in game seven. But Toronto played its strongest game of the series in wrapping up another Stanley Cup championship with a 4-0 victory back in Toronto. "That fluke goal by Baun in overtime is what killed us," Gordie Howe acknowledged. "It gave the Leafs the momentum they needed for this game and seemed to take a lot out of us."

Howe, Gadsby and many of the other Wings would never again get so close. But for Sawchuk, there was more Stanley Cup glory still ahead.

## Chapter Eleven

### A NEW LEAF

**EARLY** that June, Sawchuk was in his backyard repairing a fence when he received a call from a reporter telling him that he'd been claimed by Toronto in the annual intra-league waiver draft. "I'm shocked, quite shocked," Terry stammered into the phone. "I had a hunch this would happen, but what are you going to do?"

In the third round of the draft held in Montreal, Sid Abel selected young goaltender George Gardner from the Boston Bruins. Every club was allowed to protect eighteen players and two goalies. Abel, who had protected Sawchuk and Crozier to that point, elected to drop Terry in favour of Gardner, making Sawchuk available to any of the five other NHL clubs for the $20,000 waiver price.

"This was a complete surprise," recounted Leaf boss Punch Imlach, who had the next pick. "Actually, I was prepared to take Gump Worsley on the round before when Montreal left him unprotected. On a whim or something I decided to wait another round."

The Toronto delegation started clapping the moment Abel announced that Sawchuk had been removed from Detroit's list. When league president Clarence Campbell indicated that it was Toronto's turn, Imlach immediately shouted "Sawchuk!"

"Sawchuk will help us," said Imlach gleefully. "With Terry and Johnny Bower rotating in the nets we'll be tough to beat." Added King Clancy, "This gives us the two goalies who fought it out for the Stanley Cup. What more could we ask?"

Toronto's coup rocked the meeting. No one could fathom

213

why Abel had taken Terry off Detroit's list to protect an untried twenty-one-year-old who the previous season had toiled in obscurity for the Bruins' Minneapolis farm club in the CPHL. "If the Red Wings wanted to go with Crozier, why didn't they try to trade Sawchuk?" asked Chicago coach Billy Reay. "They surely would have gotten something better than $20,000."

The general reaction was best summed up by Abel's fifteen-year-old daughter, Linda, who placed a long-distance call to her father the minute the meeting ended. "Dad, what are you doing?" she demanded.

"I think she thought somebody had hit me on the head with a hammer because I let Terry go," Abel said. "We hated to lose Terry, especially in view of all that he has done for the Red Wings. But Terry's thirty-four and he only played a little more than half the season for us each of the last two years and we had to make the move. Roger Crozier is our goalie and he's certainly proved he belongs in the National League."

Abel's math was more than a little off. The past season Sawchuk had played in fifty-three games of the seventy-game schedule, and the season before that he had made forty-eight appearances. The plain truth was that Abel felt that at that point in their respective careers, Crozier was both a better and more reliable netminder than Sawchuk. Abel projected Crozier to play almost every game for the Wings the next season, with only occasional relief help from a similarly youthful understudy (Gardner perhaps).

In fact, Abel expressed relief that Toronto had drafted Sawchuk. "It may have solved a problem for us because we may have had to ask Terry to play at Pittsburgh next year and this is something we would not have wanted to do."

Unlike Abel, Punch Imlach was undeterred by Sawchuk's high mileage and advancing years. Imlach had built his success on rejuvenating the careers of aging stars. The roster of the Stanley Cup champions included such grizzled veterans as Allan Stanley, thirty-eight; Tim Horton, thirty-four; Red Kelly, thirty-six; George Armstrong, thirty-three; Ron Stewart and Andy Bathgate, both thirty-one; and Johnny Bower, thirty-nine. In the first round of the waiver draft, Imlach claimed Dickie Moore, thirty-three, who had quit hockey the year before with aching knees. Imlach intended to talk him into making a comeback.

Comedian Johnny Wayne joked that Imlach's Leafs were the only team in the history of professional sports to have their dynasty threatened by prostate problems.

"I tell my players to tear up their birth certificates and I'll tell Terry Sawchuk to do the same thing," Imlach said. "Good old guys like Kelly, Bathgate, Horton, Bower and Sawchuk don't deteriorate as fast as ham-and-eggers. Being former All-Stars they can come down a long way and still be better than most."

Terry didn't even try to hide his disappointment at having to leave his Union Lake home and the Red Wings for a second time. "I'm not happy about this, but I'll report. I had a good year last season and never believed Detroit would leave me unprotected."

The last time the Wings let Sawchuk go he had just won the Vezina; this latest transfer came after Detroit writers had voted him the team MVP for 1963-64, ending Gordie Howe's reign of eight straight years. After three Stanley Cup championships, the shutout record and so many other accomplishments as a Red Wing, Sawchuk had trouble understanding why he wasn't permitted the luxury of finishing his career in Detroit. Alex Delvecchio would enjoy that privilege; so would Gordie Howe, at least until his first retirement. "I think it really bothered Terry that, despite all he'd done for the team and his great record, he wasn't considered in the same untouchable category as those other guys," says Johnny Wilson.

Having both Sawchuk and Bower, two future Hall of Famers, on the same championship squad seemed to many an embarrassment of riches. "What's Imlach going to do with Sawchuk?" asked Howe. "He has a great goalie in Johnny Bower." Indeed, the Leaf incumbent was coming off a season in which he had posted a goals-against average of 2.11 in fifty-one games, the best individual mark in the league.

"I was probably more confused about the drafting of Sawchuk than anyone," Bower recalls. "I found myself wondering why they thought they needed him. Did Imlach think that I was starting to slip? Remember, I was the oldest goalie in the league at the time, almost forty. At that age it's not safe to take anything for granted."

But the more Bower thought about it, the clearer Imlach's logic became. "All Imlach was suggesting was a platoon situation. I'd play a few games until I got tired, then Terry would take over until he got tired. No way would I have wanted a young goalie breathing down my neck. But I knew that no matter how well Terry played, at some point he'd need a rest. I remember going to Imlach and telling him that he'd just bought himself a Stanley Cup."

In Union Lake, a still-dazed Sawchuk told a reporter that he had no objections to sharing the Toronto netminding job with the man he called the best goalie in hockey. "I don't think that either Bower or myself can be at our best for seventy games any more."

Terry drove all night from Detroit to make it to Peterborough, Ontario, in time for the start of the Leafs' training camp on September 4. His arrival was a novelty on a Toronto squad whose line-up had hardly changed during the championship years. It took ten minutes for him to make his way through the swarm of autograph seekers to the ice for the opening seventy-five-minute skating session.

Afterwards, Terry and Bower lingered in the dressing room talking shop. Someone asked if it bothered Sawchuk to wear Number 25 (he later switched to Number 30) instead of his customary Number 1, which on this team belonged to Bower. "You don't stop pucks with numbers," he snapped.

Life at the Leaf camp proved a far cry from what one writer called the "*dolce vita*" training habits of the Red Wings. During the Stanley Cup final the previous spring, much had been made of the contrasting philosophies of Imlach and Abel. The day after the opening game, which Toronto won 3-2, Imlach had ordered the Leafs back on the ice at noon for a workout. The easy-going Abel, meanwhile, had instructed the Wings to sleep late. That afternoon Abel chartered a bus to take them sightseeing and then on to the Fort Erie racetrack to play the ponies.

"I'm in business. That's why we practise every day," barked Imlach. "When the playoffs are over we'll go sight-seeing."

Imlach believed that hard-grinding workouts every morning from the start of training camp to season's end cul-tivated a corporate-like attitude and were essential in main-taining the conditioning of a veteran team. Often he frustrated his players by holding practices where all they did was skate, never once touching a puck. "I skated more here in the first five days than I did in Detroit in five years," Sawchuk grumbled. Toronto played eighteen exhibition games in a month—including eight matches in fourteen days—and travelled an exhausting 12,000 miles during Terry's first camp.

Every exhibition, every practice, was conducted with the

serious intent of a regular-season match. "I was with a guy from Detroit once, watching a Leaf practice," recalled Lou Cauz, who covered the Leafs for *The Globe and Mail*. "He sees Baun take a run at someone. Then Shack fires one past Bower's ear. There's a couple of fights. Vicious body checks all over the place. He turns to me and says, 'Jesus, these guys practise harder than the Red Wings play in a real game.'"

"I couldn't do a lot of the things he does," Sid Abel said of Imlach. "I think he practises his team too much. It's just not my system, but I'm not saying he's wrong. He's doing one thing we're all paid to try to do—win Stanley Cups."

Profane and irascible, the bald-pated Imlach had worked miracles ever since he'd arrived in Toronto at the age of forty following a long apprenticeship in the minor leagues. One of his first acts as general manager was to fire Billy Reay and name himself coach of the last-place Leafs in December of 1958. "My guys are gonna rise up like Lazarus," he announced to startled reporters. "In fact, if Lazarus isn't under contract I might like to sign him for the stretch run." By spring, the Leafs were in the finals battling Montreal for the Cup. Three years later, Toronto won it for the first of three consecutive seasons.

Certainly many of his players felt Imlach worked them too hard—but it was tough to argue with success. "We blame the system when we're losing," Red Kelly said, "but when we're winning, we think it's excellent."

Watching Sawchuk work out in camp, his former defenceman Bob Goldham, who had started out as a Maple Leaf, made what would prove to be an amazingly prescient prediction. "I know Terry hated to leave Detroit at thirty-four after so many years with the Wings," Goldham said, "but he'll have a better team in front of him and that should add three years to his career."

For the time being, Terry took nothing for granted.

Having been let go by the Wings for a second time, he felt more insecure than ever about his abilities. Sawchuk constantly reminded reporters that he would first have to beat out Don Simmons (Bower's primary understudy for the past three seasons) and promising minor leaguer Gerry Cheevers to prove that he should share the job with Bower. "I think I belong in the big league, but the Leafs could farm me out to the minors. If that happened, I'd have to think a lot about whether I'd go."

Of course, there was never the slightest doubt that he would be staying in Toronto. "That was just Terry being Terry," says Johnny Bower. "I don't know if he really worried about being sent down to the minors or if he was just having fun with the reporters. But the rest of us knew that he wasn't going anywhere." Imlach hadn't landed the great Terry Sawchuk to play goal for the Rochester Americans.

Bower got the start on opening night in Detroit and played strongly in a 5-3 Toronto victory. But what made the evening memorable was the return of thirty-nine-year-old Ted Lindsay in a Detroit uniform. The day before, Terrible Ted had announced the end of his four-year retirement. A crowd of 14,323, the largest ever to see a Detroit home opener, welcomed Lindsay home with a thunderous two-minute standing ovation.

Lindsay had never stopped pining for the Red Wings. Sid Abel urged his former left winger to try a comeback after Lindsay was the best player on the ice in a charity match between Detroit and the Red Wing old-timers. Against Toronto, Lindsay signalled his return by decking rugged Tim Horton with an elbow to the head. Whistled to the penalty box, Lindsay spewed invective until referee Vern Buffey slapped him with an additional ten-minute misconduct. Just like old times.

Sawchuk made his debut as a Maple Leaf two nights later in New York. For the first forty minutes he had little to do and Toronto jumped out to a 2-0 lead. But then his forwards mysteriously stopped checking. In the end, it took several sparkling saves by Terry to preserve a 3-3 tie.

His first game against the Wings came November 11 in Toronto. Sawchuk kicked back thirty-one shots—including two tremendous saves on Gordie Howe—in a 3-1 triumph that halted a nine-game Detroit unbeaten streak. "I had a soft night's work with Brewer, Baun, Stanley and Horton playing so well on defence," Terry said modestly. "Man, did they belt those Wings."

It must have been tempting, but Sawchuk refused to gloat a few weeks later when he and his new teammates crushed Detroit 10-2 in what was Roger Crozier's first bad outing of the season. Afterwards, in the corridor leading to the dressing rooms at Maple Leaf Gardens, Terry pulled Crozier aside, put his arm around the little goalie's shoulders and whispered a few words of encouragement in his ear before sending him on his way with a slap on the seat of the pants. "I told him to forget it," Sawchuk said. "Start over Sunday against Montreal…. He's a good kid, a real good kid. That can happen to any of us and I just thought he could use a pat on the back."

Imlach got everything and even more than he'd hoped from Terry when he selected him back in June. Sawchuk didn't lose his first game until November 25 in New York, allowing only eleven goals in nine games to that point. After the 10-2 blowout of the Wings on December 5, his record stood at 8-2 with three ties.

By the first week of January, Sawchuk and Bower led the Vezina race. They made a pact that if either of them won the award, they would share the $1,000 prize money equally. "It seemed only fair," Bower says. "Why should one guy get all the cash when he might end up playing only a handful of games more than the other." To encourage their teammates to continue focusing on defence, Terry and Bower announced that they would pay for a season-ending team party should they win the Vezina.

Terry sat out most of that first month of 1965 with an injury his old platoon partner feels slightly sheepish about to this day. "Terry was playing so well that Imlach started him almost every game," Bower says. "I was getting frustrated, and one day I jokingly mentioned to Eddie Shack, who had a very heavy shot, that he should fire a high hard one at Terry during practice. I told Eddie that maybe that would shake Terry up a little and I'd finally be able to get in a game. But I was just *joking*.

"Anyway, that crazy Shack took me seriously. During our next shooting drill Eddie came down on Sawchuk and caught him off guard, breaking a finger on his catching hand. Terry was mad as hell at Shack, cursing him a blue streak. But Eddie just skated over to me with a big grin on his face and told me I owed him a steak dinner as his reward."

Sawchuk was proving to be just as much of an enigma to his new teammates as he had been to the Red Wings. Bower tried perhaps harder than anyone to get close to Terry. Warm and outgoing, with the kindly, open face of a favourite uncle, Bower numbered among the most popular men in Canada during his heyday with the Leafs. But he had little success in attempting to befriend Sawchuk.

"I'd admired Terry ever since we'd first played against one another when I was with Cleveland in the American League," Bower says. "It just seemed natural to me that we get to know one another better, us both being goalies and having been around so long." Early on when Pat visited her husband in Toronto (she and the kids stayed behind in

Union Lake while Terry shared a house that season with teammate Ron Stewart), Bower and his wife invited the Sawchuks over for dinner. "It was a pleasant evening," Bower recalls, "but the relationship never went any further than that. I don't really know why."

Terry seemed uninterested whenever Bower tried to engage him in a conversation about a topic other than hockey. "I could never figure out what made Sawchuk tick," he says. "It was hard to get a smile out of him. Someone would tell a joke that the rest of us thought was hilarious and Terry would hardly react. He'd give a small grin and that was it."

When the Leafs went out to a restaurant for a bite to eat and a beer after a game or practice, Sawchuk might come along—but he always sat off by himself at a separate table. It was the same when they rode a train to another city. Terry sat by himself reading a book, hardly saying a word to anyone.

"You know, I was a loner in Cleveland, too," Bower continues. "But I grew out of it. Most goalies start out as loners. But Terry never changed. More and more the guys on the team just left him alone. Nobody wanted to risk saying anything that might upset him. He was still a great goalie and we needed him."

Like his players, Punch Imlach took special care with Sawchuk. For three years he carefully stroked Terry's fragile ego. "I've got the best two goalies in hockey," Imlach repeated like a mantra. Whenever Sawchuk slumped, he would excuse his performance by saying that his goalie was tired, or that he had been playing so well for so long that, after all, he was entitled to a bad game or two. Even Bower, whom Imlach genuinely admired, was sometimes criticized by his boss in the press. Not Sawchuk. Imlach didn't dare risk it.

But some things never change. Shortly after Terry's return to the line-up from the broken finger, he played dreadfully in a 6-3 loss to first-place Chicago. This prompted the inevitable talk of retirement. "I am not getting any younger and I am pretty tired," he complained to George Gross of the *Toronto Telegram*. Terry added that he had recently received a job offer from a group building a sports centre in Pontiac. "It is a tempting proposition with good pay." Gross had been on the hockey beat long enough to wait for the familiar retreat. "But I still would like to play at least another season—perhaps two," Terry said.

Sawchuk and Bower, together with their superb defence, provided the bright spots in a Toronto season otherwise marred by injuries and the severe depression that hospitalized the team's scoring star, Frank Mahovlich, for a month. The Leafs dropped from third the season before down to fourth, thirteen points behind the first-place Red Wings, who captured their first Prince of Wales Trophy since 1956-57.

Dire predictions to the contrary, the Wings managed quite nicely with the diminutive Crozier guarding their cage. Crozier withstood the daily grind to become the only goalie to play all seventy games and was named the league's outstanding rookie. Ullman, Howe and Delvecchio finished among the league's top five scorers. But the spark, the intangible element that had been missing from the Wings for so long, was provided by Ted Lindsay. Many mornings that winter Lindsay awoke so bruised and sore that he could barely force his middle-aged body out of bed. Nonetheless, he suited up for sixty-nine games, scored fourteen goals, and served 173 minutes in penalties. With Lindsay leading the way, the Wings won twenty-five of their last thirty-nine games.

Detroit had already clinched the pennant when they met Toronto for a home-and-home series on the final weekend

of the season. Still to be decided was the outcome of the
Vezina race. Crozier, attempting to become the first rookie
since Frankie Brimsek to capture the award, trailed Sawchuk and Bower by a single goal at the weekend's outset.
His opponent both nights would be Bower, whom Imlach
wanted tuned-up for the start of the playoffs.

To that point, Sawchuk had worked in thirty-six games to
his partner's thirty-two. Terry's edge in games played meant
that it was his name that would go on the Vezina should
Bower manage to hold onto the lead. But Sawchuk had
recently announced that he would refuse to accept the award
unless the NHL agreed to declare Bower his co-winner.

Crozier leaped from one goal behind to two in front of
the Leaf tandem when Detroit downed the Leafs 4-1 on Saturday night at the Gardens. Too nervous to watch the action
the next night at the Olympia, Sawchuk, in full goalie's
gear, spent the first two periods in the dressing room. He
finally forced himself out for the concluding twenty minutes, taking a seat in the corridor near the Toronto bench.

Bower played magnificently in turning aside thirty-seven
Detroit shots. Toronto already led 3-0 when Dave Keon slid
a final goal into the Wing net with three seconds left on the
clock. Sawchuk climbed atop his chair and raised his arms
while, at the same moment, Bower tossed his stick into the
air. Moments later the partners embraced on the ice.

"I was rooting and making every move with him in the
last twenty minutes," Terry said. "What reflexes. He was like
a teenager. I never saw anything like him. He eats that puck."

Bower's goals-against average of 2.38 was the lowest
individual mark in the league, while Sawchuk's 2.56 placed
him fifth-best in a season that saw most teams regularly
employ two goalkeepers. Only Crozier and Boston's Eddie
Johnston were solo acts.

Someone asked Terry if the Vezina win meant more

coming as it did at the expense of the Red Wings. "You're darn right I'm happy the way it happened," he answered. "Yeah, there was a little more satisfaction doing it against them. But there's the guy who won it. They can put Bower's name on the thing."

They did. That June the league governors amended the rules to allow for Vezina co-winners, provided that both goalies appeared in a minimum of twenty-five games. Sawchuk and Bower each received a commemorative plaque and had their names engraved on the original trophy.

Sawchuk was also the catalyst for a rule change which took effect in time for the start of that season's playoffs. The governors decreed that all teams must dress two goalies so that the substitute would be ready for immediate action should the starter be injured or pulled by his coach for ineffective play.

Chicago owner James Norris, Jr. began agitating for the change the year before when on several occasions the pinched nerves in Sawchuk's aching shoulder forced the interruption of semi-final matches between the Hawks and Wings. Each time the crowd and players waited impatiently while Champoux or Crozier changed out of their street clothes and into uniform. Originally intended to cover only the playoffs, the edict was so clearly an improvement on the old system, which can only be described as bush-league, that the governors extended it to include regular-season games starting the next season.

After the initial euphoria, even the Vezina win didn't seem to cheer Sawchuk, who presented a particularly dour face to teammates and reporters at the start of Toronto's semi-final against second-place Montreal.

Terry felt lousy after taking blasts from Frank Mahovlich and Tim Horton on an already tender right arm in practice. The arthritis in his back was also kicking up. "I guess I'm just too old," he said. "Next year I won't have these problems any more. I don't think they'll even protect me in the summer draft. They still have Johnny, who is good for another ten years, and Gerry Cheevers in Rochester." Sawchuk added that he still hadn't ruled out that job offer with the sports complex in Pontiac.

Montreal edged Toronto 3-2 in a brawl-filled opener at the Forum. Bower played well and was slated to start the second game. But a freak pre-game mishap placed Sawchuk between the pipes instead.

Before every game, Bower would rub oil of wintergreen on his legs and body to help him warm up. This time, forgetting to wash his hands afterwards, he unthinkingly touched his face and eyes. "Boy, did I get a jolt," Bower said. For a while he couldn't see, and there wasn't the slightest chance of his playing that night.

Though the Habs completely dominated the action, thanks to Sawchuk the score was knotted at 1-1 into the last minute of play in the second period. Already he had made twenty-nine saves, including at least a dozen difficult chances. Montreal finally took the lead when, during a power play, Jean Béliveau fired Henri Richard's rebound over Sawchuk's shoulder and into the net.

A third-period bloop goal by Henri Richard completed a 3-1 Montreal victory. Lofted from eighty feet out, the puck bounced in the opposite direction of Sawchuk's slide. "He was lucky," Terry groaned. "That puck was on its edge. Otherwise he couldn't have lifted it past me from that distance. I just don't live right, I guess."

Backed by a clear-eyed Johnny Bower in net, Toronto rebounded to even the series with 3-2 and 4-2 wins. Bower's superlative netminding prompted Punch Imlach to declare, "From now on I don't believe in miracles or ghosts.

Now I only believe in Santa Claus, and I pronounce his name Johnny Bower."

But Montreal, who hadn't been in a Cup final since Rocket Richard's retirement in 1960, would not be denied. They outhustled and outshot Toronto for a 3-1 decision in game five. Claude Provost's backhander past Bower at 16:33 of extra play in game six completed a 4-3 victory and ended the Leafs' three-year reign as champions. Montreal went on to defeat Chicago in a seven-game final to claim their twelfth Stanley Cup championship.

Terry and Bower held the party they had promised their teammates at a suburban hotel owned by former Leaf great Charlie Conacher. Both partners chipped in $250 to cover the cost of the festivities.

Bower recalls that for that one night the gloom that Sawchuk wore like a shroud magically lifted away. "He was just one of the boys. Terry played cards and was laughing and joking. Maybe it was because the season was over and the pressure was off. All his cares seemed to have suddenly disappeared.

"You know," Bower continues, "in the three years we played together, that's the only time I can ever remember seeing Terry have fun."

It was only natural for Sawchuk, a well-worn thirty-six on his next birthday, to fret about his future in the game. But Punch Imlach had won three Stanley Cups with a veteran squad and saw no reason to start checking birth dates now. That June, to Terry's surprise, Imlach stood pat with his Vezina twins while allowing Don Simmons and Gerry Cheevers, who many figured was the Leafs' goalie of the future, to slip away.

"The odds against Johnny Bower and Terry Sawchuk

going over the hill together, or being hurt at the same time, are so great," Imlach said, "I don't even think of it."

He did, however, recognize the need to shake up a squad that had grown complacent with success. "I guess we thought we were a lot better than we were," captain George Armstrong acknowledged after the playoff defeat. Early that off-season Imlach and Sid Abel completed one of the biggest deals of the decade. Toronto parted with Andy Bathgate and Billy Harris in return for a package that included Marcel Pronovost, Larry Jeffrey and Ed Joyal. In a separate deal, Imlach moved Terry's housemate Ron Stewart to Boston for rugged Orland Kurtenbach.

Sawchuk, who surprised no one by deciding to continue with his hockey career, was naturally delighted to be reunited with his old pal Pronovost. "Ukey was here for three years and never made what you'd call a friend," a former Leaf teammate recalled at the time of Terry's death. "The only one was Marcel Pronovost, who'd been with him in the good days at Detroit."

The new-look Maple Leafs were no better than a fourth-place team for most of the first half of the season. Sawchuk started strongly, but by late January he was struggling through his first prolonged slump since joining Toronto. In his first seventeen starts, he surrendered fifty-nine goals, two more than Bower allowed in his first twenty-four appearances.

Teammates rushed to Terry's defence when the press unfavourably compared his performance to Bower's. "It makes no difference who's in there," said centre Bob Pulford. "If you check back, you'll find Bower was in goal when we went ten games without losing. He was there when we got hot. That's all."

"Sawchuk will be all right," insisted Imlach after Terry allowed eleven goals in weekend matches against Boston and New York. "The problem is he didn't expect to play on the weekend. And he wouldn't have if Bower hadn't hurt himself in a warm-up Saturday. Sawchuk doesn't bear down in practice the way Bower does and, as a result, he's not sharp unless I can let him know ahead of time when he's going to play."

Compared to the energetic Bower, Terry's practice habits appeared more lackadaisical than ever. "I've never seen two goalies who were so opposite in their work habits," recalls Billy Harris, who had left the Leafs for Detroit in the big summer trade. "We practised at 11 and Bower would be out on the ice at 10:30—unlike Sawchuk, who waited until the very last minute. While Bower worked away at one end, Sawchuk was in the other net doing the absolute bare minimum. Sawchuk rushed off the ice the second practice ended. Bower would stay behind if anyone wanted to work on their shot, and stick around as long as they wanted him."

An exasperated Imlach once called Sawchuk into his office and demanded to know why he didn't try harder in practice. "I figure I only have so many saves left in me," Terry deadpanned, "and I want to save them all for the games."

Sawchuk's slump continued until Marcel Pronovost noticed that his friend had abandoned his famous crouch. So often in the past Pronovost had seen the same thing happen. Whenever Terry played several bad games in a row, it was usually because he had unconsciously straightened up.

Returning to the crouch, Sawchuk recorded his first shutout of the season (the ninety-eighth of his career) against the Rangers in Toronto on February 9. Several more strong performances followed before a pulled hamstring forced Terry out of action and precipitated the catastrophe that Imlach had scoffed would never happen. Both Sawchuk and Bower, who had gone out earlier with a pulled groin, were unavailable for duty at the same time.

Summoned from the Rochester farm, young goalie Gary Smith briefly saw action before he too was injured. Then Imlach threw junior Al Smith into the fray. Bower rushed back, but almost immediately tore ligaments in his ribs. And then, on the eve of his own return, Sawchuk re-injured his hamstring in practice. "I really fixed it good this time," he grimaced, holding an ice pack over a nasty-looking bruise. "I just kicked and away it went. And brother, it's painful."

Just in from Tulsa of the CPHL, scar-faced twenty-seven-year-old Bruce Gamble got his chance next. The laconic loner, whose long sideburns inspired the nickname "Paladin" after the TV western hero, had seen the bright lights of the NHL before. Gamble played two games with New York in 1958-59, and a total of eighty with Boston between 1960 and 1962.

Four shutouts in his first six games, only twenty-one goals allowed in ten outings—few goaltenders have made Gamble's sudden impact. Sparked by his pinch-hit performance, the Leafs quickly grabbed third place from Detroit, challenged Chicago for second and even briefly flirted with the idea of overtaking the front-running Habs.

Gamble's hot streak lasted until March 16, when he pulled a hamstring in action against the Canadiens. Fortunately, by this point Bower was ready to come back. Sawchuk felt well enough to gingerly start skating.

Bower raised Imlach's ire by playing poorly in a 3-1 loss to Montreal on March 30 that all but killed the Leafs' chances of climbing any higher than third in the standings, which was where they eventually landed. Imlach, a notoriously sore loser, stomped out of the dressing room and, instead of boarding the team bus, drove alone to the Toronto airport, where a plane waited to take the Leafs to Boston. "They gave it away," Imlach snarled to a reporter.

He remained in his foul funk the entire flight—slouching in his seat, scowling endlessly into the darkness outside his window. When a flight attendant approached and asked for permission to serve the players their meal, Imlach curled his lips into a sneer. "Yeah, you can give them something now," he said in a voice loud enough for most in the plane to hear. "Give them poison."

That was classic Imlach. "A short, explosive and profane cockatoo of a man," in the words of the authors of *Net Worth*. "At any one time Imlach's stable admired, loathed, revered, respected or resented him—often all at once."

"I blow up easily," Imlach said. "There are nights I call them every no-good thing there is in the world, but I get over it just as quickly. I tell them at the start of the season we'll disagree, we'll fight, we'll argue. But when it's all over I'll still be their friend and I hope they'll be mine."

Most of the older veterans on those Leaf squads remain solidly in Imlach's corner to this day. His faith in their abilities and insistence that they remain in peak physical condition helped prolong every one of their careers. "We owe him a debt of gratitude," says Allan Stanley, who turned forty that season. "It's hard not to respect a man who believes in you the way Imlach believed in most of his older players. And then there was all that playoff money he made for us. You don't forget that either."

It was with the younger players that Imlach encountered most of his problems. A second lieutenant in the Canadian Army during World War II, Imlach ran the Leafs like a military regiment. He had no sympathy for malingerers. Nor, with the notable exception of Sawchuk, who Imlach figured had earned the right to be eccentric, did he allow for differences in human nature.

High-strung individualists Carl Brewer and Frank Mahovlich both exasperated and baffled Imlach. Brewer was so intense that during the hockey season he would lose handfuls of hair from stress. But the All-Star defenceman's greatest frustration came during contract negotiations at the start of training camp. Every year Brewer threatened to quit over the niggardly raises Imlach offered. Finally, before the start of the current campaign, he had walked out in disgust and returned to university.

Johnny Bower, an otherwise unabashed Imlach admirer, still bristles when he remembers how Imlach completely mishandled Mahovlich, the team's scoring star. An introspective, almost other-worldly figure at times, The Big M ("The Big M stands for Big Mystery," wisecracked Toronto sportscaster Joe Morgan) withdrew into a shell whenever Imlach employed his usual intimidation tactics. Twice during his eleven-year career as a Leaf, Mahovlich entered hospital suffering from a combination of fatigue and depression.

"It was just crazy," Bower says. "Imlach should have spent his time encouraging Frank instead of constantly criticizing him. How do you think that made Mahovlich feel? Here was this great player who Imlach kept saying wasn't living up to his potential. Pretty soon the fans got on Frank, too."

Yet, despite his many faults, Punch Imlach knew how to win. He had resurrected the Leafs "like Lazarus" and then led them to three Stanley Cups. Behind the bench, Imlach had an uncanny knack for almost always making the right move.

In his autobiography, Conn Smythe recalled Imlach's first days as the Leaf coach. For years Smythe, while seated in his private box halfway up the stands, had been in the habit of sending frequent notes to the Toronto bench. "I would see a line that wasn't working, a player below par, all the things I had been seeing for years and telling coaches about—except that with Imlach, before I could get the message down to him, he would have done exactly what I wanted him to do.

"He was the best coach I ever saw," Smythe wrote. "It was as if he were a mind reader."

Looking ahead to the playoffs, Imlach, the master strategist, made certain that all three of his goaltenders saw action on the final weekend of the season. In a 3-3 draw with New York on Saturday night, Sawchuk (who hadn't played a complete game since February 16) and Gamble alternated at approximately five-minute intervals. On Sunday in Detroit, in another 3-3 tie, Bower worked the first period, Sawchuk the second, and then Gamble, who had been watching from the Olympia press box, came down and suited up for the third. Teams were allowed to carry three goalies, but they could dress only two.

Despite his elaborate preparations, Imlach left no doubt as to whom he pinned his hopes on in the semi-final against first-place Montreal, victors over Toronto in six games the year before. "Bower's the big boy for us," he said, putting aside his recent disappointment in his long-time ace. "I don't care how old he is. If he locks them out, we'll win."

But two hours before the game, Bower, sick with the flu virus that was sweeping through the team, informed Imlach that he couldn't play. Sawchuk took over and looked a little rusty—though by no means terrible—in a 4-3 Montreal victory. "If I had played well we'd have beaten Canadiens instead of losing," he said, as always his own harshest critic. "But I didn't get the feel of things until the third period. Then I felt good."

Sawchuk started again in Bower's place in game two.

This time he responded with a standout performance through two scoreless periods. His one, ultimately fatal, mistake came midway through the third period when Claude Provost and Gilles Tremblay broke in on the Leaf net during a Montreal power play. Provost faked a pass, then fired the puck from a severe angle. His shot caught Terry by surprise and trickled in off his goal pad. Bobby Rousseau put away the game 2-0 on a conversion of a Ralph Backstrom rebound that Terry had little chance on.

Their ranks ravaged by influenza, the Maple Leafs proved no match for Toe Blake's hard-driving Canadiens. A still wobbly Bower was in net when Montreal completed the sweep with 5-2 and 4-1 decisions at Maple Leaf Gardens. The Habs went on to capture their second-straight Stanley Cup with a six-game victory over Detroit in the finals. The Conn Smythe Trophy, awarded to the outstanding player in the post-season, went to Roger Crozier.

Punch Imlach seemed strangely resigned to his team's fate. Or possibly he was still feverish from his own bout with the flu. "Aw, they're a bunch of bums," he said fondly of the Leafs. "But they're my bums so that settles that."

## Chapter Twelve

# CENTENNIAL PROJECT

FOR years now, Sawchuk had been trying his best to ignore, or at least learn to live with, the excruciating, almost constant pain in his lower back. Only the painkillers that he used to mask this as well as so many other physical complaints kept him in the game.

Shortly after the end of the 1966 playoffs, his bad back finally rebelled. "I thought I had suffered a stroke," Sawchuk recalled of the day when the entire left side of his body suddenly went numb. Doctors diagnosed two herniated discs and recommended immediate surgery. They told Pat that her husband would be lucky to ever play hockey again.

And yet, at first, Sawchuk's recovery went amazingly well. A week after surgery he began a program of swimming exercises, and a month after that he felt well enough to take an eight-mile hike with his son Gerry. Before leaving for Peterborough and the start of training camp, Terry was playing thirty-six holes of golf a day.

"I feel like a new man," Sawchuk told a reporter. "You wouldn't believe the change it has made in me. For the first time in two years I don't have headaches every day. My temperament is much better now. Why, I even play around the house with my kids."

He even walked taller as a result of the operation. "I remember George Armstrong asking Terry if he had high heels on that first day of training camp," says Johnny Bower. "His old slouch was gone. It looked as if he'd grown a couple of inches over the summer."

Sawchuk's optimism about making a successful comeback from his surgery ended with his first full practice session. Afterwards, his back felt stiff and he could barely move from exhaustion. When he felt just as badly the next day and for a week or more after that, he decided to pack up and go home. "I was tired and discouraged," Sawchuk recalled. "There seemed no point in staying around any longer."

This time Terry really did mean to quit. The doctors had said he would probably never play again and they had obviously been right. It was time to get on with the rest of his life.

He broke the news to Imlach, who tried to talk to Terry like a father, arguing that he wasn't being fair to either himself or his family. Sawchuk went away and thought things over—and came back just as determined to end his career. Then Imlach tried flattery, insisting that Terry could once again be one of the best in the game and that, if the season were starting the next day, he would want him there in the Toronto cage. Imlach even offered to let him get into shape at his own pace, with occasional days off and missed practices. After thinking it over some more, Terry, reluctantly, decided to give it another try.

Despite his persuasive words, Imlach knew all too well that for Sawchuk, as well as the rest of Toronto's prized collection of greybeards, time was rapidly running out. Red Kelly was thirty-nine that season; Tim Horton turned thirty-seven; George Armstrong was thirty-six; Allan Stanley turned forty-one; and Johnny Bower turned forty-two. A few months before, the NHL had announced that the league would double in size in 1967-68. Come the expansion draft the following June, Imlach would have no choice but to let some of them go in order to protect younger players.

But there was still this season. With luck, Imlach believed that the old gang might have it in them to lead the Leafs to one last Stanley Cup. Which was why he talked so long and hard to prevent Terry from retiring. Together, Bower and a healthy Sawchuk remained hockey's most imposing goaltending tandem.

Around this time, Imlach refused the opportunity to trade Sawchuk away. The offer, which had to have been tempting considering the status of Terry's back, came from New York general manager Emile Francis, who hoped to pair him with young Ed Giacomin in the Ranger net. "Yeah, I wanted Sawchuk," Francis recalled. "And I was willing to offer full value for him. I know how much a great goalie can lift a team and Terry was still a great goalie."

Slowly, Sawchuk's condition improved and by the start of the season he was thankful that Imlach had talked him into staying. An injury to Bower on the opening weekend forced Terry to come back sooner than he would have liked, but he played strongly in a 3-2 decision over the Red Wings and was named the game's first star.

One standout performance followed another through October and November. Even when he returned to the line-up, Bower spent most of his time on the bench. "That's the problem of keeping two goalies in shape," Imlach said. "One guy was going so well we couldn't play the other." On the first Saturday of December, Sawchuk and the Leafs beat the Wings 5-2 to take sole possession of first place.

Another victory Sunday night over rookie phenomenon Bobby Orr and the Boston Bruins prompted an unusually happy and relaxed Sawchuk (whose 2.11 GAA led the league) to make the familiar joke that his good fortune couldn't possibly last. Terry was still euphoric the next day when the Leafs arrived in Montreal to prepare for a Wednesday-night date at the Forum. He cracked up team-mates and newsmen with quips about his former walking style—back and shoulders hunched forward with his rear end thrust back. "If you'd been bending over for twenty years like I have you'd probably be walking the same way."

Everyone who saw him play during this period agreed that Terry had rarely looked sharper. "Our goaltending is the reason we're in first place," Imlach said. "Sawchuk has been fantastic. I think he's playing the best hockey of his career right now. Even better than when he was playing with Detroit in the fifties."

Of course, Sawchuk was right about his luck being too good to last. He had foolishly ignored a few tell-tale twinges of pain in his back after the Boston game. Against the Canadiens, Terry played horribly in a 6-3 defeat—fanning on a low drive by Bobby Rousseau from a bad angle; left paralysed by a hundred-foot slap shot from Yvan Cournoyer. He allowed five of Montreal's six goals before Imlach sent Bower out to replace him in the third period.

While Terry showered after the game, a sudden jolt of back pain sent him tumbling to the floor. Tim Horton gently carried his groaning teammate back to the dressing room and helped him to get dressed. The next day, after spending the night in agony on the train, Sawchuk entered Toronto General Hospital. Teammates noticed that he was walking with his familiar slouch when he got off the train.

Terry placed a call to Pat from his hospital room. "She cried when I told her what had happened," he said. "She pointed out that these things always seem to happen to me when things are going well. It seemed at the time I'd need another operation and we both knew that would finish me."

After eleven days of examinations, Sawchuk's Toronto doctors concluded that additional surgery might not be necessary after all. They ordered him to return home and take complete bed rest for a month. "Then I'll come back to Toronto and hope for the best," Terry said. "It's too bad it had to happen to me when I thought I was playing my best hockey of the past ten years."

While across the border Canadians exuberantly celebrated one hundred years of Confederation by ushering in the New Year with fireworks, bonfires, bell ringing and one-hundred-gun salutes, Sawchuk rested uncomfortably in his bed at Union Lake.

The news from Toronto was not good. During a special Christmas holiday practice in front of 7,000 screaming youngsters, Frank Mahovlich unleashed a slap shot that broke Johnny Bower's catching hand. His replacement, Bruce Gamble, had used up all his miracles the year before. The Leafs began a freefall that would see them lose ten games in a row. Even Bower's return to active duty on January 28 didn't help.

Sawchuk, meanwhile, returned to Toronto following his month in bed and began his rehabilitation by swimming endless laps at the War Amps' pool. Water-logged after a week, he convinced Imlach to let him start skating, even though the doctors insisted that it was still too soon. On February 7, two months to the day since he had collapsed in agony in the Forum dressing room, Sawchuk suited up for his first full workout.

When he had checked into hospital, the Leafs stood atop the standings. They had since plunged to fourth, just one point ahead of fifth-place Detroit. But Terry adamantly rejected suggestions that his absence had caused Toronto's fall. "I couldn't have played any better than these two guys," he said of Bower and Gamble. "I don't think our problems have been in goal."

Nor were the origins of Toronto's woes found on the defence or up front among the attackers. Simply put, the trouble with the Leafs was Punch Imlach. Many of his players, especially the younger ones, had reached the end of their endurance under his dictatorial rule.

His overweening ego, his constant criticisms, the never-ending practice sessions—they were sick to death of it all. Following a loss in Chicago, the Leafs' seventh of the current winless string, Imlach drove his exhausted and demoralized troops through four practices in a span of just thirty hours. When they dropped the next game in Montreal, he threatened to make them all walk back to Toronto. Never once during the entire crisis was he heard to utter an even remotely encouraging word.

"With Punch, it was always push, push, push," says Brian Conacher, a rookie winger on that Leaf team. "But, you know, that only works for so long. Punch made our lives so darned miserable and oppressive that we lost our focus. Maybe a handful of the veterans, the guys who had been with Imlach a long time and had gotten used to him, could take that constant aggravation. But the rest of us started to tune him out and became lethargic. Imlach's sourness and negativity got us to the point where we hated to come to the rink in the morning."

Imlach tried everything to get the Leafs back on track. He shipped slumping young winger Jim Pappin to the minors for two weeks. Larry Hillman was promoted from Rochester and given regular work on the blue line. Imlach went from using three lines to four, then back to three, and tried a dozen different player combinations in the process.

Relentlessly prodded by Imlach and rallied to the cause by the core of veteran stars, the Leafs finally regained their focus and, at Maple Leaf Gardens on Saturday, February 11, fought Chicago to a 4-4 draw that ended the losing skid at ten games. Toronto beat Boston the next night and pounded New York 6-0 three nights after that.

Leaf fans everywhere breathed easy again. But all the

losing had taken its toll on Punch Imlach. Some nights when the Leafs were on the road, he stayed up drinking and brooding until dawn, wound so tight that often he forgot to eat. The Saturday after the breakthrough victory, Imlach complained of pain in his left side and a knot of tightness in his chest. Team doctors checked him into the hospital for tests and complete bed rest. The diagnosis was acute exhaustion brought on by stress.

King Clancy coached the team to a 5-3 victory that night over Boston and stayed behind the bench for the next three weeks while Imlach regained his strength. For the Maple Leafs, who won their first six games under Clancy's direction, the loveable little Irishman was like an early breath of spring air. Clancy constantly cracked jokes and gave them pep talks and pats on the back. "He was a rare character," said Allan Stanley, "a man who saw the best in everybody." Imlach had already managed to turn the team around before his illness. Now, with Clancy at the helm, the game became fun again.


"I was so jittery, you wouldn't believe it," Terry confided after his return to action in Detroit on Thursday, February 23. "I wasn't sure whether they'd score two or ten."

Not that his nervousness showed. Sawchuk stopped thirty-eight shots and looked as good as new in a 4-2 Toronto victory. The win moved the Leafs into third place, a point ahead of the Canadiens and six up on the fading Red Wings.

Sawchuk knew his back would hold up after Gordie Howe slammed into him in the first period. "I loosened up after that and played my normal game," he said. Two of his saves in the third period bordered on the unbelievable. On the first, Sawchuk, though caught off balance at the other end of the net, managed to thrust out his stick and deflect a drive from Dean Prentice. The second came when he was down on the ice and Andy Bathgate drilled a shot that looked like a certain goal—until Terry's hand, in the words of one reporter, "darted out like a snake's tongue to smother the puck."

He picked on Detroit again two nights later in Toronto for the ninety-ninth shutout of his career. He stopped thirty-nine shots in a 4-0 final, took a bow as the game's first star, and afterwards optimistically declared: "I've got my own Centennial project now. Play long enough and get a hundred shutouts."

In fact, he had only to wait one week for the career milestone. The date was March 4 and once again Maple Leaf Gardens provided the setting. His victims were the first-place Black Hawks, the NHL's highest-scoring club.

Terry later called it one of the easiest games he played all season. So tight was his defence that Hull, Mikita and the other Hawk snipers managed only twenty-two shots on the Leaf net. The Golden Jet's best chance came on a power play during the second period. Hull broke across the blue line and let rip a low slap shot that Sawchuk just managed to deflect into the stands with the toe of his skate.

By the third period, Toronto led 3-0 and everyone in the audience of 15,981, most of whom had been there for shutout number ninety-nine the week before, knew what was at stake. The Leafs pounced on every loose puck and backchecked furiously. With ten seconds left on the clock and the puck deep in the Chicago zone, the fans began the countdown. Sawchuk raised his arms wide moments before the buzzer sounded and then was mobbed by his teammates.

Selected the game's first star by Foster Hewitt, Terry, close to tears, stepped back onto the ice for a final bow. He was still fighting his emotions during the post-game interview on nation-wide CBC-TV, and later as he walked slowly around the Leaf dressing room, shaking his teammates' hands. "Man, were they coming back tonight," he said. "They were really checking for me."

Reporters pressed him for a memorable quote, something to sum up the occasion. At first Terry was at a loss. But then he hit on what seemed like the perfect end note to the evening. Grinning widely, he observed, "The first hundred are the hardest."

Before the start of the season, Punch Imlach had expressed the conviction that by "adding a couple of kids to some old pappies," Toronto would have an excellent chance of winning back the Stanley Cup.

Youthful forwards Jim Pappin, Brian Conacher and Pete Stemkowski all contributed impressively to the stretch drive. Recently, Stemkowski and Pappin had been teamed with Bob Pulford on what instantly became the Leafs' most dangerous line. In the last twenty games of the season, Pappin scored fifteen goals, seven of them game-winners.

The team moulded by Punch Imlach and then rejuvenated by King Clancy won six of its last nine games to finish in third place with seventy-five points, two back of second-place Montreal. Far out in front of the pack, with ninety-four points, were the awesomely powerful Hawks. Chicago scored a record 264 goals for the season and were thought by many to be the NHL's most dominating squad since the Canadiens of the late 1950s. Emile Francis's resurgent New York Rangers finished comfortably in fourth, fourteen points in front of fifth-place Detroit.

"I'm satisfied where we are right now," said Imlach, who took back the reins from Clancy in mid-March. Almost all indicators read positive as the Leafs prepared for their first-round confrontation with heavily favoured

Chicago. Johnny Bower shone in season-ending victories over New York and Boston. No defence in the league was playing it tighter than Horton, Stanley, Pronovost, Hillman and Baun. And of late the offence had scored in bunches, putting ten goals past the Rangers and Bruins on the final weekend. But perhaps the most promising sign of all came when Dave Keon and Bob Baun engaged in a stick-swinging duel in one of the last practices before the start of the playoffs. The Leafs were *ready*.

Well, everyone that is, except Sawchuk. Terry was depressed and talking retirement again as the season drew to a close. "Three more games, then the playoffs and that's it," he said in Montreal the last week in March. "Twenty years is a long time. I want to start spending more time with my family. You know our seventh is on the way this summer."

He made his comments to *The Globe and Mail*'s Lou Cauz while killing time in the lobby of his hotel before the start of a Wednesday night game at the Forum. "They're not going to protect an old guy like me with a bad back," he said of the Leafs. "It'll be Bower or one of the younger guys."

The only way he would play the next season, Sawchuk told Cauz, was if a deal could be worked out that would send him back to Detroit, where he could be with his family. It seemed that his heart still belonged to the Red Wings.

Terry's performance that night in a crucial match against the Canadiens (the battle for second place had yet to be decided) reflected his mood. He constantly bobbled shots and coughed up fat rebounds. "Something is the matter with him," observed Jacques Plante in the Forum broadcast booth. "He's not sharp. Funny, this place was the spot he used to be terrific." Montreal led 4-2 when Imlach sent Bower out to replace Sawchuk midway through the second period. The Habs went on to win 5-3.

On Friday morning, *The Globe* ran Cauz's story, in which he quoted Terry about his plans to retire unless he somehow landed back in Detroit. Later that day Cauz and a couple of other reporters were in Imlach's office at the Gardens.

"Punch is up on the exercise bicycle, pumping away, when in clomps Sawchuk, still wearing his face mask," recalls Cauz. "He was angry as hell, and started yelling at me for misquoting him in the newspaper about the retirement story, basically denying everything that I had written. Then I remember him waving that big goal stick of his around like he was going to take off my head. All the while Imlach is still riding his bike, laughing and egging Terry on. 'Yeah, you give it to him Ukey. You tell him.'

"By this time I'm getting pretty steamed myself. 'You sure as hell did say those things to me,' I yelled back at Sawchuk. 'I've got everything here in my notes.' It was a pretty crazy scene."

Like the Detroit writers before them, Lou Cauz and the other scribes on the Leaf beat had little choice but to put up with Terry's mood swings. They had no way of telling which side of his personality they were likely to meet—the Jekyll, the Hyde or, sometimes, both.

Still a staple in Toronto press circles is the story of Sawchuk's encounter with the late Bob Pennington, a dignified Englishman who wrote a sports column for the old *Toronto Telegram*. Sawchuk abruptly interrupted a question from Pennington by telling him to "Fuck off." The Englishman, with exquisite politeness, replied, "Very well, Terry, if that's how you feel, I shall."

Pennington's response completely flustered Sawchuk. "Hey, okay, come back," he stammered after the retreating reporter.

Most of the writers have stories about how Sawchuk

would rebuff them only to come back later and apologize. "I get so wound up at times I don't know what I'm saying," he once tearily told Jim Proudfoot of *The Toronto Star*. As Proudfoot would write, "On balance, most people were willing to forgive him for being irritable. Life seemed to be an ordeal for him."

Terry's treatment of fans was similar. He met autograph hunters with barely concealed contempt. When he was in a particularly foul mood, he would shout at them to leave him alone. And yet, occasionally, when he was playing well and the team was winning, he could be disarmingly gracious and charming. He had a particular soft spot for anyone he perceived as an underdog, especially children who were handicapped or sick. Having been in hospitals so often himself, he understood their suffering.

That season, following a victory in which Sawchuk starred against the Black Hawks, a teenaged boy in a wheelchair was pushed into the Leaf dressing room at the Gardens. Bob Pulford saw him first and took the kid over to Terry's corner. It was late and the players were hurrying to catch a flight to Chicago for the return match.

"I was just another awestruck fan," remembers David Onley, the polio victim in the wheelchair. "The security guard got permission to let me in the room and, suddenly, there I was talking to Terry Sawchuk, who had always been one of my idols. Sawchuk told me a couple of stories and even vividly demonstrated a save he had made that night against Bobby Hull. The trainer was telling everyone to hurry up but Terry kept talking. Then he grabbed Pulford's game stick and took me around the room, introducing me to the players and making sure each one signed his autograph."

By then it was late and the team had to go. Sawchuk patted Onley on the head and told him to keep exercising, to keep plugging.

"You know, like a lot of people, I've heard stories about how Sawchuk could be a nasty piece of work," says Onley, who today is the education and science reporter for Toronto's City-TV. "But he couldn't have been any nicer to me. One night a couple of years later, after Sawchuk had moved on from the Leafs, I waited for him at the players' entrance at the Gardens. By then I was out of my wheelchair and using a cane. Maybe he was just being polite, but he said that he remembered me. He shook my hand and again told me to hang in there and keep plugging.

"I remember how upset I was when I heard that Sawchuk had died," Onley says. "My impression of him was that he was a kind and good man. Though I only met him twice, he definitely made a difference in my life."

Punch Imlach fondly called Johnny Bower Toronto's "big boy." But just like the year before against Montreal, when Bower had been kayoed by the flu, it was Sawchuk who found himself in net for the opening game of the semi-finals. During the Leafs' final scrimmage (their sixth practice in three days) before the start of the series in Chicago, a Pete Stemkowski drive shattered the little finger on Bower's right hand, leaving him unable to grip his goalie stick.

Terry felt none too spry himself. Since his return to the line-up in February, he had lost more than twenty pounds, dropping down to a skeletal 160. Like Bower, Sawchuk had also recently taken a direct hit. Old nemesis Eddie Shack nailed him with a slap shot, leaving a tender purple welt the size of a hockey puck on his collarbone and left shoulder.

In the privacy of their dressing room, the Leafs conceded that the Hawks were the more talented hockey club. But Chicago relied perhaps too heavily on superstars Stan Mikita and Bobby Hull (who finished one-two in the scoring race) to orchestrate their offence. If the Leafs could check them to a standstill, taking away their ability to manoeuvre and forcing them to pass off the puck, then they had a chance.

The theory was sound. Putting it into practice proved more difficult, especially during the Thursday-night opener at a packed and rowdy Chicago Stadium. Both Hull and Mikita, the pivot for Kenny Wharram and Doug Mohns on the famed Scooter Line, scored single goals in a 5-2 Chicago romp. Throughout the entire lopsided affair, Toronto appeared awkward and a full step slower than the stylish Hawks.

Denis DeJordy, that year's co-winner of the Vezina with Glenn Hall, easily outshone Sawchuk, who admitted he should have stopped at least two of the Chicago scores. Of the opening goal by Wharram, he said, "I got the puck between my arm and body: If I don't move my arm, the puck stays out." Hull's goal, which put Chicago ahead 3-1 in the second period, deflected in off Tim Horton's stick. In reaching for the puck, Terry knocked it into the net himself.

"I thought the difference was in goal," said Hawk coach Billy Reay. Even if Imlach agreed, he knew better than to voice any criticism of the goalkeeper he was counting on for at least one more start in Bower's absence. "It's in the book how good Sawchuk is," Imlach said firmly, "and I feel like the book says. He's been good an awful lot of times. If Terry's bad once in a while, he's entitled to be."

No one had to make excuses for Sawchuk in game two. Big saves on Bobby Hull and his kid brother Dennis early in the action, followed soon after by an even more spectacular steal on Eric Nesterenko, stalled Chicago's momentum. The Leafs outmuscled and outhustled the Hawks in a 3-1 triumph. Only Mikita, who like Hull was almost constantly frustrated by Leaf checkers, managed to beat Terry, spoiling the shutout bid with a thirty-five-foot snap shot at 8:45 of the third period.

Sawchuk looked so sharp that Imlach told Bower to relax and rest his hand a while longer. In game three at Maple Leaf Gardens, Terry again frustrated the Hawks by producing key saves in the opening period. On two occasions he sacrificed his body to block full-force blasts by Hull. The first caught him on the inside of his calf; the second on the meat of his catching arm. Hull finally did manage to score, but not until late in the third period, when he converted a Lou Angotti rebound for Chicago's only goal in another 3-1 Toronto win.

"Our guys made the ice look like a minefield out in front of me," lauded Sawchuk, who stopped thirty-six shots and sported bruises over most of his body. Even Bower, who by now was ready and anxious to play, felt that Imlach had to stick with Terry. "You don't take out a hot goaltender," he said. "There's too much riding on this series."

Two nights later, the Hawks changed tactics and tried to beat the Leafs with brawn. For three thrilling, exhausting periods the combatants butted heads like rams in heat. Observers wondered how much the eventual winner of the series would have left to give in the finals against the Canadiens, who had already swept aside the Rangers in four-straight.

Kenny Wharram equalled Gordie Howe's record for the fastest playoff goal when he beat Sawchuk on a feed from Mohns after just nine seconds. Before the eleven-minute mark, the Leafs and Hawks had two goals apiece. Chicago gradually took control of the match, but Sawchuk kept the Leafs in it with tremendous saves on Doug Jarrett and Red Hay. In the second period, he stopped a Bobby Hull bomb, and then stoned Mikita on a breakaway.

Nesterenko finally put Chicago ahead 3-2 at 2:31 of the third stanza when, after repeated jabs at the puck, he managed to force it over the goal line. Sawchuk raged that the goal was illegal. "I had it twice," he shouted at referee Bill Friday. "I had it once, and they jabbed it clear. I got it again and they whacked my entire arm into the net."

Just over six minutes later, Hull beat Terry with a hip-high forty-foot slap shot for what proved to be the winning goal in a 4-3 decision. Chicago and Toronto stood even at two wins apiece.

Leaf Brian Conacher recalls that by this point in the series Sawchuk had taken such a beating that most of his teammates were amazed that he was playing at all, let alone so brilliantly. "I've got a picture of Sawchuk taken during the playoffs. The guy looks like he was 104 years old. Terry had an awful lot of hard miles on him by that stage of his career and he'd had a phenomenally tough series. He was bruised and beat up from head to toe—and obviously he was completely exhausted."

Nonetheless, he was still Imlach's choice for the pivotal fifth game Saturday afternoon in Chicago. "I'll play if he wants me to," Sawchuk said without enthusiasm. But before the start of a match that has since become one of the cornerstones of his legend, Terry went to Imlach and asked to sit out in favour of Bower.

A huge audience saw that game—the 20,000 fans jammed into every corner of Chicago Stadium, with millions more watching on CBS in the United States and on nation-wide CBC-TV in Canada. Slush puddles dotted the ice surface on an unseasonably muggy afternoon. By game time, the temperature in the arena was already in the eighties and cigarette smoke hung in the air like a stale fog.

Toronto and Chicago split the scoring in a savagely contested opening period: rookie Mike Walton and Frank Mahovlich on power plays for Toronto; Bobby Hull and Lou Angotti for Chicago when both teams were a man short. Bower, who hadn't played in almost two weeks,

frequently juggled the puck, always a sure sign that he
was off his game. Imlach called him over to the bench.
Bower admitted he was shaky, but said he wanted to at
least finish out the period. Then Imlach consulted Sawchuk, seated at the end of the bench. Terry agreed with
Bower that it would be better to wait until the start of the
second period if he had to go in at all.

During the intermission, Imlach made the decision to
switch goalies. The second period had barely begun when
Allan Stanley drew a charging penalty, forcing the still-cold
Sawchuk to face down the Hawk power play. The puck
came to Bobby Hull, positioned about twenty feet to Terry's
left, almost parallel to the goal. Hull unloaded a high blast
that struck Sawchuk flush on his sore left shoulder, knocking him down as if he'd been poleaxed.

Many in the hushed crowd thought that he had been hit
in the head. Trainer Bob Haggert slid across the ice and
broke through the huddle of Leafs standing silently over
Sawchuk.

"Where'd you get it?" Haggert asked Terry.

"On my bad shoulder."

"Think you're all right?"

"I stopped the shot, didn't I," Sawchuk answered sarcastically. He reached for his stick and gloves and slowly
climbed back to his feet.

"I almost died when that shot landed," Imlach said later.
"But he came back—you saw it. Words can't describe the
marvellous game he played for us." Everyone watching was
awed by Sawchuk's phenomenal performance during the
final two periods of game five.

Five times Terry turned aside smoking drives from
Bobby Hull. Stan Mikita and his Scooter Line constantly
buzzed the Leaf net. At one point, Mohns cut in front and
attempted a deke. Terry flashed out a hand and smothered

his shot. During a power play, Mikita redirected a Hull slap shot from the left point. Sawchuk left the crowd gasping with that save. In the third period, Stemkowski and Pappin scored to give Toronto a 4-2 lead. The Hawks, frantic now, fired twenty-two shots (out of a total of thirty-seven handled by Sawchuk) during the game's final twenty minutes. More blanks.

"The Chicagos may have the better shinny club, as everybody claims," wrote Milt Dunnell. "They certainly were the better club Saturday afternoon. But the Leafs had Sawchuk. He was the old equalizer. Against him, the Hawks were like kids with new airguns, blasting away at Fort Knox."

"I saw him make those saves," Bobby Hull said, "but I still can't believe it. That was the most frustrating experience of my career. I've never seen such goaling."

"He gave us nothing, not a rebound," added Pierre Pilote. "That, my friend, is perfect goaltending."

Punch Imlach cast his memory all the way back to high-school history class for a parallel that would do justice to his goaltender's heroic performance. "Sawchuk was like that guy on the bridge, you know, Horatio," he said, referring, in fact, to the Roman general Horatius. "He was fantastic."

Smoking a cigarette and slowly sipping on a Coke, Terry sat alone in the dressing room for a long time after the game. "I feel fifty-seven, not thirty-seven," he sighed. "I'd like to leave hockey like that. In good style."

Still later, brushing aside autograph seekers as he made his way out of the arena, Terry once more talked of quitting. "I'm going out while still on top, with them saying, 'He could have played four or five years.' Who needs this aggravation? I'm just one great big aching bruise." But by the next day, after a few beers to unwind and a full night's sleep, he was a new man. "I feel pretty good," he said cheerily. "I know for sure my back is okay. I'll be a lot stronger next season. I may just come back again if the money is right."

The victory in game five changed everything for Toronto. Chicago, the highest-scoring club to that point in hockey history, had thrown everything it had at them and been brought to the brink of elimination. With Imlach's battered Horatius as their rallying point, the Leafs believed themselves capable of anything.

Toronto controlled the play in game six from the opening whistle. Only a strong performance by Glenn Hall kept the Hawks' hopes alive. Conacher opened the scoring at 5:06 of the first period, locating an opening between Hall's legs for his first goal in twenty-three games. Chicago tied it just over nine minutes later when Pat Stapleton's shot deflected off Horton's stick and over Sawchuk's shoulder into the cage.

Terry made thirty-five saves, but compared to game five the pace seemed almost leisurely. Probably his biggest stop came in the scoreless second frame when he raced fifteen feet out of his net to snare the puck away from Dennis Hull. In the third period, Conacher scored his second of the night and Stemkowski added one for insurance to put away the game 3-1 and nail shut Chicago's coffin.

Oddsmakers pegged Montreal as 2-to-1 favourites over Toronto in the finals. In the Leafs, Hab coach Toe Blake had exactly the match-up he'd been hoping for all along. Montreal beat Chicago only twice during the regular schedule, but they split their season series with Toronto, winning six, losing six and tying two. And because they finished ahead of the Leafs, Montreal enjoyed the advantage of playing the opening two contests at the Forum as well as, if necessary, the fifth and potentially decisive seventh.

No one picked Toronto to win except the squad they'd just beaten, the Black Hawks. Said Bobby Hull, "The kind of hockey they beat us with—positional play, close checking, balanced lines, hitting—that's what it takes to beat Montreal."

"If the Leafs aren't hurting too badly, they'll win it," forecast Doug Mohns.

Together the Leafs and Canadiens had won the Cup eighteen of the past twenty-four seasons. The confrontation that spring between hockey's arch-rivals would become a cherished memory of Canada's Centennial celebrations. No matter what their loyalties, fans across the country took comfort in knowing that Lord Stanley's silver bowl would stay on Canadian soil.

A letdown was all but inevitable for Toronto after the intensity of the Chicago series. In the Thursday-night opener at the Forum, the Leafs didn't skate, lacked drive, and were even outhit by the Canadiens, who usually preferred finesse over brawn. One Toronto writer compared it to watching a Sopwith Camel against a jet fighter. A three-goal effort by Henri Richard paced the Habs to an embarrassingly easy 6-2 victory.

Sawchuk, complaining of fatigue, looked old and slow, his shortcomings made all the more obvious by the youthful bounce and confidence of twenty-one-year-old Rogatien Vachon in the Hab net. The rookie, after wresting the starting job away from veterans Gump Worsley and Charlie Hodge, had sparked the Habs to their current eleven-game winning streak, which now included victories in five straight playoff games.

Before the start of the series, in a laughably transparent attempt to rattle the youngster, Imlach derided Vachon as a "Junior B goalie." Vachon's performance in the opener prompted Imlach to generously upgrade his assessment.

"He's still Junior B," Imlach said. "But he's the best damn Junior B in the country."

Montreal led 5-2 early in the third period when Imlach mercifully lifted Sawchuk in favour of Bower, who looked sufficiently sharp the rest of the way to earn the start in game two.

"I tried to warn them," Toe Blake said angrily, pacing the floor of the Canadiens' dressing room. "They did it to Chicago, played a bad first game and bounced right back. I tried to warn our guys but…"

Game two Saturday afternoon saw the return of the snarling brutes in blue who had upset Chicago the week before. "The checking was so close we felt like we each had a twin for a shadow," said Jean Béliveau. Even when a Canadien did break free for a shot on goal, he was met by an impenetrable Johnny Bower, who made thirty-one saves in a 3-0 Toronto victory that evened the series at one win apiece.

It was gritty, hard-slamming, old-fashioned playoff hockey all the way. Though the Habs didn't score, Bower took a beating nonetheless. Three times Montreal enforcer John Ferguson crashed into his crease. "The first time he got me on the forehead," said Bower, seated beside Sawchuk in the dressing room after the game. The second, Larry [Hillman] lifted his stick and it took the bark off my nose. The third time he caught me on the collarbone."

Blood still seeped from the nick on Bower's sizeable beak. "Nothing serious," he said happily. "It's like Punch Imlach says, a hurting nose doesn't hurt anybody. Right, Terry?"

"Not unless you get knocked out," answered Sawchuk with a smile.

Bower returned for more of the same in game three when the series resumed in Toronto, matching Vachon save for save through three heart-stopping periods of end-to-end hockey, and then on for another twenty-eight minutes and twenty-six seconds of overtime. The end finally came when Stemkowski snapped a pass from behind the Montreal net to Pappin, who fed it to a waiting Pulford. In an instant the puck was behind Vachon for a 3-2 Toronto victory.

Sawchuk watched it all in perfect contentment from his perch on the end of the Leaf bench. Still nursing wounds from the Chicago series, he had no desire to be out there in Bower's place. Every time he moved, a large welt on his hip, a souvenir from a Bobby Hull slap shot, sapped his ambition.

He and Bower weren't close friends, but they liked and admired one another. Terry was always pleased by his partner's success. Maybe, as Bower has said, it would have been different if one of them had been a much younger goalie, anxious to make his mark. But neither felt threatened by the presence of the other. Each knew that together they still made one great goalie.

The next morning Bower happily held court before a mob of reporters at Maple Leaf Gardens. "John loves every minute of it," Sawchuk said, looking on from across the room. "I'd sooner be over here enjoying peace and quiet. It's nice to be the centre of attraction. But those interviews can get tedious, especially when a dozen different guys troop up and ask you the same questions over and over again."

The way Bower was playing, Sawchuk figured his season was over. After practice he left the Gardens and strolled to a bar he frequented on nearby Church Street. He ordered a drink, and then another and another. What did it matter any more? He sat there getting sloshed until the bar closed at one o'clock the next morning.

Some people who were close to the Leafs in those days insist that Sawchuk was still hung over when he showed up at the Gardens the next night for game four. But the only man who can say for certain is in his grave. If things had turned out differently, the hangover story would have made a colourful addition to the Sawchuk legend; hockey's equivalent of the oft-told baseball tale of how a bleary-eyed Grover Cleveland Alexander emerged from the Cardinals' bullpen to finish off Babe Ruth and the Yankees in the 1926 World Series.

Late in the pre-game warm-up, Bower reached for a puck and snapped a hamstring in his left thigh. He was through for the night and probably the season. Like old Grover, Sawchuk stepped reluctantly into the breach.

"I've had better nights, and I've had worse nights," he would say, "but real early I found out what kind of night this would be." Terry lay flat on the ice when Ralph Backstrom shot high for the opening goal. A Béliveau pass—a *pass*, not a shot—struck his skate and trickled in for the second goal. Next he muffed an Henri Richard floater. Some in the crowd began booing, apparently having forgotten that without him the Leafs would never have gotten past Chicago into the finals. Montreal won 6-2, the same score as in the opener—except, if anything, Terry played even worse this night.

One thing that could always be said for Sawchuk was that he never tried to make excuses after a bad game. "I've got one thing to say, gentlemen," he addressed the assembled reporters. "I just didn't have a good night."

He'd been hurt by the jeers of the crowd. But what stung even more was a telegram he received after the game from a Leaf fan in the Maritimes, who wondered, "How much money did you take to throw the game?"

"How can people say those things?" Terry asked. "I tried just as hard."

Like the Toronto fans, the Canadiens appeared to have forgotten what Sawchuk had only recently done to the Hawks. They returned home to Montreal convinced that the Cup was as good as won. "We were in the driver's seat again," defenceman Terry Harper recalled to author Stephen Cole. "We had home-ice advantage. We were two and two, and as far as we were concerned, Bower had beat us those two games as much as anything else. Now we had Sawchuk again and he'd looked pretty shaky. There wasn't a guy on the team who wasn't sure, absolutely sure, we were going to beat the Leafs at that point."

The Habs came out with guns blazing in game five Saturday afternoon, trying to put the game and probably the series away right then and there. On the very first shift, centre Ralph Backstrom broke in on the Leaf goal, made the deke and fired for the corner. Sawchuk kicked out his right leg and deflected the puck wide.

Horatius was back on the bridge. Next he robbed Cournoyer, then Béliveau and J.C. Tremblay. The blitz continued until, finally, the Canadiens managed to slip one through. On a feed from ex-Leaf Dick Duff, Leon Rochefort slapped a shot that ricocheted off Tim Horton and past Terry into the net.

Rochefort's goal snapped the Leafs out of their shell-shock. They quickly regrouped to form what one writer described as "a veritable line of scrimmage at the blue line." Soon Toronto controlled the play and before the period ended Jim Pappin tied the score, beating a suddenly shaky Vachon with a wrist shot from forty feet out.

Toronto scored three more unanswered goals in the second period. Brian Conacher converted a Red Kelly rebound. Marcel Pronovost beat Vachon on another long shot. In the period's final minute, smooth-as-glass Dave Keon, whose indefatigable two-way play would earn him the Conn Smythe

Trophy, stole the puck from J.C. Tremblay and passed off to a charging Tim Horton. His blast bounced off Jacques Laperriere and back to Keon, who deked Vachon out of his longjohns before backhanding the puck into the net.

Sawchuk met every test. Backstrom tried his luck again early in the second period only to have Terry shift suddenly and deflect the shot off his stick arm. Later, during a Canadiens' power play, he robbed Jean Béliveau on a short slap shot.

Montreal outshot Toronto 38-29, but the margin didn't reflect the play after the opening onslaught. By the start of the third period, when Gump Worsley replaced Vachon in the Canadiens' net, the Leafs focused only on defence. Montreal never again mounted a serious threat and the score remained frozen at 4-1 until the final buzzer. Toronto stood only one victory away from hoisting the Stanley Cup.

No one could have blamed Sawchuk for crowing a little, not after the beating he'd taken from the fans and press. Instead he quietly talked about how he had approached the game with the simple, hard-won philosophy gleaned from a lifetime of stopping vulcanized rubber: "If I do good, I do good. If I don't, well, I've tried."

He did, however, use the opportunity to point out that this was exactly the same approach he had taken going into the disastrous fourth game. "To be honest, I felt as sharp today as I did on Thursday," Terry said. "I tried just as hard Thursday as I did today. That's all you can do."

He knew that his teammates and millions of Leaf fans across the country were counting on him to shut down Béliveau, Cournoyer and the rest one last time. In the end, it always came down to the man in goal. On Tuesday morning, just hours before the start of game six in Toronto, Tim Horton acknowledged that the Leafs' fate was in the hands of God and Terry Sawchuk. "Know what they say, goalkeeping is like pitching. If Sawchuk is like Koufax tonight, we win. If he isn't, well, as they say in Montreal, '*C'est la guerre.*'"

Every save he made that night he made in fear. "I was scared witless," Terry said. "Scared every time they got near me."

Punch Imlach figured that if Toronto didn't clinch on home ice then they wouldn't win it at all. The Leafs hadn't played well at the Forum during the regular season. The fact that they had managed to win two games there in the finals was close to a miracle. Neither Imlach nor anyone else was willing to bet on their winning a third time.

Addressing the team before the start of the game, he instructed his younger players to remember the example of Bill Gadsby, who had played twenty-one seasons without winning a Stanley Cup. They might never get this close again.

Imlach directed his next remarks at the veterans. "Some of you have been with me for nine years. It's been said that I stuck with the old ones so long we couldn't possibly win the Stanley Cup. For some of you it's a farewell. Go out there and ram that puck down their throats."

It was Sawchuk who was forced to eat rubber in the opening minutes of play. Terry made seventeen of his forty saves in the first period alone. Béliveau tested him twice and both times went away shaking his head in frustration. Cournoyer, Backstrom and Rochefort were likewise turned aside with sensational stops. "There were three or four shots in the early part of the game you could usually count as goals," Béliveau said.

Tallies by Ron Ellis and Jim Pappin put the Leafs up 2-0 in the second period. Gump Worsley, working only his second full game since injuring a knee in early December, had little chance on either one. At the other end, Sawchuk foiled the finish of a pretty three-way passing play between Terry Harper, Bobby Rousseau and Béliveau. Twice he reacted with split-second timing to stop deflections off the stick of John Ferguson. Then he robbed Dave Balon after a perfect set-up by Henri Richard.

"It's almost superhuman the way he's getting in front of some of those Canadien shots," exclaimed ex-Leaf great Joe Primeau from his perch in the press box. "He made a dozen stops that I regard as next to impossible."

Dick Duff finally got one back for Montreal, weaving around Horton and whipping a backhander that hit the twine behind Terry just inside the left goalpost. With 14:32 still to play in regulation time, the Canadiens intensified their attack. Sawchuk turned back tries by J.C. Tremblay and Ted Harris. Paced by the checking of Dave Keon, George Armstrong and Bob Pulford, the Leafs managed with difficulty to contain the uprising as the clock counted down.

Fifty-eight seconds remained when an off-side call led to a face-off to the left of Sawchuk in the Leaf zone. Toe Blake pulled Worsley for an extra attacker. Then Imlach shocked the crowd by sending out a line-up of "old pappies" to finish the kill—Armstrong, Stanley, Kelly, Horton and the fuzzy-cheeked youngster of the group, Bob Pulford, just thirty-one.

Stanley muscled Béliveau off the puck on the draw. Kelly snared the loose puck and passed to Pulford, who lateralled to Armstrong. The Leaf captain took aim and fired an eighty-foot wrist shot into the empty Montreal net.

There are no photographs of Sawchuk joyously celebrating the Stanley Cup victory on the ice with his teammates. When the buzzer rang, he made straight for the dressing room, where he sat alone for several minutes, his head bowed in exhaustion. Even when the party caught up to him, he remained apart. "I don't like champagne and I'm too tired to dance around," he said, sipping slowly on a Coke as his teammates carried on around him.

Sweat still poured off him. "It may sound corny," Terry said softly, "but this has to be the greatest thrill of my life. I've had a lot of wonderful moments in hockey and other Stanley Cups, but nothing to equal this. It would be nice to go out a winner, the first star in a Cup-winning game. I have a wife, six kids and another on the way. And I miss them very much during the hockey season. I'm not saying this was my last game, but I'm going to give it a lot of thought in the next few weeks."

Much later, after Sawchuk had showered and dressed, he went to a phone and called Pat and the kids. Then, as one observer remembered, he walked alone into the night, looking for some place to have a quiet drink.

# Chapter Thirteen

## OVERTIME

**AT** precisely 10:01 a.m. on June 6, 1967, NHL president Clarence Campbell reached his hand into the Stanley Cup and drew the name of the new team that would pick first in the historic expansion draft. The lucky winner, Campbell announced to the hushed crowd in the massive second-floor ballroom of Montreal's Queen Elizabeth Hotel, was the Los Angeles Kings.

Rising to his feet, Jack Kent Cooke, the Kings' flamboyant Canadian-born owner who had become a multi-millionaire through his vast publishing and radio interests, unhesitatingly announced, "Los Angeles drafts Terry Sawchuk from Toronto."

In return for their two-million-dollar entry fees, the six new franchises—Philadelphia, Oakland, Pittsburgh, St. Louis, Minnesota and Los Angeles—were permitted to pick like scavengers from the cast-offs of the original six teams. The only quality to be found in the draft was among the goaltenders made available. The established clubs could each initially protect one goalie and eleven skaters, with the first two of the draft's twenty rounds devoted exclusively to goaltenders. Chicago Black Hawk mainstay Glenn Hall landed in St. Louis; Bernie Parent and Doug Favell, both former Bruins, went to Philadelphia; Charlie Hodge, like Hall and Sawchuk a former Vezina winner, departed Montreal for Oakland.

Despite Terry's heroics during Toronto's Stanley Cup drive, there never was the slightest doubt that it would be him and not Bower whom the Leafs would set free. "I had to go with Bower," Punch Imlach explained. "He had been with me longer. Sawchuk was the one who had to leave."

Terry knew as much—and expected nothing less. The pattern for his farewells had been established long before. When Detroit first traded him, he had just won the Vezina; when the Red Wings let him go the second time, he was coming off a year in which he had been the team MVP. Nine days after the expansion draft, Terry would be named the winner of the J.P. Bickell Memorial Trophy as the outstanding Toronto Maple Leaf for the past season.

It should be noted that Imlach tried his best to regain the rights to Sawchuk during the draft meeting in Montreal. Terry's name cropped up during a bitter public squabble between Imlach and Los Angeles over the rights to Red Kelly.

Kelly, assuming that he had the approval of the Leafs to end his playing career, had signed on with Los Angeles as coach. But Imlach wanted the Kings to draft Kelly, allowing Toronto the advantage of selecting another player to fill his spot. Growing impatient by the end of the tenth round of the draft, Imlach put Kelly back on Toronto's protected list.

"We'll give them Kelly," Imlach said, "for Sawchuk. We'll even throw in another goalie."

"I was so dang mad, I almost went across the room and punched Punch on the nose," fumed the usually placid Kelly. "I had a verbal agreement with him, that he wouldn't stand in my way of becoming a coach. He knew I did not intend to play during the 1967-68 season."

After the Kings had filed formal complaints against Imlach, the two sides finally sat down and Toronto agreed to accept a number fifteen draft choice, unheralded defenceman Ken Block, in return for the rights to Kelly. Sawchuk stayed the property of Los Angeles.

Many writers and long-time fans condemned the expansion draft as a farce and the ruination of hockey. "Doubling their size overnight—a more swift growth than that in any other expanding sport—the NHL incumbents were forced to surrender more quantity than any other league," noted *The Hockey News*. "They made up for it by giving up less quality."

Most of the new teams selected a nucleus of veterans—players like Andy Bathgate (Pittsburgh), Billy Harris (Oakland) and Elmer Vasko (Minnesota) who, though well past their primes, were at least known to the hockey public. Insisting on having the final say in the Kings' selections, Cooke opted, after choosing Sawchuk first, for youth instead. Terry was the only player on the roster who had spent all of the previous season with a big-league club, and even those with NHL experience had never been better than fringe players. Los Angeles was widely held to have emerged from the draft in worse shape than any other team.

"The Los Angeles Kings, at this moment, are clowns," opined Dick Beddoes of *The Globe and Mail*. "Can you visualize Gordon Labossierre, Bob Wall, Eddie Joyal, Paul Popiel, Terry Gray and Bryan Campbell in big league uniforms as playmates of Terry Sawchuk?"

Sawchuk felt flattered at having been selected first in the draft, but said he still wasn't certain that he wanted to continue his playing career. Later that June, he shot a round of golf with the Kings' newly appointed general manager, Larry Regan, a teammate of Terry's during his aborted second season in Boston. "He made an offer and I said what I wanted," Sawchuk recounted. "Nothing has been decided and we're still dickering. I hope we'll be able to come to terms. It's a tough decision though, taking seven kids away from their home."

In the end, Terry found the money offered by the Kings impossible to refuse. Like so many veterans of the old six-team NHL, he had been grossly underpaid throughout his career. Expansion not only instantly doubled the number of big-league jobs from 120 to 240, it sent players' salaries soaring. Sawchuk and Regan finalized the details of his contract when he reported to training camp in Guelph, Ontario.

Asked to sit in on that meeting was Sawchuk's old friend Johnny Wilson, who had joined the Kings' organization as coach and general manager of the American League's Springfield Indians. Cooke had purchased the Indians from Eddie Shore as the first step in building a farm system. "Regan and I had already gone over Sawchuk's old Toronto contract," Wilson remembers. "He had been making just $18,000 with Toronto. Regan shook his head. 'That's a real shame,' he said, 'A guy who's been a Vezina winner and won the Stanley Cup.'

"Regan offered Terry a three-year deal—$41,000 the first year, $39,000 the next year, and somewhere around $37,000 the third year [the final year of the contract was not guaranteed]. Regan figured that, at his age, Terry would play fewer games each year. Well, Terry could hardly believe what he was hearing. His eyes filled up and he said, 'I never made that kind of dough in my life.'"

The Kings considered Sawchuk's salary a sound investment in the future of the franchise. It was hoped he would provide the backbone for a youthful and largely untalented squad. Cooke, whose holdings included the basketball Lakers, also counted on Terry to help fill a grandiose new sixteen-million-dollar arena, dubbed the "fabulous Forum," he was building in time for a December 30 opening. Sawchuk was a name player and that sold tickets in image-conscious California.

"If we get forty games from Terry we'll be right in there," Red Kelly said of the Kings' chances in the West Division, composed entirely of the new teams. At the conclusion of an interlocking regular schedule, the East, comprising the original six clubs, and West would conduct separate playoffs, the winners then meeting in the Stanley Cup final.

"Terry can cover up the mistakes of a young expansion team," continued Kelly. "He won't shut out everybody or cover for all the mistakes, but he comes up with key saves. That's all we can ask. The goalie has to come up with four or five great saves in the game. Terry does. That's why I am optimistic about our season."

All the hype surrounding his selection and signing embarrassed Sawchuk—"I've been beat 9-0 a couple of times too," he reminded everyone—but he was anxious to start life in sunny California. For the first time, Pat and the kids accompanied him to a new city. The family settled happily into a large, rented house at Hermosa Beach, within sight of the ocean. Visited by a reporter at his home that November, Terry contentedly waved at the Pacific and said, "This sure beats retirement."

If only his life at the rink could have been so carefree. The trouble started a couple of days before the season opener, when he was hit on his bad right elbow by a shot in practice. The elbow puffed up and haemorrhaged, forcing him to sit out the first four games of the season. Terry's understudy, twenty-five-year-old Wayne Rutledge, who had played the previous season for Omaha in the CPHL, performed superbly in his place. Los Angeles beat Philadelphia and Minnesota at home, then tied Oakland and St. Louis on the road.

Sawchuk fared well enough in his first start as a King, a 5-3 decision in Chicago that handed the stumbling Black Hawks their sixth consecutive loss. But then he lost 4-2 to the Leafs in Toronto, and the Rangers bombed him 6-1 in his home debut. Red Kelly openly criticized Terry's play after that game and again following his next outing, a 3-1 loss to Chicago. Soon Rutledge, a big man for a goalie, six foot two and two hundred pounds, was getting most of the starts, even against the six established teams, assignments originally intended to be Terry's exclusive preserve.

Already Sawchuk was feuding with the LA writers. When an article appeared gently needling him about not playing regularly, Terry responded, "If they don't know anything about hockey, they shouldn't be writing about it." He rebuffed one reporter by saying that he didn't give interviews after a game; he told another that he wouldn't answer questions before a game. "My first thought," wrote Bill Libby, who covered the Kings for *The Hockey News*, "was that this left only the games, themselves, during which to interview him…. It seems surprising that Sawchuk, the highest paid and most prominent player in the ranks of a team seeking to find a following, should be doing the sort of public relations job in LA that Al Capone did in Chicago."

Red Kelly, in spite of his own criticisms of Sawchuk's play, defended his old friend. "This is a long year," he said. "And when that Stanley Cup playoff comes around, you'll see Ukey out there." Kelly added that Terry was helping the team in ways that the writers and fans couldn't see.

During practices, Sawchuk gave Rutledge tips on how to position himself when the other team had the puck behind his goal or in the corners. And before every game, he went over the opposing forwards with the rookie, discussing their favourite moves and where they were most likely to take their shots.

"The young players we have all look up to him as the real pro," Larry Regan said of Terry. "He was their hero when most of them were learning how to skate. You've got to remember that our kids are learning a completely new system of hockey, and a fellow like Sawchuk is aware of the importance of developing an organization. He sets the example for others, who look up to him. He's always giving them pointers."

Los Angeles surprised everyone by holding first place in the West until late November. Budding stars Bill White and Dale Rolfe, both acquired in the Springfield purchase, anchored the defence. Up front, previously unheralded shooters Eddie Joyal, Bill "Cowboy" Flett and Lowell Mac-Donald sparked a surprisingly effective attack. Playing a wide-open style, the Kings scored two hundred goals, which led the West, but was topped by all the original teams.

A string of injuries hampered Sawchuk through the season. His elbow had barely healed when, in December, he pulled a hamstring. Early that February, he went out with an eye injury. Pit Martin of the Black Hawks fired a shot from close range that jammed Sawchuk's mask against his face. Both of his eyes swelled shut and he missed several games.

By the last weeks of the campaign, many in hockey were ready to write Terry off as a front-line performer. "He was the greatest goalie ever, but now he has no speed left and his reflexes are shot, and anyone observing him realistically could see how vulnerable he was," wrote Bill Libby. "He got by only as long as the Kings threw a blanket of protection around him. When the Kings' defencemen fell apart, he was a sitting duck."

The Kings finished second in the West, one point back of Philadelphia. Libby and others believed that it was Red Kelly's insistence on using Sawchuk in the big games down the stretch that cost Los Angeles the pennant. In thirty-six appearances, Sawchuk posted a 3.07 GAA, compared to Rutledge's mark of 2.87 in forty-five games.

But who could blame Kelly for continuing to believe in his thirty-eight-year-old goalie? He had been there during the playoffs the year before and so many other times in the past when Terry had worked his miracles. Thumbing his nose at the critics, Kelly announced that Sawchuk was his man for the opener of the semi-finals against fourth-place Minnesota.

For two games, it was almost like old times. Terry turned aside the North Stars 2-1 in the opener. Most of the thirty-one shots fired Sawchuk's way by the anaemic Stars were of the routine variety. But he did make several excellent stops and only a point-blank blast by Dave Balon in the third period denied him of the twelfth playoff shutout of his career.

That came in game two, a 2-0 decision in which Minnesota taxed Terry with only eighteen shots. The North Stars looked so laughably inept that Kelly was moved to say, "We should never lose to this club."

"We must have helped Sawchuk to another year," said a disgusted Wren Blair, the Minnesota coach and general manager. "I'll bet he's never had such an easy couple of games. Just ask him." Terry refused the bait. "There's no such thing as an easy shutout," he replied. "They had some good shots—not many, but enough."

Kelly had been too quick to dismiss the North Stars' chances. When the series switched to Minnesota for game three, the Stars blasted Sawchuk from the net with five goals by the end of the second period. Rutledge finished out a 7-5 loss that put the Stars back in the series. In game four, with Terry back in the cage, Minnesota edged the Kings 3-2 to pull even.

Sawchuk came down with a virus and Rutledge took over for game five, a 3-2 victory in which he made several outstanding third-period saves to preserve the Kings' advantage. Rutledge played well again in a 4-3 overtime loss three nights later that sent the series back to the coast for a seventh-game showdown.

Kelly had gotten two strong efforts out of Rutledge. But he went back to Sawchuk for the finale, a decision based more on loyalty and blind faith than a clear-headed examination of recent events. "After the two games Rutledge gave them, I couldn't believe the Kings would turn back to Sawchuk, but when we saw him in the nets it gave us a lift and I think it let down the Kings," Wren Blair would say. "It would have been hard to yank him after his great career, but I guess the team should have come first."

Rarely had Sawchuk looked worse than he did in taking a decisive 9-4 pasting that night at the hands of the North Stars. Terry barely reacted on any of the shots that beat him. Within a span of just four minutes and fourteen seconds in the second period, Minnesota scored four unanswered goals. Things got so bad that following the North Stars' eighth goal, the crowd of 11,214 turned on Sawchuk and began chanting, "We want Rutledge!"

Then they started throwing things at him—programs, wads of paper, popcorn boxes and soft-drink containers. Terry Sawchuk, the all-time great who was supposed to help sell the game of hockey in California, stood there and took it all without any visible sign of emotion. The refuse bounced off his head and his shoulders. Carefully, he swept up the mess with his goal stick and returned to his famous crouch, waiting for the action to resume.

"I've been knocked around by reporters and booed before," he said when the humiliation had finally ended. "All I can say is I tried."

"It would be nice to go out a winner, the first star in a Cup-winning game," Terry had said just twelve months before. Given the marked decline in his abilities, that opportunity had almost certainly disappeared for good. Bill Libby recalled running into a visiting coach in Los Angeles after the Kings' defeat.

"Is Terry Sawchuk retiring?" asked the coach.

"He should," answered Libby, "but he still has another year to go on a fat contract."

"Then he'll play," said the coach.

The Kings began shopping Sawchuk around and that spring, in the annual intra-league draft, they picked up promising young goalie Gerry Desjardins, who had starred with Cleveland in the American League the past season. Terry was left off the Kings' original protected list. But there were no takers.

He was still with the team at the start of training camp, which had been switched from Guelph to Barrie, Ontario. In an obvious attempt at fence-mending, Terry sat down to lunch with Kelly, Regan and several of the writers covering the team. "No, last season was not all I hoped for," Sawchuk acknowledged. "I had some good games, but I had some bad games. I ended on a dismal note. But I figure I have one more year left, and I plan to make it a good one."

Terry regretted his problems with the press. "I was under a lot of pressure last season and perhaps I wasn't as co-operative as I should have been, but I think things will be better this year... A good deal was expected of me, personally. It was a really tough proposition."

"I wouldn't write him off yet," Regan added. "He wouldn't be the first goaltender everyone figured was washed up who bounced back."

It was all window dressing. Shortly before the end of camp, Los Angeles dealt Terry to Detroit in return for twenty-four-year-old Jimmy Peters, Jr., a journeyman centre whose father had been Sawchuk's teammate on the Wings in the early 1950s. The trade and another even less flattering offer from Toronto vividly demonstrated just how far Terry's stock had fallen in one season. The Maple Leafs, who like Detroit had missed the playoffs, tendered a straight-cash bid of $20,000 for Terry. But Jack Kent Cooke wanted a player and accepted the Detroit offer instead.

Sawchuk had mixed emotions about returning to the Wings. Red Kelly remembered that Terry broke down and cried when told about the trade. Sawchuk felt badly about letting the Kings down, and he and his family also had regrets about giving up their new life at Hermosa Beach. But then there was that side of him that was never happy out of a Detroit uniform. The Wings new coach, Bill Gadsby, said that when he had run into Terry that summer, the goalie had "prodded" him several times about getting him back in a trade.

"I'm happy to be coming back to Detroit," Terry said. "You know there are only two places I really wanted to play and Detroit is number one if I had to leave Los Angeles. Sure, I'd heard rumours that Toronto wanted me, and I really figured that's where I'd wind up. But the Kings sure did me a favour by getting me back to Detroit. This is where my home is and it's where I got my start in the NHL…and it will be nice to finish my career here."

Gadsby and general manager Sid Abel saw Terry as strictly a back-up and mentor to Roger Crozier and Roy Edwards, who had shared the goaltending job. Crozier was to be Terry's personal project. The year before, when the Wings had finished out of the playoffs for the second year running, the high-strung little netminder had quit the team and hockey for three months, returning to his home in Bracebridge, Ontario, to work as a carpenter. It would be the job of Sawchuk, the moodiest and most volatile goaltender of his era, to help Crozier keep his emotions in check.

All of which was more than a little ironic. Detroit had once been in the enviable position of owning both Crozier and Sawchuk, back in the days when Terry was still at the top of his game. Now the veteran goalie was being asked to

provide the type of leadership that he could have been
giving Crozier and the Red Wings all along. No wonder Sid
Abel found himself being increasingly criticized in the
Detroit press for the team's woeful standing.

Around this time, Terry started talking about the possibility of his becoming a coach one day. He had won praise
for his work in helping Wayne Rutledge the season before
and there was no denying that he possessed the credentials
and the charisma demanded by the profession. Gadsby
soon lauded the impact that Terry had made on Crozier.
"You know how jittery Roger can get," he said. "Well,
since Ukey has been working with him he has really
calmed down. I think, for probably the first time in a long
time, Roger's really enjoying playing goal."

Still, given Sawchuk's temperament and his well-known
contempt for the press, it's difficult to imagine anyone in
pro hockey ever entrusting him with a job as a head coach.
More likely Terry, in the manner of his contemporary Glenn
Hall, would have become a special goaltending instructor
for an NHL franchise, a job for which he was eminently
qualified but which didn't come into vogue until several
years after his death.

Friends were happy to see Sawchuk looking to the
future. But all his plans came crashing down that January
when Pat filed for divorce, citing in her suit "extreme and
repeated" cruelty. Despite their often stormy marriage,
Terry had never imagined that he might one day lose the
only woman other than his mother that he had truly loved.
Even when the divorce went through several months later,
he never stopped loving Pat or hoping for a reconciliation.

His drinking, which had become progressively heavier
with the passing years, got worse following the separation.
He became more irritable and even less tolerant of
reporters, fans and anyone else outside his select circle of

friends. His desire to play the game deserted him along with his talent.

Lefty Wilson remembers that when Gadsby would announce which one of his three goalies was playing that night's game, "the other two guys would laugh like bastards. They were just happy they didn't have to play."

Once again the Wings missed the playoffs, staggering home fifth in the East Division, seven points behind the fourth-place Maple Leafs. Terry appeared in just thirteen games, winning three, losing four and tying three. He posted a 2.62 GAA.

Under mounting pressure to make changes to his line-up, Sid Abel announced that the Wings would use only two goalies the next season. Obviously, at age thirty-nine, Sawchuk would be the one to go. Terry had talked of retiring at the end of the campaign. But now, burdened by the weight of support payments for seven children, he had no choice but to keep playing as long as someone would have him.

This time the only bidder was New York Ranger coach and general manager Emile Francis. A former NHL goalie himself, Francis had long been an admirer of Sawchuk's and had earlier tried to pry him loose from Toronto. Francis still needed someone who could fill in occasionally for Eddie Giacomin. His sights were also set on the next round of playoffs. Giacomin, despite first- and second-team All-Star selections, had proven a disappointment in the post-season. New York had lost its last eight playoff matches. Francis hoped that Sawchuk still had it in him to play one or two standout games when it counted most. At the very least, his presence might spur Giacomin to an improved performance.

On June 20, 1969, Francis and the Wings cut a deal that sent Sawchuk and minor-league winger Sandy Snow to New York in return for Larry Jeffrey, a left winger developed in the Detroit system whose chronically sore knees limited him to duty as a penalty killer.

"All we want from Terry is twelve or fifteen games," Francis said. "Just enough to give Ed Giacomin an occasional rest." When informed of his duties, Sawchuk answered, "That's fine. I'm old and tired. I don't want to be—can't be—number one any more."

Terry made eight appearances in a season that saw the Rangers, who held down first place from November 16 until March 1, wilt under an avalanche of injuries and then have to scramble to narrowly edge out the Canadiens for the final playoff spot. Montreal's elimination ended a twenty-two-year string of Habitant playoff appearances.

Even when he played well—as on occasion he still could—Sawchuk always needed reassurance that it was his talent and not just dumb luck that had carried the day. "I didn't embarrass anyone out there, did I?" he would ask reporters after a game.

"The next day, however, he would often be surly and unapproachable," remembered Gerald Eskenazi of *The New York Times*. "Many times he would sit in the lobby of a hotel doing *The Times* crossword puzzle in ink and motioning questioners away."

Eskenazi described watching the Rangers leave their practice arena after a Christmas morning workout that drew a large crowd of vacationing school kids. One boy eagerly held out his pad and pencil to Sawchuk. "You don't want my autograph," Terry brushed him off. "I'm washed up."

Sawchuk enjoyed a last hurrah of sorts on February 1 in New York. Against Pittsburgh, he posted his first shutout in almost two years and the 103rd of his NHL career. By the final thirty seconds of the 6-0 decision, the fans at Madison Square Garden were on their feet applauding and counting down to the final buzzer.

Defence star Brad Park reached him first and kissed Sawchuk's forehead. "We wanted to show he's not washed up, as some guys have been saying," Park said of a Ranger blue-line corps that, in the words of one writer, shielded Terry "as if he were an egg about to crack."

"I don't think we tried extra hard on defence to protect him, though," Park continued. "Well, maybe we did just a bit. We know what he can do, and we wanted everyone else to see what he can do."

But by this point, not all of the Rangers were as star struck by Sawchuk as Brad Park. Terry's moodiness was off-putting to some and still more were angered by his refusal to work hard in practice. Sawchuk's old philosophy that if he stopped the puck during the games, somebody else could stop it during workouts hardly seemed appropriate now that he was nothing more than a spot starter.

New York entered the semi-finals against the powerful Boston Bruins still battered by injuries. Key performers Vic Hadfield, Rod Seiling, Donnie Marshall and Arnie Brown all sat on the sidelines. Injured though still playing were Brad Park and fellow defenceman Jim Neilson. When the Bruins slammed five goals past a shaky Giacomin in the first two periods of the opener, Emile Francis sent in Sawchuk, who allowed three more in an 8-2 rout.

Desperate, Francis started Terry in game two. But a self-admittedly "washed-up" forty-year-old backstop and his shorthanded mates were no match for a Boston squad led by Bobby Orr and Phil Esposito, the league's top two scorers. The Rangers fell 5-3 for a record-equalling tenth straight playoff defeat.

With Giacomin back in net, New York rallied to win the next two games and even the series. When the press, who had been quick to write off the Rangers' chances, swarmed into the New York dressing room after game four, Terry sarcastically told them all to "Go on over to the Bruins where you can cut the gloom with a knife."

Sawchuk made what would prove to be the final appearance of an unparalleled career in game five on April 14. Sadly, he went out with something less than a storybook ending. The Bruins led 3-2 late in the third period at Boston Garden when Emile Francis stunned the crowd by removing Giacomin from the net and sending Terry out in his place. But it was simply a delaying tactic. The Bruins, who had been carrying the play, were forced to wait around while Terry took his warm-up shots. League rules stipulated that a new goalie must remain in the net for sixty seconds, or until a face-off. When Brad Park quickly forced an icing call, Giacomin skated back out. Boston held on for the victory and then clinched the series with a 4-1 decision in game six. The Bruins went on to win their next eight-straight over Chicago and St. Louis and claim their first Stanley Cup in twenty-nine years.

In all his life, Terry had never felt so low. On April 2, he'd received news from home that his seventy-one-year-old father had been involved in a near-fatal car accident. Louis Sawchuk lay in a Pontiac hospital wrapped in a body cast. Terry's mother, Anne, had died in 1966.

Trent Frayne recalled his final meeting with the goalie whose life and times he had chronicled for two decades. Frayne spotted Sawchuk as he left Boston Garden after one of the playoff matches. "It was the first time I'd seen him in two or three years, and our relationship had always been cordial," Frayne wrote. "So I hailed him and went through the crowd to shake hands. I could see then that he didn't recognize me so I mentioned my name. His face contorted. 'Won't you sons of bitches ever leave me alone?' he said, wheeling. 'Fuck off!' He disappeared in the crowd, an anguished man."

## Chapter Fourteen

# FINAL DAYS

SAWCHUK and his Ranger teammate Ron Stewart shared a house that season at East Atlantic Beach on Long Island, a summer resort that offered homes for rent during the off-season. Most of the Rangers, few of whom lived year-round in New York, settled in the area for the winter. One resident characterized the community "as a quiet place where everyone minds his own business." Their next-door neighbours didn't even know that Sawchuk and Stewart were hockey players.

The two were old friends, having enjoyed a similar domestic set-up during Terry's first season with the Maple Leafs. Both men were divorced, had the same dry sense of humour, liked to drink, and were long-term NHL survivors. Stewart, known as one of the game's cleanest players and still a smooth, effortless skater at age thirty-seven, had broken in with Toronto seventeen years before. The past season with the Rangers the right winger had scored fourteen often crucial goals and had specialized in bedevilling opponents in short-handed situations.

Both men also shared a reputation for losing their tempers when under the influence of alcohol. An argument that flared between the friends while they were drinking in a local pub began the series of events that shocked and mystified the hockey public and which led ultimately to Sawchuk's death.

The E & J Pub was a favourite Ranger hangout in Long Beach, a sister community of East Atlantic Beach. Terry and Stewart were there on the night of April 29 (thirteen days after the Rangers had been eliminated from the playoffs) when they began quarrelling over how much responsibility each had to clean up their house before handing the keys back to the owner. Stewart also insisted that Sawchuk owed him money for household expenses.

According to witnesses, the two began shoving one another at the bar. The bartender ejected them, but outside on the sidewalk they continued arguing. Finally, the bartender came out and insisted that they go home.

Each drove his own car to the house at 58 Bay Street. There the dispute resumed outside in the yard in front of two witnesses: Rosemary Sasso, Stewart's twenty-four-year-old girlfriend; and Benjamin Weiner, a close friend of Sawchuk's who was the manager of Cooky's, a well-known area restaurant. Weiner reportedly tried to intervene, pulling Terry away. But the two men tripped, possibly on a barbecue grill, and tumbled to the ground on top of Stewart.

In the fall, Sawchuk hit his stomach heavily on either the barbecue or Stewart's knee, no one was certain which. He was obviously in tremendous pain. Sasso, a registered nurse, called Dr. Denis Nicholson, a family physician for many of the Rangers. "They told me there had been a fight," recounted Dr. Nicholson, who quickly arrived on the scene. "He [Sawchuk] was in shock. He was pale and had extremely low blood pressure. The shock must have been from the pain."

An ambulance rushed Sawchuk to Long Beach Memorial Hospital. Tests revealed that he had sustained serious damage to both his gall bladder and liver. Soon after his admittance, Terry underwent surgery for the removal of his gall bladder. A few days later, a second operation was performed to remove blood from his lacerated liver.

Dr. Nicholson, though no longer directly involved in the case, visited Sawchuk at Long Beach Memorial after his first operation. The veteran goalie was clearly in bad shape—plugged into intravenous feeding tubes, his arm hanging limply over the side of the bed. The two talked of the events leading up to Sawchuk's injury. "Terry told me that Stewart had been bugging him all year, and he had gotten fed up," Nicholson said later. He quoted Sawchuk as saying, "I punched him and knocked him down."

The doctor continued to quote Terry. "They kicked us out of the bar and I hit him again—I just kept knocking him down. At the house, I tagged him again and knocked him down again. I jumped him, and I fell on his knee. I started it and I finished it."

Sawchuk lay in hospital for more than three weeks before his condition became known to the public. The strange silence surrounding his hospitalization and the unusual circumstances leading to it inevitably sparked rumours that the New York Rangers and possibly even the local police had been involved in a concerted cover-up of the facts. "How does an internationally known personality get admitted to hospital, suffering critical injuries, without causing at least some slight quiver of curiosity on the part of the cops?" Milt Dunnell asked typically. "And remember, this didn't happen at Baffin Island or Tuktuk, it happened on Long Island, a bedroom of New York."

In fact, local police did briefly question Sawchuk soon after he was admitted to hospital. He told them that he and Stewart had simply been horseplaying on the lawn and that he had "tripped" over his friend. Since there was no hint of foul play, the interviewing policeman had not filed an official report.

Two weeks or so after Terry entered hospital, rumours began circulating in New York that a prominent athlete lay seriously ill in a small hospital on Long Island. Gerald Eskenazi checked his sources and broke the story of Sawchuk's injuries in *The New York Times* on May 22. What no one could understand was why the Rangers hadn't made news of their goalie's hospitalization public the moment it happened. The usual procedure, at least during the hockey season, would have been for the team to issue a press release about the situation.

The cover-up theory gained even more credence when Ron Stewart, who in the meantime had returned to his home in Barrie, Ontario, at first denied any knowledge of Sawchuk's situation. "It's news to me," Stewart told a Toronto reporter who knocked on his front door. Asked if he remembered fighting with Sawchuk, he answered, "Certainly not."

A beleaguered Emile Francis tried his best to justify the team's silence. "I did not know and the Rangers did not know that Terry had been injured until a week, a good week, maybe eight or nine days, after it had happened," he explained shortly after Sawchuk's death. "We found out when a doctor at the hospital phoned my office to tell us that one of our hockey players was in the hospital and had already undergone two operations.

"I was in Quebec at the time on a scouting trip and I did not know any of my players were still in New York, let alone a hospital. I flew back to New York immediately and went to see Terry."

Sawchuk had just come out of the intensive care unit following his second operation. Francis asked him what had happened. "He found it hard to come up with an explanation. But said finally that he and Stewie had had a tussle. He also said there was no way Ron Stewart should be blamed for what happened....

"'I was the only one to throw a punch,' he told me and said, 'I missed him with that one. That was when we were in front of the bar.' He then went on to say that they went to the house they shared together and then pushed some more."

According to Francis, Sawchuk said, "'I went to grab Ron and my friend [Ben Weiner] grabbed me from behind and we fell forward on top of Stewart and that was when I knew I was hurt and told them to call a doctor.'

"I then asked him, 'Terry, why weren't we informed?' and he explained that his father, who had been injured in a car accident on April 2, was in bad shape in a hospital in Detroit and he hadn't wanted the fact that he was in the hospital to get out." Francis said that Sawchuk specifically requested that he maintain the secrecy about his situation.

Reaction to Gerald Eskenazi's story in *The New York Times* was even stronger than Terry had feared. The hospital switchboard lit up with calls from writers demanding to talk to Sawchuk. Terry hung up on one Toronto reporter three times without speaking.

In the little more than a month from the day he was injured until his death, Sawchuk talked to just a single member of the press—and he had to be tricked into that. Immediately after the story broke, Shirley Fischler, a New York freelance writer and radio host married to the well-known hockey journalist Stan Fischler, found her way to his hospital room and then used her maiden name, Walton, to fool Terry and gain his confidence. At no time did she reveal that she was a reporter after a story. The next day, May 23, Fischler's story of her meeting with Sawchuk ran in *The Toronto Star* under the headline: "Terry Sawchuk: 'Can Never Come Back From This.'" Fischler provided a more complete account of their visit in the November 1970 issue of *Hockey Illustrated* magazine, in which she boasted of being the last journalist to see the game's greatest goalie alive.

Getting in to see Sawchuk, she said, was surprisingly easy. Armed with a bouquet of flowers, she simply walked right into his semi-private room. "The first thing I saw was a very old man in the first bed. He seemed to be very ill and coughed constantly. Then I peeked around a yellow curtain dividing the room and there was Terry Sawchuk, gazing out of his large window overlooking Reynolds Channel."

Terry, so pale and thin that Fischler hardly recognized

him, seemed startled to have a visitor. She told him that she was Shirley Walton, a die-hard Ranger fan who had come to the hospital to see how he was. "All of which was true," Fischler noted.

Sawchuk was eager for company. His room was bare except for a couple of pop bottles left behind by his two oldest sons, who had come from Michigan to visit him. Terry's hand clung for support to the railing at the side of his bed. He complained of the constant coughing of his neighbour, and the fact that the old man didn't want the windows open or the air-conditioner turned on.

"I can't even tell you if this is a good hospital or not," Sawchuk said wearily. "I've been doped up for so long, I don't know.... They still don't know if I'll recover from this. And it was so bad for a while that I really didn't care. I'm still full of tubes and my back is bothering me from lying here so long."

As they talked, Fischler found herself forgetting the Saw-chuk she had watched after hockey games. "The Terry Saw-chuk who ignored reporters and admirers alike. The Terry Sawchuk who rudely shoved young autograph hounds from his path. I saw Terry Sawchuk the lonely man, ill and weak in a hospital bed. The Terry Sawchuk who was eager for company and flowers. And I was suddenly sorry that I had come."

But she stayed, gently coaxing Terry to answer her questions. She asked him how he felt about the press coverage of his situation. "It was just a fluke," he said of his original injury, "a complete fluke accident. Those writers, they'll do anything to make up those stories."

Before the accident, there had been speculation that Terry was on the verge of being traded to St. Louis as part of a three-way deal that included Jacques Plante's transfer from the Blues to Toronto. When Fischler mentioned this possibility, Sawchuk shook his head.

"I'm retired, man," he said raising a pencil-thin arm. "Look at me. I can never come back from this."

The scarred and battered body that Terry had pushed so hard through twenty NHL seasons grew weaker by the day as blood continued to collect in his damaged liver. Four days after Fischler's visit, Sawchuk was moved back into the intensive care ward. On Friday, May 29, his doctors transferred him to New York Hospital, a major Manhattan infirmary overlooking the East River that specialized in acute illnesses. The new hospital had an arteriogram, a piece of equipment not available in the Long Island facility, that could determine exactly how much internal damage he had suffered.

By this point, only Emile Francis and Terry's brother Gerry, who had flown in from Detroit, were permitted to visit Sawchuk. "He was bleeding internally and they conducted about five hours of tests on him," Francis remembered. "When the tests were over they held a meeting.... They told him he had a very serious problem and that they were going to have to operate as soon as possible."

Before his surgery early Saturday evening, Terry asked to see a priest. "About an hour later they wheeled him into the operating room," said Francis. "That was about six in the evening. I was in the hospital and when he went by me he took a ring off his finger and gave it to me. It was a Detroit Red Wing ring...."

Dr. Frank Glenn, the hospital's surgeon-in-chief, performed what was described as "acute abdominal surgery" on Sawchuk's bleeding liver. The first forty-eight hours following his operation were considered crucial. Late Saturday night, Terry briefly regained consciousness. But he faltered through the early hours of Sunday, May 31, and at 9:50 a.m. he slipped away in his sleep. An autopsy

conducted that day by a New York City coroner revealed
that the exact cause of death was a blood clot that had travelled from a vein into a pulmonary artery.

"His heart just stopped beating because he was so generally weak," said a hospital spokesperson. "It was a case of
his being in such bad shape when he was brought here and
our not being able to revive him."

Following the autopsy, Emile Francis was asked to go to
the morgue on Second Avenue and identify the body. "They
didn't know who I was and they didn't know who he was,"
Francis recalled to Dick Irvin, Jr. "A chap came out and
said, 'Is there anyone here named Francis?' I identified
myself and he told me to follow him. We went down a couple of flights of stairs and he opened the door and there
were about thirty bodies lying there and the first thing that
hit me was that they were in bags just like the bags we used
to carry hockey sticks in. And there he was, his head out of
one end of the bag with a tag around his neck. They had
'Terry Sawchuk' written on the bag."

Even before Sawchuk's death, homicide detectives in Long
Island's Nassau County, spurred on by the publicity and
speculation surrounding his original injuries, had launched
an investigation into the case under the personal direction
of District Attorney William Cahn. On the day of Terry's
final operation, the Rangers, acting on Ron Stewart's
behalf, retained the services of Long Island's most noted
defence attorney, Nicholas Castellano. When news came of
Sawchuk's passing, speculation ran rampant that Stewart
would face a charge of involuntary manslaughter.

On Tuesday, June 2, Cahn announced that a grand jury
hearing the following Monday would determine whether a
crime had been committed in Sawchuk's death. Ron Stewart, having returned from Barrie the day before, was among

those subpoenaed to appear, as were Emile Francis, Rosemary Sasso and Benjamin Weiner.

The next day, a sombre, obviously shaken Stewart met with the District Attorney for preliminary questioning. He was accompanied by his lawyer and Rosemary Sasso. "I spoke with them for nearly an hour and they were most co-operative," Cahn said after the meeting. "They answered every question put to them and they agreed to return on Monday to testify and sign a waiver of immunity."

Later that day, Sasso, in an interview with the *New York Post*, created a stir by saying that she had detected symptoms of an illness in Sawchuk beginning about two weeks before his clash with Stewart. "Terry was spitting up blood," she said, "and I was pleading with him to see a doctor, but he wouldn't."

Sawchuk's friend, Ben Weiner, corroborated Sasso's story. "He was at our house one night during playoff time, and he mentioned that he had been spitting up blood, but he didn't know what it was," Weiner said.

Ron Stewart also spoke at length to the *Post*, expressing his incredulity and shock over the events of the past few weeks. "It just doesn't make any sense," he said. "All his lifetime Terry took much worse falls on the ice and he always bounced back...and then he trips on top of me and suddenly his life is ended. A fall like that, just like a thousand he's taken on that hard ice and nothing ever happened to him.... It's all like a bad dream when I look back now."

Stewart said the quarrel in the bar started when he insisted to Terry that they had to clean up their rented house before moving out. "Terry laughed about it," Stewart said. "He didn't take me seriously. But I told him, 'We've got to get busy.' His answer was, 'The hell with it.' And then I said, 'No, we've got to get the house back into the shape the owner gave it to us.'"

According to Stewart, the exchange grew more heated

when he brought up the topic of money he felt Sawchuk owed him. "I told Terry that I'd paid out $184 and some change for bills on the rental that made him blow his top. He pulled out a roll and handed me $190 and told me to 'shove it.'"

At the house, Sasso tried to stop the dispute, but "pretty soon Terry and I were wrestling each other again," recalled Stewart. "She tried to step in and separate us but I told her to get into the house. When a couple of monsters like us go at it, a girl can get hurt."

Ben Weiner, who had also been at the bar, arrived around this time, ordered Sasso inside, and then grabbed Sawchuk around the middle from behind, trying to keep him off Stewart.

"But Terry just kept coming after me," Stewart said. "I backed away and tripped over a metal barbecue pit that had been lying on the lawn from the day before when it fell over. It was dark at the time and when Terry came after me, with Weiner still holding on, he caught his foot in my leg and fell on top of me...but I think he hit himself against one of the protrusions on the cooker—or possibly against my knee."

At first Stewart thought Sawchuk was acting when he groaned in pain and clutched at his groin. "But I soon realized he wasn't putting us on. I called Rosemary out of the house and told her to phone Doc Nicholson.

"Terry almost had a fit," Stewart continued. "He didn't want the doctor. 'I don't need a doctor,' he said. His biggest fear was that word would get back to his father in Detroit and that he would worry.

"We all went to the hospital with Terry. Terry was kidding all the time about being brought there. 'You guys are crazy,' he kept saying, 'there's nothing wrong with me.' That's what we thought, too, and then when they removed his gall bladder I figured that was what his trouble was. Just a bad gall bladder. But when the days and weeks passed and they kept operating on him, it just didn't make sense to me."

Stewart blamed himself for not ignoring Sawchuk when he wanted to fight; for not fully realizing how despondent Terry was after his return from a recent visit to Detroit, where he had visited his father and unsuccessfully attempted to reconcile with his ex-wife. "I can't tell you how sorry I am that I didn't turn away. The guy had real problems. When I think of it I'm ready to go out of my mind.

"You don't know how much Terry loved that woman," Stewart said of Pat. "He was crazy about her. And his heart just melted over those kids of his…. Terry was broken-hearted. You got to understand the guy. You got to know him the way I did to realize how badly he felt. He was very sensitive and, as tough as he might have been on the rink, he was really soft where it counted—in the heart."

In Union Lake, Pat Sawchuk took strong exception to Stewart's inference that the failure of a reconciliation attempt had left her former husband broken-hearted and in the mood to lash out at his housemate.

"The last time I saw Terry was at Pontiac General Hospital when he came to visit his father in early April," Pat said. "We talked at the hospital for two or three hours and then we picked up the kids and went out and had dinner together. Terry said that after the season he'd like to take the kids to Florida and wanted me to go along to take care of them—I think in his mind he felt it was the final chance for a reconciliation. He kissed the kids goodbye and we were on the best of terms."

During Terry's hospitalization, she sent him a letter, a card and photos of the children. She wrote that she hoped he'd be out of the hospital soon and signed it, "Love, Pat and the kids." After returning from visiting his father, young Gerry said that the card and pictures had given his dad a big lift.

Pat acknowledged, however, that the reason she didn't go

to New York or telephone Terry during his hospitalization
was "because I was told he didn't want to talk to me."

Speculation about Sawchuk's death and the role played by
Ron Stewart continued to build until the grand jury convened
as scheduled in a courthouse in Mineola, Long Island. After
hearing testimony from nine witnesses over a three-hour
period, the jury deliberated less than half an hour before rul-
ing that the goaltender's death was "completely accidental."

District Attorney William Cahn told reporters that the
testimony indicated that Sawchuk and Stewart had been
involved in a "childish and senseless verbal argument, with
a lot of pushing and shoving.... Apparently Stewart fell
backward over an obstacle in the yard and Sawchuk and
one Ben Weiner, who had hold of Sawchuk, fell and the
injuries which caused the embolism leading to the death of
Sawchuk occurred."

Cahn said the grand jury had received no substantiation
for published reports quoting Rosemary Sasso (and Ben
Weiner) as saying that Sawchuk had been spitting blood for
two weeks prior to the altercation. Nor, despite what Terry
had reportedly told Dr. Denis Nicholson shortly after the
accident, was evidence given by any of the witnesses that
blows were actually struck.

The grand jury exonerated Stewart of any responsibility
in his friend's death. Cahn pronounced the investigation
into the "tragic, senseless, bizarre death of Terry Sawchuk...closed so far as any further criminal investigation by
this office is concerned."

Leaving the courthouse, Ron Stewart declined to comment further to the press about the case. It is a silence that
he has steadfastly maintained ever since.

*Epilogue*

# THE LEGEND GROWS

THEY came out of the church and back into the sunlight—
Tommy Ivan, Terry's first coach with the Red Wings; former Canadiens great Bernie Geoffrion; Ed Giacomin, Jean
Ratelle and Rod Seiling of the Rangers; Bruce A. Norris,
owner of the Wings; Stafford Smythe and Harold Ballard,
majority shareholders of the Toronto Maple Leafs; and Bob
Kinnear, the old scout who had discovered Sawchuk on the
outdoor rinks of Winnipeg. All told, ten of the fourteen
NHL clubs sent representatives to the memorial service.

Johnny Wilson, then the coach of the Los Angeles Kings,
was one of those who travelled with the funeral cortège to
Pontiac's Mt. Hope Cemetery, not far from the house in
Union Lake where Sawchuk had lived with Pat and the kids.
The procession was originally scheduled to pass by Pontiac
General Hospital, where Terry's father lay gravely ill. But
the day before, an ambulance had taken Louis to the funeral
home for a private visit, and the route had been changed.

Wilson watched as they laid Sawchuk to rest near the
grave of his mother, Anne. "Like everyone else," he
remembers, "all I could think about was what a waste it
was. It was tough to think of those seven kids having to live
their lives without their father."

Today, Wilson is an automotive-parts salesman in the
Detroit area. He drives past Mt. Hope Cemetery three or
four times a week while making his rounds. "Old Uke's
grave is right by the side of the road," Wilson says. "Every
time I go by I think about him and wonder how things
might have turned out if he'd lived. It's funny how hockey
fans seem even more interested in Terry now than when he
was alive."

Sawchuk's legend has grown larger with every passing year since his death. In 1971, he was posthumously awarded the Lester Patrick Memorial Trophy—for "outstanding service to hockey in the United States." Also that year, voters waived the usual three-year waiting period and elected Sawchuk to the Hockey Hall of Fame. By the 1980s, hockey cards and other memorabilia relating to his career had become among the most expensive and sought after on the market. Terry had emerged as hockey's greatest cult figure.

Then, in 1994, came the honour that would have pleased him the most. On March 6, his beloved Red Wings officially retired Sawchuk's Number 1 and a commemorative banner was hoisted to the rafters of Joe Louis Arena by his family members. It hangs with the other retired numbers of Gordie Howe (9), Ted Lindsay (7) and Alex Delvecchio (10).

"The Uke was the best goalie I ever saw, everything that a goalie should be," Gordie Howe said that night.

"Of course, Terry would have felt uncomfortable about all the fuss," Johnny Wilson says. "You know how he hated publicity. Still, it's a darn shame he didn't live to see it. But what people should remember is that Terry Sawchuk led a hell of a life. Nobody can say he didn't."

# ACKNOWLEDGMENTS

THIS biography of Terry Sawchuk was completed with the help of many people, including several of the goaltender's former teammates and closest friends—but not, unfortunately, with the participation of the Sawchuk family. Gerry Sawchuk, Terry's eldest son, made it clear from the outset that family members did not wish to be interviewed. Respectful of his wishes, I at no time—when seeking interviews or other information—presented this work as anything other than an unauthorized biography.

Among those who consented to be interviewed on the record, I would especially like to thank Sawchuk's former teammates Johnny Wilson, Benny Woit, Lefty Wilson and Johnny Bower, whose insights were invaluable. Of those I talked to who knew Sawchuk during his early years in Winnipeg, a special thank you to his boyhood chum Biff Fliss.

This is the first published full-length biography of Terry Sawchuk. But literally hundreds of magazine and newspaper articles have been written about him through the years. And, of course, the authors of other hockey titles have devoted considerable space to his exploits.

I drew upon many of these resources during my research. It was a particular joy to go back into the various newspaper archives and reread the game reports and columns of the likes of Milt Dunnell, Jim Proudfoot, Dick Beddoes, Scott Young, George Gross, Lou Cauz, Red Fisher, Dink Carroll, Red Burnett, Marshall Dann, Paul Chandler, Joe Falls, John Walter, Gerald Eskenazi and many others. Though Terry Sawchuk never had much use for reporters, I found that these writers invariably tried their sympathetic best to present this troubled and often difficult man in the best possible light.

I am particularly indebted to veteran Canadian sports-writer Trent Frayne, a personal hero, who knew Sawchuk well and chronicled his life and times in articles that appeared in a variety of magazines, as well as in several books of his own authorship.

Equally essential to my research were back issues of *The Hockey News*, which I reread on microfiche at the Metropolitan Toronto Reference Library. The only problem with this source was that I became so engrossed in reliving the glory days when Howe and Lindsay and Kelly and Sawchuk were winning Stanley Cups for Detroit that I spent far more time than I could afford in front of my viewing screen.

Several dozen books were consulted in the writing of this book, many of them pulled from the shelves of the Hockey Hall of Fame's library. Among the most essential: *Net Worth: Exploding the Myths of Pro Hockey* by David Cruise and Alison Griffiths (Penguin Books Canada, 1991), to my mind the single most important hockey book ever written; all the titles edited by Dan Diamond, but especially *Years of Glory: 1942-1967* (McClelland & Stewart, 1994); *In the Crease: Goaltenders Look at Life in the NHL* by Dick Irvin (McClelland & Stewart, 1995); and *The Last Hurrah: A Celebration of Hockey's Greatest Season '66-'67* by Stephen Cole (Penguin Books Canada, 1995).

I would also like to extend my appreciation to Phil Pritchard and Craig Campbell of the Hockey Hall of Fame for both their assistance and unfailing generosity.

Thanks also—and especially—to my wife, Sharon McAuley, who always gets the all-important first read and pencil edit.

Finally, a special note of gratitude to my publisher and editor, Cynthia Good of Penguin Books Canada, who believed in the project from the start—and who delivered stirring pep talk exactly when I needed it most.

Abel, Linda 214

Abel, Sid 1, 25, 30, 32, 34, 35, 39, 43-45, 51, 60-61, 64, 74, 78, 84, 178, 179, 184-186, 189, 191, 192, 194, 199, 201-204, 206, 208, 211, 213-214, 217-219, 228, 273-275

Adams, Charles 58

Adams, Jack 9, 11-16, 21, 24, 27, 28, 30-35, 42-48, 50, 51, 53-58, 60, 66, 71-74, 76, 79-83, 86, 90, 91, 93, 96-99, 101, 104, 105, 109, 114, 115, 118, 119, 122-123, 125, 127, 129, 130, 133, 135-139, 143, 151, 164, 170-176, 179, 180, 182, 183, 189, 202

Agar, George 18

Alexander, Grover Cleveland 257

Almas, Ralph 15

Angotti, Lou 249, 250

Armstrong, Bob 53, 142, 155

Armstrong, George 215, 228, 235, 236, 261

abando, Pete 26, 27, 110

ackstrom, Ralph 204, 234, 257-260

alfour, Murray 187

allard, Harold 291

alon, Dave 261, 270

arilko, Bill 46

arkley, Doug 195, 208

assen, Hank 175, 185-189, 191, 192, 01, 206

athgate, Andy 145, 205, 215, 228, 242, 65

uer, Bobby 89

uer, Hank 86

un, Bob 198, 210, 211, 218, 220, 244

Beddoes, Dick 265

Béliveau, Jean 104, 107, 116, 130, 204, 226, 255, 257, 261

Bentley, Max 65

Berger, Howard 120

Berra, Yogi 86

Bionda, Jack 155

Blair, Wren 271

Blake, Toe 132, 134, 145, 161, 191, 192, 234, 253, 255, 261

Block, Ken 264

Boisvert, Gilles 135

Bonin, Marcel 117-118, 123, 135

Bouchard, Butch 133

Boucher, Frank 57, 61-63

Bower, Johnny 1, 22, 25, 26, 48, 184, 185, 187, 198, 213-239, 243, 244, 247-251, 255-258, 263

Brewer, Carl 198, 220, 231-232

Brimsek, Frank 24, 37, 62, 139, 199, 224

Browne, Dr. Edward R. 148-151, 156

Broda, Turk 22, 24, 37, 38, 40, 52, 65, 100, 101, 160, 161, 199, 208

Brown, Arnie 277

Brown, Walter 57, 120, 143, 154

Bruneteau, Modere "Mud" 17

Bucyk, Johnny 136, 173-175

Buffey, Vern 219

Burnett, Red 65, 129

Caffery, Jack 155

Cahn, William 286, 290

Cain, Herbie 32, 39

Campbell, Bryan 265

Campbell, Clarence 57, 123-127, 158, 213

Capone, Al 268

Carroll, Dink 130
Carse, Bobby 25
Castellano, Nicholas 286
Cauz, Lou 218, 244, 245
Chabot, Lorne 199
Chadwick, Bill 45
Champoux, Bob 207, 225
Chandler, Paul 36
Cheevers, Gerry 219, 226, 227
Chevrefils, Real 135, 144, 145
Clancy, King 116, 202, 203, 210, 213,
  241, 243
Conacher, Brian 240, 243, 250, 253, 259
Conacher, Charlie 227
Connell, Alex 199
Cooke, Jack Kent 263, 265-266, 272
Cooper, Carson 138
Corcoran, Norm 135
Costello, Murray 144
Cournoyer, Yvan 238, 258-260
Cousy, Bob 142
Creighton, Dave 115
Crozier, Roger 202-203, 206-209, 213-
  214, 220, 223-225, 234, 273-274
Cruise, David 13, 172
Curry, Floyd 44, 70, 107, 108, 133

Dann, Marshall 23, 164, 180
Davis, Lorne 135
Dea, Billy 153
DeJordy, Denis 248
Delefice, Norman 149, 151, 153, 167
Delvecchio, Alex 50, 70, 82, 85, 97, 117,
  129, 130, 132-133, 175, 180, 186, 196,
  208, 215, 223, 292
Desjardins, Gerry 272
Dewsbury, Al 28
Dineen, Bill 99, 101, 117
Douglas, Kent 198
Douglas, Les 25
Duff, Dick 198, 199, 258, 261
Dumart, Woody 88-89
Dunnell, Milt 49, 147, 161, 252, 281

Durnan, Bill 22, 24, 37, 40, 62, 139, 159,
  199

Eagleson, Alan 175
Edwards, Roy 273
Ellis, Ron 261
Eskenazi, Gerald 276, 281
Esposito, Phil 277
Ezinicki, "Wild Bill" 35-36

Falls, Joe 3, 4, 119
Favell, Doug 263
Ferguson, John 204, 255, 261
Ferguson, Lorne 144
Fischler, Shirley 283-285
Fischler, Stan 283
Flaman, Fern 64, 142
Fleming, Reggie 209
Flett, Bill "Cowboy" 269
Fliss, Biff 6, 9-10, 19
Fonteyne, Val 184, 195
Fontinato, Lou 180, 186, 195
Francis, Emile 2, 237, 243, 275, 277-
  278, 282, 285-286
Frayne, Trent 14-15, 136, 173, 278
French, Lenny 7
Friday, Bill 250

Gadsby, Bill 176, 183, 195, 210, 211,
  260, 273-275
Gamble, Bruce 230, 233, 239
Gamble, Dick 115
Gardner, Cal 100, 141
Gardner, George 213
Gavel, George 56
Gee, George 50
Gelineau, Jack 37
Geoffrion, Bernie "Boom Boom" 44-4,
  68-70, 100, 103, 104, 106, 108, 116,
  124, 129-133, 186, 205, 291
Giacomin, Ed 236, 275, 277, 278, 291
Giesebrecht, Jack 19
Gillooly, Jim 159

Glenn, Dr. Frank 285
Glover, Fred 21, 25, 50, 56
Godfrey, Warren 135, 137
Goldham, Bob 28, 30, 53-54, 72, 77, 87, 93, 100, 101, 107-108, 218
Gray, Terry 265
Griffiths, Alison 13, 172
Grimes, Bill 120
Gross, George 223

Hadfield, Vic 206, 277
Haggert, Bob 251
Hainsworth, George 2, 6-7, 62, 199
Hall, Glenn 41, 48, 50, 82-83, 88, 91, 96-97, 118-119, 122, 135-136, 138-139, 141, 144, 146, 160, 170-174, 185, 188, 193-195, 202, 248, 253, 263, 274
Harper, Terry 258, 261
Harris, Billy 228-229, 265
Harris, Ted 261
Harvey, Doug 44, 99, 110, 130, 138
Hassard, Bob 115
Hay, Red 249
Hayes, George 124
Hayley, Len "Comet" 183-184
Heller, Ott 20, 48
Henderson, Johnny 139
Henderson, Paul 206
Henry, "Sugar" Jim 28, 50, 53, 63, 67, 87-88, 90, 139, 167
Hewitt, Foster 6, 242
Hillman, Larry 240, 244, 255
Hodge, Charlie 200, 254, 263
Hollingworth, Bucky 137
Horeck, Pete 27
Horton, Tim 198, 215, 219-220, 225, 236, 238, 244, 253, 258-261
Horvath, Bronco 136, 138, 174
Howe, Colleen 97
Howe, Gordie 1-2, 13, 25-26, 32-34, 36-37, 39, 43-44, 63-64, 66, 68-70, 74, 78-79, 83-85, 88-91, 93, 97-104, 106, 116-117, 123, 131-133, 141, 153, 169,

171, 173, 175, 180, 184, 186-187, 196-197, 199-201, 204-205, 208, 211, 215, 220, 223, 241, 249, 292
Howell, Harry 145
Hull, Bobby 188, 196-197, 205, 209, 242, 246-252, 254, 256
Hull, Dennis 248, 253
Hunt, Sammy "Golfbag" 59

Imlach, Punch 1, 183-184, 197, 213-220, 222, 226-234, 236-241, 243-245, 247-255, 260-261, 263-264
Irvin, Dick Sr. 29-30, 33, 41, 67, 71, 76, 85, 100, 107-109, 117, 133
Irvin, Dick Jr. 104, 286
Ivan, Tommy 20-21, 24, 30, 45, 51, 77, 79-81, 88-90, 98, 101, 109, 111, 114, 116, 137, 170, 173, 187, 291

Jarrett, Doug 249
Jeffrey, Larry 206, 228, 275
Jessiman, Harvey 15-16
Johnson, Chet 22
Johnson, Tom 69, 107, 138
Johnston, Eddie 224
Joyal, Ed 206, 228, 265, 269
Juzda, Bill 35

Kaese, Harold 147
Kelly, Red 1-2, 26, 30, 36, 39, 43, 53, 64, 77, 79, 85-91, 93, 99-100, 103, 106-107, 109, 141, 177, 182-184, 195, 198, 215, 218, 236, 259, 261, 264, 266-270, 272-273
Kennedy, Ted 26, 57, 63, 65
Keon, Dave 198-199, 224, 244, 259, 261
Kerr, Davey 71, 199
Kinnear, Bob 7-10, 291
Klukay, Joe 88
Koufax, Sandy 210, 260
Kurtenbach, Orland 228
Kyle, Gus 53

Labine, Leo 90, 141-142
Labossierre, Gordon 265
Lach, Elmer 45, 63, 69, 71, 87
Langelle, Pete 6
Laperriere, Jacques 259
Laycoe, Hal 53, 124, 139, 142
Leswick, Pete 25
Leswick, Tony 50-51, 69, 87, 93, 101, 106, 110, 116, 128, 135, 159-160
Libby, Bill 268-269, 271-272
Lindsay, Ted 2, 13, 25-26, 32-37, 39, 43, 51, 64, 69, 72, 74-75, 78-79, 82, 84-86, 88, 90-91, 93, 97-98, 102-106, 111, 115-117, 123, 125, 128-131, 133, 138, 141, 169, 172-173, 175, 219, 223, 292
Litzenberger, Ed 115, 130
Long, Dr. E. Clarkson 165
Lopez, Al 22
Louis, Joe 118
Lumley, Harry 15, 21-22, 24, 26-30, 37-38, 47-48, 75, 82, 98-102, 117, 127-129, 141, 160-161, 199, 203
Lunny, Vince 110

MacDonald, Lowell 269
MacDonald, Parker 196, 200, 209
MacGregor, Bruce 195
MacKay, Cal 42, 25
Mackell, Fleming 87, 89-90, 141
Mahovlich, Frank 1, 184, 198, 202, 205, 223, 225, 231-232, 239, 250
Mantle, Mickey 86
Marshall, Don 277
Martin, Clare 23, 27, 50
Martin, Pit 206, 269
Masnick, Paul 70, 115
Mazur, Eddie 107
McCool, Frank 71-72, 159
McCormack, Johnny 68, 107
McCreedy, John 6
McDonald, Bucko 55
McFadden, Jim 50
McIntyre, John 87

McKenney, Don 141, 155
McNab, Max 18, 50
McNeil, Gerry 22, 37, 41-45, 69-70, 85, 107-110, 159-160
McNeill, Billy 153, 183, 200
Meger, Paul 44, 70
Melnyk, Jerry 184
Mikita, Stan 188, 193, 205, 242, 247-249, 251-252
Mohns, Doug 248, 251, 254
Moore, Dickie 68, 71, 104-106, 131, 154, 215
Morenz, Howie 58
Morgan, Joe 232
Morrison, Don 28
Mortson, Gus 56, 100
Mosdell, Kenny 45, 68, 108, 132
Mosienko, Bill 25
Mowers, Johnny 15
Mutcheson, Len 19

Neilson, Jim 277
Nesterenko, Eric 177, 197, 248-249
Nevin, Bob 198
Nicholson, Dr. Denis 280-281, 288, 290
Norris, Bruce 60, 189, 291
Norris, Eleanor 60
Norris, James D. Norris, Sr. 11-12, 58-60, 78, 115
Norris, James Norris, Jr. 59-60, 78, 91, 114, 225
Norris, Marguerite 60, 78, 189
Northcott, Baldy 10

O'Brien, Andy 181-182
Olmstead, Bert 44, 85, 103, 107
Onley, David 246-247
Orr, Bobby 237, 277

Pappin, Jim 240, 243, 252, 256, 258, 26
Parent, Bernie 263
Park, Brad 276-278
Patrick, Lester 139

Patrick, Lynn 23, 88, 138-139, 141, 144, 146, 152-153, 157, 161-163, 166-171, 173-174, 177

Pavelich, Marty 51, 69, 79, 81, 88, 103, 130

Peirson, Johnny 29, 87

Pennington, Bob 245

Percival, Lloyd 31-32, 47-48

Peters, Jimmy Sr. 27, 50

Peters, Jimmy Jr. 272

Piersall, Jimmy 159

Pike, Alfie 6

Pilote, Pierre 188, 252

Pinckney, Fred 138

Plante, Jacques 48, 107, 130, 133, 138, 146, 159, 185, 191, 203, 244, 284

Poile, Bud 115

Popiel, Paul 265

Prentice, Dean 241

Primeau, Joe 56, 261

Pronovost, Marcel 1, 3, 24, 53, 77, 100-101, 107, 109, 120, 133, 175, 180, 184, 195, 228-229, 244, 259

Proudfoot, Jim 119, 207, 246

Provost, Claude 227, 233-234

Prystai, Metro 25, 28, 30, 51, 71, 79, 86

Pulford, Bob 193, 228, 243, 246, 256, 261

Quackenbush, Bill 27, 53, 67, 137, 142

Quackenbush, Max 25

Raglan, Clare 50

Raleigh, Don 63

Ratelle, Jean 291

Rayner, Charlie 6, 23, 26, 37, 52

Reaume, Marc 183

Reay, Billy 43-45, 68, 209, 214, 218, 248

Regan, Larry 265-266, 268, 272

Reibel, Earl "Dutch" 99, 103, 106, 117, 122, 128

Reid, Gerry 21

Reise, Leo 26, 30, 32, 34, 39, 42, 53, 74, 77

Richard, Henri 226, 254, 257, 261

Richard, Maurice "Rocket" 29, 33, 40-45, 51, 63, 67-69, 71-72, 76, 83-84, 100, 103-108, 116, 124-129, 131, 176, 179, 186, 188, 199, 227

Rickey, Branch 86

Riggin, Dennis 182, 191, 201

Rizzuto, Phil 65

Rochefort, Leon 258, 260

Rolfe, Dale 269

Rollins, Al 22, 37-40, 46, 51, 63, 65, 98-100, 161

Rope, Don 8-9

Rousseau, Bobby 234, 238, 261

Ruth, Babe 257

Rutledge, Wayne 267-271, 274

Sandford, Ed 87, 125, 135

Sasso, Rosemary 280, 287-288, 290

Sawchuk, Anne 5, 49, 94, 114, 164, 278, 291

Sawchuk, Gerald 5, 285

Sawchuk, Gerald Thomas 114, 135, 179, 235, 289

Sawchuk, Jo Ann 179

Sawchuk, Judy 5

Sawchuk, Katherine 179

Sawchuk, Louis 5, 10, 165, 278, 291

Sawchuk, Mike 5-7

Sawchuk, Pat 1, 95-98, 114, 135-136, 140, 144, 153, 155, 162, 165-167, 173, 178-179, 181-182, 207, 221, 235, 238, 262, 267, 274, 289-291

Sawchuk, Roger 5

Schmidt, Milt 63, 88, 136, 140-141, 146, 153, 155-156, 161-162, 164, 167

Seiling, Rod 277, 291

Selke, Frank 57, 126

Shack, Eddie 117, 183, 199, 218, 221, 247

Shaw, Minnie "Ma" 33

Shoalts, David 138
Shore, Eddie 168, 177, 266
Silverman, Al 62
Simmons, Don 168-169, 185, 191, 219, 227
Sinclair, Reg 74, 78, 89
Skinner, Alfie 11
Skinner, Jimmy 115, 117, 125, 144, 174, 178, 189
Skov, Glen 71, 135
Sloan, Tod 63, 66
Smith, Al 230
Smith, Floyd 208
Smith, Gary 229
Smith, Sid 29, 63, 65
Smythe, Conn 52, 54, 57, 64, 67, 100, 103, 232
Smythe, Stafford 291
Snow, Sandy 275
Spoelstra, Watson 86
Stanley, Allan 155, 162, 169, 198, 215, 220, 231, 236, 241, 244, 251, 261
Stanowski, Wally 6
Stapleton, Pat 253
Stasiuk, Vic 135, 145, 174, 186
Stemkowski, Peter 243, 247, 252, 256
Stewart, Gaye 28, 30, 50, 110
Stewart, Jack 9, 28, 123, 137
Stewart, Nels 84
Stewart, Ron 1-2, 215, 222, 228, 279-282, 286-290
Storey, Red 30, 101, 106, 120, 131
Sutphin, Al 57

Tannahill, "Ma" 34
Thompson, Cliff 124
Thompson, Tiny 199
Thomson, Jim 102
Tobin, Bill 57
Toppazzini, Jerry 144
Tremblay, Gilles 233
Tremblay, J.C. 204, 258-259, 261

Ullman, Norm 136, 175, 196, 223

Vachon, Rogatien 254-255, 259
Vasko, Elmer "Moose" 177, 265
Vecchio, Rev. E.A. 1
Vezina, Georges 53, 62
Voss, Carl 120

Waldmeir, Pete 194
Wall, Bob 265
Walter, John 120
Walton, Mike 250
Watson, Harry 65, 83, 115, 151
Wayne, Johnny 215
Weiner, Benjamin 280, 282, 287-288, 290
Wharram, Ken 248-249
White, Bill 269
Williams, Ted 142, 158
Wilson, Johnny 1, 3, 14, 50, 65-66, 69, 77, 88, 101, 108-109, 121, 135, 143, 175, 216, 266, 291
Wilson, Lefty 20, 23, 121, 182, 191, 200, 275
Woit, Benny 3, 20-21, 25, 50, 53, 74-75, 77, 105, 107, 120, 130, 135, 143
Worsley, Lorne "Gump" 22, 48, 145, 185, 213, 254, 259, 261
Worters, Roy 199

Young, Howie 186-187, 195-196, 202
Young, Scott 19, 195